John Bratt

*Taken at the age of seventy-three, a year and six months
prior to his death*

Trails of Yesterday

BY JOHN BRATT

Introduction by Nellie Snyder Yost

UNIVERSITY OF NEBRASKA PRESS
LINCOLN AND LONDON

⊚ The paper in this book meets the minimum requirements of American National Standard for Information Sciences—Permanence of Paper for Printed Library Materials, ANSI Z39.48-1984.

First Bison Books printing: 1980
Most recent printing indicated by first digit below:
2   3   4   5   6   7   8   9   10

Library of Congress Cataloging in Publication Data
Bratt, John, b. 1842.
Trails of yesterday.
Reprint of the first ed. published by the University Publishing Co., Chicago.
1. Bratt, John, b. 1842   2. Frontier and pioneer life—Nebraska.
3. Nebraska—History.   4. Cattle trade—Nebraska—History.
5. Pioneers—Nebraska—Biography.   I. Title.
F666.B82   1980   978.2'03   79-26411
ISBN 0-8032-6055-5 (pa: alk. paper)

Reprinted from the original 1921 edition by the University Publishing Company, Chicago.

INTRODUCTION TO THE BISON BOOK EDITION

Nellie Snyder Yost

In his introduction to the Bison Book edition of Edgar Beecher Bronson's *Reminiscences of a Ranchman*, W. D. Aeschbacher listed some notable firsthand accounts of ranching on the northern Great Plains in the 1870s and 1880s. Whether by design or accident, the list—which included E. C. (Teddy Blue) Abbot's *We Pointed Them North*, James H. Cook's *Fifty Years on the Old Frontier*, Luther North's *Man of the Plains*, and A. B. Snyder's *Pinnacle Jake*—was headed by *Trails of Yesterday*. If John Bratt's book is not so well known as the others today, the reason is simply that the original edition, published in 1921, has been out of print for many years. Rich in frontier history, this classic of cow-country literature is authentic and reliable, hence of value to scholars, and of first interest to western buffs for its down-to-earth, detailed picture of the West that was and the great days of the cattle industry.

John Bratt was born in 1842, the son of a village minister in Staffordshire, England. Well educated in his early youth and apprenticed when he reached the age of twelve to a merchant friend of his father, John went into business for himself after serving out his five-year apprenticeship. All this while he had been reading everything he could lay his hands on about America; and "the lure of the home of the free and the land of the brave, where one man was as good as another, and where I would not be obliged to bow and doff my hat to the country squire and give him three-fourths of the road" grew stronger by the day. Although he was successful in business, at twenty-two years of age he sold out and took ship for New York City, arriving in July 1864. His life had as many ups and downs as a roller-coaster for the next two years—he spent them in Chicago, New York, and New Orleans—but his real story begins in Nebraska City in May 1866, when he hired out to Captain Bass, wagon master of a train of twenty-eight ox-drawn wagons headed across the plains for Fort Phil Kearny in northern Wyoming.

The chapters devoted to the journey will be of special interest to anyone who wants to know more about the Great Platte River Road as it was when Bratt made the trek more than a century ago. He gives us a precise and vivid account of that vast stretch of country, reporting on the condition of the trail, meetings with Indians, including Dull Knife and other chiefs, and encounters with buffalo herds, which were still plentiful on the plains. There also are splendid descriptions of the few forts then protecting the long trail—Forts Kearny, McPherson, Mitchell, and Sedgwick—and of the road ranches of John Burke (whose only daughter was to become Mrs. John Bratt), Lou Baker, Jules Coffee, and the notorious Jack Morrow, among others.

At Fort Phil Kearny, Bratt met Levi Carter, the man who was instrumental in shaping his future occupation. As a Carter hay-cutter at the fort, at Sherman Station, and at Tie Siding on the Union Pacific (then building westward toward Promontory), the young Englishman lived through some exciting months, fighting off Indian attacks between stints of cutting and hauling hay. It was at this time that he began to understand the nature of the struggle then going on in the western plains and mountains. A half century later he wrote: "Citizens living in this part of the Great American Republic one hundred years hence will have no conception of the hardships experienced by the men who blazed this Northwestern trail, which hundreds of times has been sprinkled with the blood of the bravest of both men and women. If a detailed history of the many murders committed on this trail from 1866 to the Custer Massacre could be written, it would blacken all Indian history on the American continent; but while condemning their cruel mode of warfare, we must not forget the fact that they were savages fighting for home and country—yes, for very existence as they understood it."

In 1869 John Bratt was sent back to Fort McPherson to fulfill a government hay contract held by Gilman and Carter. Subsequently he entered into a ranching partnersip with Coe and Carter, and for the next twenty-two years participated in all the phases of the fast-changing cattle business, from bringing herds up the Texas trail to selling the finished beef in Omaha and Chicago. During these years he met and worked with many other well-known cattlemen: Ed Creighton, builder of the first transcontinental telegraph line; Ben Gallagher; Buffalo Bill Cody; Bill Paxton, like Creighton a pioneer Omahan; J. W. Iliff, who had ranged cattle in the western Platte Valley since the early 1860s; Major Lester Walker; M. C. Keith of North Platte, who began his stock-raising operation with five American cows; and Russell Watts—men whose names, as James C. Olson says in his *History of Nebraska,* "are woven securely into the fabric of the old West." Also among Bratt's respected ranching friends was Nebraska's first cattle queen, Mrs. Alexander Randall of North Platte. *Trails of Yesterday* provides invaluable information about these people, most of whom were unable, too busy, or disinclined to write of their experiences.

At this time the western third of Nebraska was mostly unorganized territory; it had not achieved statehood until March 1, 1867. Lincoln County, site of Bratt's headquarters, had been organized in 1860—originally it had been called Shorter County, but the name was changed in 1866—and North Platte, the county seat, was laid out in the latter year. Because it was difficult to control or oversee affairs fifty or more miles from North Platte, John Bratt corrected the situation in his area by presiding over the creation of a new county.

"On January 18, 1872," he writes, "being anxious to make a stock country south of the Platte . . . we organized Frontier County." The night was bitter cold, with snow on the ground. The organization had to take place at the site of the proposed new county seat, Stockville, fifty miles distant, before six o'clock the following evening. During the long and hurried night journey, one of the intended officials of the new county was almost fatally injured in a buckboard upset, but nonetheless the organization was accomplished on time, in the tipi of a squaw man, Henry Clifford. In order to fill all the required county offices it was necessary to recruit almost every white man living in the designated area.

John Bratt built his sod ranch headquarters four miles south and east of North Platte, and constructed extensive corrals of cedar logs cut in the adjoining canyons to the south. His cattle ranged over most of the western part of the state, as far as the borders of Colorado and Wyoming. During his ranching years he was in the saddle more often than not, sleeping wherever night overtook him, "often in the open with my saddle for a pillow and slicker and saddle blanket for my bed." Alongside his men he battled blizzards and prairie fires, swam flooded rivers, and stood night herd when on roundups.

Fair-minded and progressive, Bratt was one of the pioneers in organizing livestock associations, which were needed very early to formulate workable range rules and control thieving and other depredations on their far-flung herds. He served as president of the first association formed at North Platte and at various times worked with the state organization.

Mr. Bratt relates that in the winter of 1872 small, thieving bands of Sioux had "killed, not for the meat but for pure, unadulterated meanness," several hundred head of his range cattle, "all because they did not happen to run across any buffalo." Accordingly, he put in a claim against the government for four hundred head and eventually received $13,000 in payment. Some years later, however, this judgment was overturned. According to the Indians' testimony in the case of the government against John Bratt for the return of the money paid to him for the butchered cattle, they had killed a very few head in order to survive the severe winter. They rest, they said, had "winter-killed" in the deep snow and extreme cold. The government won the case and Bratt had to refund most of the money.

This was one of the last occasions Indians were to be on the winning side. A few more years and the struggle between the white man and the red for control of the great grassy plains and river valleys was over. Cattlemen, no longer threatened by marauding Indians, developed one of the greatest cattle empires in history on the open ranges. But their reign was brief, covering a span of little more than twenty years, and, as the Indians had given way to the ranchers, so the ranchmen had to give way to the influx of homesteaders, the men with plows, barbed wire, and fence posts. In time, as most of the rangeland proved its unfitness for farming, the big ranches would take over again, but under fence and new range management. The day of the open range was gone forever.

Moving with the times, Bratt sold out his ranching interests and moved his wife and four daughters into North Platte, where he built a commodious and comfortable frame house. The old sod ranch buildings have long since returned to the earth from which they came, but a huge corner post and some of the cedar corral poles, still in good condition after one hundred and ten years, are now on display at the Lincoln County Museum in North Platte, along with a Bratt circle branding iron.

After his move into town, John Bratt opened an office and established a real estate, insurance, and loan business. At the turn of the century the young city was considered "loose," with gambling a recognized vocation, saloons operating wide open, and taxes soaring out of control. As a successful businessman who neither drank,

IN LOVING MEMORY

THE wife and four daughters of a most beloved husband and father have endeavored to carry out his wishes to publish his autobiography, so that his friends and relatives may read the story of his very eventful life correctly told.

Often when urged by his family to publish this he would remark, "Some day when I have more time I will rewrite it and put on the finishing touches."

But this time never came. Being in comparatively good health, he enjoyed his business activities, in which he continued until three days before his sudden and unexpected death.

His original writings have not been disturbed, so it is hoped that the readers will overlook some repetitions which could not have been avoided, considering the manner in which it was written. As he himself says: "Sometimes these were written under difficulties in tent, wagon box, ranch, or on the open prairie, if not on my field desk; perhaps on a cracker box, the cook's bread box, the end gate or seat of a wagon, the skirts of my saddle, or on an ox yoke. These facts are what I have seen and done in years of activity, often at the risk of my life."

The many temptations that confronted the early frontiersman have often made his friends marvel that he remained a clean moral man; though he professed no orthodox creed, yet he had an unfailing trust in a protecting God.

The writer's description of frontier life as cowpuncher and cowboy, with its buffaloes, Indians and untold hardships, will ever be of interest to the reader.

The automobile and the Lincoln Highway have taken the place of the ox train, the immigrants and the Oregon

Trail; yet so vivid are the descriptions that even now as you travel over parts of Colorado and Wyoming, where there are miles and miles of nothing but sagebrush, you find yourself almost looking for the Indian and horseman to appear and are somewhat disappointed because they do not. But they have disappeared with the wilds of the country and nothing but memory and imagination can take you to them now.

THE PIONEER

To-day we enjoy the beautiful West,
    Its rivers and mountains and plains;
Let a thrill of thanksgiving heave in the breast
    For the pioneer and his trials and pains.

With a knife in his boot
    A gun at his side,
His law was "Do right,"
    And his conscience his guide.

He knew not God through religion or creed.
    But out in the open, the stars overhead,
A stick for a pillow, the dew for a spread,
    He felt a Protector that met every need.

With the courage of soldier in battle,
    No fear in his heart or dread,
He succeeded in blazing the trail
    Where we now thoughtlessly tread.

The sage brush, the sunshine and rivers
    Are there and the lofty pine tree,
But pioneer, bullwhacker and cowboy,
    A thing of the past is he.

                G. B. G.

Where the Writer First Saw the Light of Day

CHAPTER I

Advent into the World—Birthplace—Bread Riot

ON the 9th day of August, 1842, in the town of Leek, Staffordshire, England, the writer of this book first saw the light of day, at the time the bread riots were so prevalent in many parts of England. I have often heard my parents speak of those exciting days and say that my advent into the world at that particular time was probably the means of saving our home from destruction, because father, in his capacity of minister of the gospel, had incurred the enmity of the mob. He had remonstrated against lawless and violent acts in the destruction of life and property, and the angry rabble, enraged at this, set upon and beat him into insensibility, after which they started to demolish our home in which lay my poor sick mother with a two-day old babe in her arms. When this became known to them, it appealed to their better nature and our home was spared.

CHAPTER II

Childhood Memories—Sunshine and Clouds—The Ministry is Not My Calling—Early Education

UNDER the kind fostering care of good and pious parents, loving sisters and brothers, my child life developed into boyhood with the usual incidents of joy and sorrow attending it; part sunshine and part clouds.

While in short dresses I remember joining some neighboring children in a hunt for blackberries in nearby woods, and in my anxiety to keep up with the others, I took off and laid down my skirt, which I failed to find when ready to return home.

I remember going in swimming with some other boys and all our clothes being stolen, so that we had to wait until dark before we could return to our homes.

I remember my first attendance at Sunday school, also at day school, the latter kept by my aunt, and how a pretty, flaxen-haired, blue-eyed miss took special pains to teach me to knit garters. I also remember sending by my father a small basket of fruit to my little instructress, for which thoughtful act I was greatly teased by my sisters.

I well remember falling into the river Churnet when it was a raging torrent. A plank, used by workmen at the silk dyehouse owned by a distant relative, had broken its fastenings, and in my boyish efforts to push it back I fell into the river. While spinning and rolling around like a chip in the swift current I thought of all the mean things I ever did. I made a grab for my Scotch cap, and as the torrent rushed me under the stone-arched bridge I wondered if the large crowd of people standing on the battlements would see me and rescue me. While these thoughts were passing through my brain I felt myself crowded against a hard substance, when the current began to whirl me around like a spinning top and my hand caught the branches of a tree, to which I clung

I Well Remember Falling into the River Churnet

St. Edward's Parish School

tenaciously and got my head above water. Then I saw that I had been washed against a pile of refuse dyestuff, up which I climbed, and thanks to my lucky star, was soon on terra firma, glad that I was out and all conceit taken out of me. I fully resolved, while picking up my bowl and stick and stealing my way home, never to bother that plank again, especially during high water. I experienced no bad effects from this ducking except a slight deafness in my left ear, which bothers me yet. Mother scolded me, made me put on dry clothes, and kept me in bed the rest of the day.

We Became Bitter Enemies

I also well remember about this time the mean tricks of a certain goat that loafed around the dyehouse stables. He seemed to take pleasure in lying in wait for me in any dark corner on my return home at night, when he would rush at me and chase me, often attacking and hurting me. The result was that we became bitter enemies and it was a source of great relief when I heard he was dead. He had simply tackled the wrong fellow and had died in his efforts to be boss.

I was not a bad boy, but I often wished that my father was not a minister, so that I could be free to act and play like other boys. My parents often advised me to be careful about my words and actions. They wanted me to be a model boy and an example to other boys of the town. Father would often invite me to accompany him to nearby villages where he would preach and en route talk about religion and encourage me to join him in his work. This was all very good but sometimes, I must confess, rather distasteful to me. I often longed to be free from the restraint that surrounded me. My parents were very strict about the company I should keep.

They had allowed me to become a fifer in a drum and fife band belonging to a temperance organization known as "The Band of Hope." I was fond of music, both vocal and instrumental. I was a singer in the Chapel Choir and sang at many entertainments before I was twelve years old. I had also been permitted by my parents to take part in the public presentation of a temperance piece known as John Barleycorn, in which I took three characters, one the part of a woman, "Eliza Brokenheart" (the wife of a drunkard), a bartender and another character.

Occasionally I was allowed to play with other boys when my parents were satisfied that they were the right kind. At one of these gatherings I became mixed up in a quarrel, taking up the rights of another boy who had been imposed upon by a larger one. The latter challenged me to fight. I tried to avoid this but a cousin, who happened to be there, gave me to understand that I must fight the boy and whip him, otherwise he would whip me. Preliminaries were quickly arranged and before taking off our coats, the fight was on in dead earnest. Under the earnest backing of my cousin and other young men present we were just getting warmed up to our work when, to my surprise and humiliation, my father appeared on the scene and marched me home where I received further punishment, together with a long moral lecture from both parents, who said that I had brought lasting disgrace upon them. This bad break on my part was no doubt the cause of my becoming fully resolved that I would never become a minister.

After attending my aunt's school I was sent to a very strict sectarian school kept by a Miss Turner, who was a prominent member of father's church and a friend of our family. What she lacked in good looks she made up in discipline. I got along nicely with her until one day one of the school boys unintentionally broke a pane in one of the windows with a snowball. Miss Turner became very angry and threatened to punish all if the guilty one did not go to her desk and acknowledge it. She finally called me up and asked if I knew who had broken the pane. I told her I thought I did. She commanded me to tell his name. I told her I could not do that. She said I must or I would receive the punishment. I replied that she could punish me but I

Father Appeared on the Scene

would not give the boy's name. At this remark, and without a moment's warning, she struck me on the side of my head and knocked me to the floor where I saw stars for a few moments. When I got up I made a rush for my books, slate and cap. She tried to prevent this but could not. I went home and told my father what had occurred. He said I ought to have told the boy's name and he ought to be punished; that he was not a manly boy or he would have acknowledged breaking the pane, especially when he saw I was being punished for his act. Father said he would see Miss Turner that evening and explain matters to her so everything would be understood in the morning. I told father that he could talk to Miss Turner if he wanted to but I would not go to her school again. He said I must not talk to him that way. I told him he could do what he pleased with me, even to cutting me up into strips, but I would never go to that school again. And I did not, but was sent to St. Edwards Parish School, taught by a Mr. Cannings, my parents paying a stipulated weekly tuition fee for this privilege.

CHAPTER III

*Ambition—An Apprentice to a Merchant—Youth in Business—
America and its Opportunities—Why Not?—Tears and
Good-bye*

I WAS in my twelfth year, had attended the Parish school
for some time, had read the Bible through, had taken an
active part in Sunday School work where I had taught a
class of little ones, sang alto in the Methodist Chapel choir
and was an active worker in the Band of Hope and other
good moral organizations. All of this had encouraged my
family, especially father, to hope that I would yet study for
the ministry, but my fight with Arthur K----- and the consequent disgrace in the minds of my parents, changed this and
assisted me materially in following my own inclinations.

It was about all father could do to support our family, yet
he would persist in aiding every poor person he knew. When I
would appeal to him for better clothes, he would tell me not
to worry—that the Lord would provide them. Sometimes,
however, I must confess, I thought the Lord had forgotten
me. It was this, combined with other circumstances, that
caused me to urge and finally persuade my father to allow me
to adopt a business career. I was accordingly bound out for
five years as an apprentice to a merchant, a friend of our
family. This merchant had two children, a son and a
daughter, the latter a little older than myself. I was taken
in and treated as a member of the family. The daughter was
a tall, beautiful girl with dark hair and eyes, and a fine form.
She was a great lover of pets, among which were a parrot and
a cat. The latter was an especial favorite and was permitted
at times to eat beside her at the table. This daughter became
very kind to me and often assisted me in my studies before
and after attendance at night school, where I was taking up
special branches. I had won the confidence and esteem of my
employer and his good wife and was permitted to accompany

the daughter to and from church and other places. In our constant association a brotherly and sisterly feeling sprang up between us. Young as I was, I could see from the actions of our parents and others interested that it would not be objectionable should this brotherly and sisterly feeling ripen into love and ultimate marriage, for perhaps unknown to either we had, in a measure, been plighted to each other by our respective parents who later on gave us to understand that at the proper time, no serious objections intervening, we would be expected to seal our friendship with our marriage vows. Occasionally when alone, the daughter—whom I will call my adopted sister, as that term better describes my own feelings in the matter—would refer to our future. She had wealth, social position and was highly educated, while I was a poor boy, trying to make my place in the world, an employee of her father. A great gulf was between us and I had fully determined, should I ever learn to love her, never to ask her to marry me until I could properly support her in the station in life to which she was accustomed. While I was her Sir Knight in every sense of the word, anticipating her every wish and doing everything in my power to please her and further the interests of my employer, yet never for one moment did I act the role of the lover, believing that such a course would be unmanly and unworthy of the confidence placed in me by her family.

I was closing my seventeenth year, my apprenticeship was ended, and I was offered a position at a fair salary by my late employer, which I declined for several reasons, contrary to the wishes of my former employer and my family. After a short vacation and a trip through the Potteries in Staffordshire, Manchester and other places, I concluded to go into business with my brother-in-law in Manchester, opening a general provision store on the Oldfield Road, Salford. A few months' trial at this proved unsatisfactory. The business was too top heavy. In other words, too many bosses for the work and the location was not the right one, so I decided to sell my interest or buy that of my brother-in-law. I bought his interest, then looked around for a better location which I soon found on Ludgate Hill. I sent for my youngest sister to come and keep house for me. Here I remained and did well until I was twenty-one years old.

I had read every book and newspaper article I could find that told anything of America. I had read "Uncle Tom's Cabin." Though opposed to slavery, my feelings went out to a certain extent to the Southern people, who, I believed, were fighting for their rights—the right to govern themselves. This sympathy was shared by seven-tenths of the English people. I had listened to the talks of Henry Ward Beecher and other Northern advocates and I became interested in the Civil War, termed in England "The Rebellion in the Northern States." Civil war was raging and it was a question at that time which side would win. War or no war I had made up my mind to close out my business as soon as I reached the age of twenty-one and go to America, that home of the free and land of the brave, where one man was as good as another and where I would not be obliged to bow and doff my hat to the country squire and give him three-fourths of the road. I had always loved America. Its large, red apples that came to my home town in barrels had made a great impression on my child mind, its republican institutions, its mighty rivers, broad prairies, gold mines, its undiscovered wealth, and its great possibilities! Who would not want to emigrate to such a free and glorious country and get out of the ruts trodden by my forefathers generations ago? I had already written my parents of my intention to close out my business and go to America. Letters arrived thick and fast, trying to persuade me from such a foolish step. Why not wait until the war was over? How foolish to give up a good business for an uncertainty! I was doing well. Mother knew I would be killed and she would never consent to my going unless I promised not to join the army or navy. Nothing but disaster was in store for me. Even my adopted sister opposed this uncalled-for step and my old employer thought there was a good opening for me to remain in England and said, "When you think of it, John, remember you are going to a new country where you have neither friend nor relative. It is being devastated by civil war, all the country under martial law. You will be drafted into the army and rushed to the front at the point of the bayonet the moment you land, if not captured by the 'Alabama' during passage. Think of the wild Indians and other lawless men you will meet. Why not think the matter over more carefully before you decide?" Many letters I received from relatives and friends who no doubt wished me well, advocating the abandonment of the contemplated move, all of which I took courage to ignore and brush aside. I finally sold my business in Manchester and took my sister home, where I bade my family good-bye. My poor mother was much grieved and would not let me go until I promised that I would join neither the army nor navy of my own free will. A special dinner was arranged for me and my parents by my old employer. Here I was for three long hours subject to all the eloquence that could be used by my parents, my employer and his family. The pictures portrayed were dark if I went. If I remained, hints were thrown out which meant a closer union than a copartnership. I could fill a chapter of very interesting reading if I gave full particulars of what occurred in that last farewell, but, with the reader's permission, I will draw the curtain here. With tear-filled eyes I bade my employer and his family good-bye. It took tact and courage to say good-bye to these good people without displaying some hidden emotions that had been fostered and encouraged by five years of uninterrupted kindness on the part of these very kind people.

latest war news from a Northern view, namely: that the Rebels, as they termed the Southerners, were whipped and all ready to surrender.

The officers and seamen of the ship had been very kind and considerate to all of us during the trip. The customary resolutions had been drawn up, adopted and presented with a present to the captain and chief officers of the Limerick. I had passed through the ordeal of bidding my relatives and friends good-bye on leaving England, but to leave and say good-bye to my newly made friends on the "City of Limerick" was almost equally as hard. No doubt the thought of being a stranger in a strange land and alone except for O'Brien, whom I had decided to help in every way possible, made me doubly sad when I bade some of my fellow passengers good-bye as we neared the landing at the ship's pier in New York on the 9th day of July. As previously stated, I had brought but little baggage—the same with O'Brien—so the Customs House officers were soon through with us. A long, last look at the old ship and we took our turn marching down the gang plank and were soon lost in the stream of humanity surging on the pier in New York City.

CHAPTER V

THE happiest and most anxious man to leave the "City of Limerick" was my friend O'Brien. We had no sooner registered and checked our baggage in one of the down-town hotels than he invited me to accompany him in search of a certain number at Fifty-third Street with a view to finding his old sweetheart, now Mrs. Katherine Ragan. We found the address but were told that Dr. and Mrs. Ragan had left there about ten days previous for parts unknown. O'Brien asked question after question about them but gained little or no information. He sat down on the curb of the walk a short distance from the house and cried like a child. He said he had nothing more to live for and wished he could die. I did all I could to encourage and brace him up. On passing the first saloon he left me abruptly, saying he would be out in a moment. After a short time I went in and found him standing by the bar draining the contents of a second glass of whiskey. After a lot of persuasion I got him into the street but had not gone far before he began to act silly like all drunken men. Fearing he would be arrested, I called a cab and took him to the hotel, where after a time I got him to sleep, during which he was very restless, often calling the name, "Katherine! Katherine!"

While I had been devoting much time to O'Brien I had not been unmindful or unobservant of the new scenes that I came across in the great city of New York; its crowded streets, its jam of traffic, its ever busy, rushing, pushing citizens full of energy, not only in the streets but at their meals. It was not an uncommon thing to see them finish a four or five-course meal while we ate our soup and fish. Its large, beautiful stores thronged with customers, its great theaters filled with enthusiastic audiences nightly, its well-filled churches and lecture halls would not indicate that not far from this great city civil war was devastating the country. The only indication of this was the "Extras" issued three or four times a day, giving the latest war news at the front, and now and then a company or regiment of troops either going, returning or being changed to different localities. I was offered $1500.00 for ninety days' service as a substitute—but, no, I could not accept it. That promise to my mother barred that. Every issue of the papers was full of war news. Yesterday Harrisburg was in danger of being captured by the Rebels—to-day Washington—to-morrow would be some other place. Such is war. Rebel and Northern spies were everywhere. Copperheads, as the Northern people called the people of the South and their sympathizers, were thick; and dozens, sometimes hundreds, of these were marched off to different forts to be kept under surveillance or shot. Martial law was supreme. All were afraid to talk to strangers, and to express sympathy for a band of sick, emaciated Southerners just captured at the front and being sent to nearby forts, meant being taken along also by the provost guard without any ceremony.

I was doing all in my power to aid and brace up O'Brien, who was evidently determined to drown his troubles in liquor. We had decided to seek employment of some kind in New York, but neither could find what he wanted, hence we decided to go to Chicago. I had sold the gold I brought with me at the highest price for paper money called "greenbacks" and the ten-cent scrip, better known as "shin plasters." Prices for everything were exceedingly high, but then I received nearly three dollars in greenbacks for one dollar of gold.

After making another fruitless search for O'Brien's Katherine, we took the train for Chicago. Our train just missed being captured by Colonel Mosby's cavalry near Harrisburg. Our route over the Allegheny mountains was interesting. The scenery was grand and impressed me with the idea that Americans, as well as Englishmen, knew something about building and operating a railroad. We finally arrived at Chicago in safety about the middle of August, 1864.

CHAPTER VI

Arrival at Chicago—A Letter from Katherine—O'Brien's Hasty Departure

AS soon as we arrived in Chicago, after securing a boarding place, O'Brien insisted on again taking up the search for Katherine. After about a month's diligent search, with no result, O'Brien received a letter from Ireland, giving the information that Dr. Ragan, who had married Katherine, had gone South and joined a certain Georgia regiment as army surgeon; that he had taken his wife with him; and that she, according to last reports, was in Columbus, Georgia, while the doctor was supposed to have gone to the front. O'Brien was elated at this information and the first mail out of Chicago carried a letter addressed to "Mrs. Dr. (Katherine) Ragan," Columbus, Georgia. The letter was brimful of sweetest sentiment, breathing eternal love and devotion. The letter did not return, neither did an answer. It might have been captured and destroyed or fallen into the hands of the censor. Another and another equally or more loving than the first followed.

In the meantime O'Brien had secured a situation as book-keeper in one of the packing houses. While he was often discouraged and in his "cups," yet I would talk to him and brace him up. I believe I did much to keep him from going to the bad. I had agreed to go with him to his church (Catholic) in the mornings and he would go with me to the Protestant church in the evenings on Sundays. Like myself, he was fond of music and enjoyed the singing. We roomed together for quite a while at a nice boarding house kept by Mrs. Dunham on Madison street. I had gone into business on South Water street and was doing well.

One evening in the latter part of October O'Brien came running into the room with a letter in his hand. His joy knew no bounds. The letter was from his long lost Katherine.

It was dated Columbus, Georgia. It commenced, "My Dear John," and went on to state that he probably knew that her parents had insisted on her breaking her engagement with him and marrying Dr. Ragan, who shortly after their arrival at a Southern port, had joined the Confederate army and after being at the front but a short time had been killed. She wrote that at present she was dependent on friends, had written home for money, expecting when she received it, to return to her home in Ireland, but that before going she wished he would come to her and that she was still ready and willing to fulfil the vows they had plighted months ago and marry the only man she ever loved. O'Brien threw himself on the bed and wept and between sobs exclaimed, "I knew she was always true to me." Poor O'Brien! My heart went out in pity for him. I gave him all the consolation I could. We sat up the greater part of the night planning how he could get to Columbus, Georgia, for which place he had determined to leave the next day, and he did. He secured the necessary papers from the British Consul, showing that he was a British subject, that his destination was Columbus, Georgia, and what his mission was. I gave him needed funds, accompanied him to the depot, saw him safely on the train and bade him God-speed and a safe, quick return. Poor O'Brien! I never heard from him afterwards, although I made many efforts to locate him and his Katherine. Perhaps he was killed in crossing the lines. If not, let us hope he found his true, loving Katherine; that they became one and inseparable; and that their lives have been continued sunshine and happiness. This is the fervent wish of the writer.

CHAPTER VII

Life in Chicago—My Wedding is Planned without my Knowledge—
Speculations on the Chicago Board of Trade—A Wreck
Investigation

AFTER O'Brien's departure I felt sad. While relieved of the constant watch I had had to keep him from indulging too freely in order to make his grief easier to bear, yet I was worried to think there would be no one to guide, brace and cheer him on his perilous trip to Columbus, Georgia, which he thought he could reach overland. I had grave doubts about his getting through the Northern army lines in safety. I could not help admiring the man for his nerve and his devotion to Katherine, for the whole world loves a lover like O'Brien. He was the only one I cared to call friend. In fact, I felt as though I had lost a brother. I had made some business acquaintances, but I felt lonesome and watched the mail closely many weeks, hoping I would receive some tidings of him, but none came.

Chicago was full of Copperheads or sympathizers of the Southern cause and there were as many or more Union spies. Like many other Northern cities, it was under martial law. At our boarding house there were some twenty gentlemen and from eight to twelve ladies. The former consisted of lawyers, doctors, lake captains, bank and other clerks. Some of the ladies were the wives of the gentlemen, others were pursuing studies of one kind or another. Still others had come from near the Mason and Dixon line in order to be safer, and a couple were holding positions in large dry goods stores. We were a happy family. Our landlord and landlady, assisted by a charming daughter who was an expert at the piano, did everything to make life pleasant and homelike. There were several musicians and good singers among the boarders. O'Brien had a splendid voice and was greatly missed when he went away. It was an extremely dull evening if we did not have singing, dancing, music or games of some kind, besides discussing the latest war news.

It was at this place that a serious joke was played on the writer by one of the lake captains. There was a neat, comely, innocent Swede girl called "Tilly" who waited on our table, and I would occasionally speak to her when arriving late for lunch. I would sometimes jokingly remark, "Now, Tilly, bring me a good lunch as soon as possible and I will look out for a good husband for you." Tilly would smile and a nice lunch would soon be before me. It was not long before I noticed that Tilly would serve me before other boarders and pay me more than common attention. It was also noticed by some of the other boarders and I was inclined to think that I had perhaps made a mistake in making so free in talking with her. I began to pay little or no attention to her outside of being polite and civil, but this did not check her preference for serving me before others. One day I noticed a smile play over a certain lake captain's face when he whispered something to Tilly. The interest of Tilly in me grew more as the days went by until one evening, when nearly ready to go to the theater, I heard a knock on the door of my room. I was told I was wanted in the parlor, which, on entering, I found full of company, among them strangers I had not seen before and to whom I was introduced by Captain Blanchard. Among these strangers was one whom the captain called Reverend Wadsworth, who had kindly, so the captain stated, agreed to perform the marriage ceremony for me and Miss Tilly, who stood there all fixed up very prettily and smiling sweetly, with a large bouquet of roses in her hands and with flowers in her hair, for this, to her, auspicious occasion. Of course, this had all been gotten up unknown to me. The Reverend (?) Wadsworth explained his mission and said that he was pleased to have the honor of uniting Miss Tilly and me in the holy bonds of wedlock. I felt like knocking him down and thrashing some others. Looking around for my friend, the captain, I found he was not there. I asked Miss Tilly who had encouraged her to carry out this deception. She stated that Captain Blanchard had come to her about a month ago; had told her I was anxious to marry her and that he had given her money to purchase her wedding clothes; that although she thought it strange I had said nothing to her about the matter, the captain assured her that I was in earnest, but being bashful, had delegated the whole thing to him. Tilly did not take the joke as seriously as I did. The affair ended by a theater party that evening at my expense.

I had become a member of the Chicago Board of Trade but did not confine my operations exclusively to articles dealt in by that body. I would buy and sell anything I saw a margin of profit in, not as a plunger but in a conservative manner. The market on staples, such as wheat, corn, oats, high wines, provisions, etc., had been almost a continual bull market and it was almost impossible to lose money on that side of the market. Everything pointed to the defeat of the Southern cause and I trimmed the sails of my little barque accordingly. I had cleaned up some fifteen thousand dollars in my few months' operation when some of my friends encouraged me to buy an interest in a vessel known as the "Western Metropolis," at that time engaged in the grain carrying business from Chicago to Buffalo. Unfortunately, shortly before Thanksgiving Day in 1864, she was wrecked near Pine Station on the Lake some twenty-two miles from Chicago. The cargo, like the vessel, was partially insured I was delegated as a committee of one to visit the wreck and report on it. This I did, or tried to do. Leaving Chicago very early on Thanksgiving Day I got the conductor of the train to let me off at Pine Station, which was nothing but a siding used as a flag station. After wandering around for some time I came across a young man who offered to pilot me to the wrecked vessel, which I found some three miles from the siding, lying near the shore, keel in, in some fifteen to twenty feet of water. Though the keel and exposed side had not been damaged greatly, it was evident from the wreckage strewn along the shore that the vessel had encountered a bad storm and was breaking up. With the assistance of the young man, who was anxious to accompany me, I succeeded in getting the top of the cabin, which lay on the beach, afloat. We picked up an oar and were soon floating from shore toward the wreck assisted by an off shore breeze. The waves beat over our little craft which commenced sinking. The young man became excited when the water came up to our knees. I told him to jump and pull for shore. He said he could not swim. We were then in over six feet of water and every minute getting deeper. Something had to be done and done quickly so I pushed him off and jumped in after him. He fought me hard and came near putting me under. Luckily I had taken off my overcoat and left it on shore, otherwise I think he would have drowned me. I finally caught him by the tail of his coat and pulled him ashore, where he started on a brisk run for home, I suppose, since he quickly disappeared in the brush. I put on my overcoat and walked around all day, hoping to find a house, but I did not. Several trains passed on the siding headed for Chicago, but it was nearly eleven o'clock that night before I got aboard one. I was still in my wet clothes when I arrived in Chicago, the result being that I took a severe cold, pneumonia set in and for over a month I was confined to my room under the care of two doctors and nurses. It was some two weeks before the doctors gave any encouragement that I was not booked for that unknown country "from whose bourn no traveler returns." But thanks to the doctors, nurses, my landlady (Mrs. Dunham) and to that good, Christian, ministering angel, Miss Percy, I pulled through. May God always bless and reward these good people for their kindness to me. My report of the wreck was not only delayed but was not a very complete one when I made it.

CHAPTER VIII

*Strenuous Times—Lee's Surrender to Grant—Assassination of
President Lincoln—I Attend Lincoln's Funeral*

CHICAGO was a hotbed of secession and many apparently respectable citizens, both men and women, some innocent, were marched off to the provost office to give an account of their actions and, if guilty, were taken to Camp Douglas, where a drum head court-martial was constantly in session passing on such cases. If found guilty, the poor fellow's soul would be before his Master before sunset. Spies, both Southern and Northern, were everywhere. It was dangerous to express ideas of the progress of the war. It was common to see a man shot down on the street. The greatest orators were engaged nightly to talk to enthusiastic audiences in the halls, theaters and churches, firing the hearts and passions of the people, advocating the Union cause and condemning slavery. Often a general right from the front would be persuaded to tell how "he did it." I had the pleasure of listening to a fiery talk by General "Fighting Joe" Hooker. Bands of music were playing war songs. The Lombard Brothers were singing them, the people joining in the chorus. All were worked up into a fever heat. These were some of the greatest scenes I ever witnessed. I shall never forget them. The war governors of the different Northern states would often visit Chicago. That great, noted, loyal citizen, John Wentworth, with his burning eloquence, could set an audience wild if he only stood on his feet. He was over six feet six inches tall and weighed nearly three hundred and fifty pounds. Henry Ward Beecher and many other noted orators of the Union's cause and the condemnation of slavery, always drew large audiences. Lee had surrendered to Grant. The streets were a blaze of light. Flags were flying everywhere. Crowds of people on the streets, in the theaters and hotels, were shouting themselves hoarse. Bands of music were numerous on the streets and one was in the Tremont Hotel where I happened to be. Cannon thundered the glad tidings from the garrison at Fort Douglas and from the Lake Front.

Yes, it was victory for the North, but what of the poor South? One-half of its manhood was in Southern graves and hospitals or in Northern prisons—its women and children starving—homes destroyed and farms ruined. These sad thoughts going through my mind made me sick as I sat or mingled in the jostling crowd in the Tremont Hotel. The Tremont Hotel was alive with people. Men in different groups were discussing the end of the war and the future of the South. Some fiery, hotheaded politicians wanted to wipe the last Rebel, his family and all his belongings off the face of the earth; but Lincoln—the patriot, the friend of the conquered South—desirous of making a united country again out of the fragments remaining, still lived and victory would be tempered with mercy. I had been in the hotel but a short time when word was flashed over the wire in the hotel that President Lincoln had been assassinated. I jumped up from my seat and joined the surging mass of men. Officers, soldiers and citizens were united in condemning the cowardly act, and yet there were some Copperheads in that crowd who were glad the deed was done. I heard one so express him-self. He made the remark that he was d—d glad of it, when an army officer, a colonel, hearing the man's remark, drew his revolver and sent a ball between the man's eyes. The man fell dead at our feet. General Sherman truthfully said that "war is hell." The Southern people as a whole condemned this assassination as bitterly as the Northern people. They knew that in Lincoln's death they had lost their best friend. What a change the next day! Flags half mast everywhere— stores, business houses and residences all draped in black! In halls and churches the following Sunday thousands con- gregated and listened to eloquent speakers and ministers who condemned the dastardly murder of the noble Lincoln. Grief and sadness were on every face. Even the would-be Copperhead had discovered he had lost a true friend in Lincoln. This manifestation of grief continued until the remains arrived in Chicago where the body lay in state. Thousands viewed it before being taken to Springfield, to which place, as a member of the Chicago Board of Trade, I accompanied it. I remember paying $175.00 for a suit of clothes to wear on this sad occasion. I could fill many pages should I attempt to chronicle one-tenth of what I saw and heard during these dark days of American history.

CHAPTER IX

Nothing Ventured, Nothing Gained—A Terrific Storm at Sea—My Small Fortune Cast upon the Waters—Heavy Hearted but Willing to Begin Again

WHILE I had been doing very well in Chicago, nearing the fall of 1865 I learned from what I considered a reliable source that a certain line of merchandise was in great demand in New Orleans. Acting on this information I closed up my business in Chicago and after securing letters of introduction and recommendations to some business firms in New York and New Orleans, I started for the former city, where I purchased my goods and on Saturday in the latter part of October, I embarked with them on the steamship "Victor" bound for New Orleans. Many of my goods arrived on board late, where I stored them on deck and covered them with tarpaulins and tied them down with ropes fastened to iron rings in the deck. While heaving anchor and feeling our way through the many vessels, preparatory to our course down the river, I noticed the freight hatchways were being well calked and things placed in quick readiness for a rough voyage, it being October, when sometimes equinoctial storms get busy and cause more or less anxiety to those who go down to the sea in ships. Though quite a few of the some two hundred passengers became seasick during Saturday and Sunday, on the whole we were a happy family on such a short acquaintance until Monday night when we were rounding Cape Hatteras. A monster black cloud commenced to show itself on the horizon. This finally lost itself in fog, rain and wind which for a time came in great gusts, the rain falling in sheets. The darkness was intense except for the continual flashes of lightning. The increasing wind was whipping the sea into huge waves which dashed against the sides and over our ship without mercy. There was one young man who, more forcible than polite, had expressed a wish to run into a storm. His every word was accompanied by an oath and he hoped we would see a d—d good storm.

It was nearly ten o'clock P. M. I was the only one left of a number of passengers who had been entertaining each other in the smoking room, which was located amidships on the deck of the "Victor." I lay communing with my thoughts, thinking of the dear ones at home. All my earthly possessions were aboard this ship with not one dollar's worth of insurance on them—just one thin plank between me and the bottom of the sea. I did not know one soul on board, neither had I any friends or relatives in New Orleans, should I get there, and I must confess that I felt blue but not entirely discouraged or forsaken. I knew that the same God who had watched over me and cared for me always would not forsake me. While occupied with these thoughts, I was suddenly pushed off the top of the table where I lay and thrown against the opposite door, which was burst open by the force of a wave which nearly washed me overboard. For a time I was nearly strangled by the salt water. As soon as I could gather myself together I groped my way to the hatchway of the cabin, which I finally found, concluding it to be a safer place than on that smoking room table. I finally tumbled into my berth but not to sleep.

By this time the wind was blowing a hurricane. The lightning was terrific and the thunder almost deafening. The sea at times would dash against the sides and over our ship with such force that every timber in her would shake like a leaf, the rain still coming down in torrents. At intervals the ship would be thrown with such violent force into the trough of the sea that it made us at times think we had been sent to the bottom, when there would come the sensation of rising with the crest of the waves to be again hurled to the bottom, making every beam in the ship tremble and quiver. What a night we spent! Some passengers weeping, some praying. The first sincere prayer offered up was by our young man who early in the evening had said he would like to see a d—d good storm. He was seeing and feeling it. I had made my peace with God and was reconciled to the worst that might befall us. Daylight on Tuesday morning came, but with it no let up in the fury of the storm. The deck over our heads had commenced to open through the center, and at intervals of every few minutes, when the waves would dash over our vessel, the sea water would pour through this opening so the passengers were saturated with salt water. During the day the partitions between the steerage and cabin passengers were torn loose and the freight commenced to shift with the motion of the vessel. Barrels of beef, lard, whiskey and boxes of merchandise were pitched and tossed around like chips and in order to be safe, passengers had to remain in their berths, where they stayed with some difficulty. Not one officer or any of the ship's crew had yet visited us, and we began to think we were abandoned to our fate. Sometime late Tuesday afternoon, for the purpose of getting a breath of fresh air, unknown to any of my fellow passengers, I had ascended the stairs leading to the deck where I soon pushed back the slide window under the skylight and found myself gazing on an awful scene. The rain was still falling. The clouds were black and rolling swiftly by and over us. The hurricane was still blowing and lashing the sea into huge waves of misty foam that dashed madly over our ship, evidently bent on smashing her to pieces and sending us to the bottom. Now and again the waves would sweep over our vessel from stem to stern, now riding the crest of a monster wave, then dashed with lightning rapidity into the trough of the sea with such force at times that it made us think we had been sent to the bed of the ocean never to rise again. The sight and feeling of this haunts me still. I had been cautiously working the sliding window backwards and forward, dodging approaching waves as they struck the bow of the ship, for some time, when I saw a monster wave coming towards me like an avalanche. The sight was grand, majestic and inspiring! I could not move when I came to my senses. I found several fellow passengers bending over me. I had been forced down the stairs by a deluge of water from that wave. My arm, shoulder and side were badly bruised in the fall and my fellow passengers gave me a severe scolding for attempting such a fool thing. It was estimated that nearly one thousand gallons of water had forced and accompanied me down the stairs.

Tuesday night was a miserable one for every soul aboard. My injuries were painful. Every hour in the black darkness seemed a day. Men, women and children were at times wrenched loose from their tight grips and thrown against the berths, barrels and boxes, some weeping, some praying, others crying from injuries received from shifting freight by continual rolling and pitching of the vessel, and shifting of broken timbers and partitions. There were twelve to fifteen inches of black, dirty, polluted sea water on a level in the cabins and every time the vessel would roll or pitch, this water followed it and not only drenched us from head to foot but at times nearly strangled us. All were hungry and famishing for a drink of pure water. Talk about the Black Hole of Calcutta! Could it be worse than this? To add to our terrors the force of the wave which struck our vessel amidships on Wednesday night smashed down every berth in the ship. Some passengers were caught in their berths and pinioned down by falling timbers and cried pitifully to be extricated. Some were screaming, weeping, praying, others moaning and a few, who had given up the fight for life, remained quiet. Words cannot paint this sad picture. To add to our fears and unbearable misery, some one later in the night cried, "Fire! Fire! Fire!" In an instant some of the stronger men without families were climbing over everything and everybody in eager haste to get to the stairs and out on deck. Luckily, the first mate, who stood lashed to the capstan near the head of the stairs, told the leaders there was no fire and to go below quickly or they would be washed overboard. What a night this was! I, and others there, will never forget it.

Daylight, Thursday morning, began to peep through the open seam in the deck, which was now widened to about six inches, through which kept pouring a stream of salt water whenever the ship would roll or pitch, thus increasing that which was already in our cabins. Shortly after daylight three of the ship's crew came down to us, but brought neither water nor food, and gave us no encouragement as to what would be our fate. They did condescend to release with ax and saw one poor fellow wedged in between two berths. We had tried to extricate him but in vain. The poor fellow was fatally injured internally. These three of the crew, in answer to our inquiries, told us that the ship was leaking, the boilers were adrift, the rudder chains broken and that we might as well prepare for the worst. They said we were somewhere in the Gulf of Mexico and on the line where some northern bound vessel might pick us up. They told us the rain had ceased, the wind was not so strong nor the sea so rough and if these favorable things continued we might be picked up yet if the vessel could be kept afloat. With these words of consolation they left us to our fate, admitting their inability to splice the broken rudder chain which they came down to fix.

The stench of our quarters was sickening. I had fully made up my mind that I would rather be washed overboard than suffocate in that dreadful hole, with women and children and some men begging and crying for something to eat and drink. We had had nothing since Monday night. I called for volunteers to assist me in getting food and water, if possible, for our fellow passengers, especially the women and children. Two Americans and a German responded and offered to go with me. We ascended the stairway and climbed on deck through the scullery hole. The sun was trying to peep out. The wind had ceased and the sea was growing calmer but at intervals of a few minutes a wave would break over the vessel, compelling us to hold on to ropes or bullrings in the deck to prevent being washed overboard. The deck of the "Victor" presented a fearful sight. One mast was left standing at an angle of about sixty degrees but split over half way up. The gaffs and spencers and much of the canvas and rigging had been carried away. The smoke and cook houses, water barrels, and apparently everything movable on the deck, including my freight that had been so securely wrapped and tied down, had also disappeared. The bulwarks of either side of the deck had been tied with heavy ropes in order to prevent the further opening of the seam in the deck. While contemplating this destruction I was startled by a voice yelling, "Hold fast there or you'll be washed overboard!" I was hanging on to a large ring in the deck when I was suddenly swung aside and buried for a time by a large body of water, which partially suffocated me and others. Thank God, though salty, the water was fresh and invigorating and made me feel like a new man. My companions had held on to some guy ropes and came out of their salt water bath better and cleaner, like myself, than when they went into it. After some time spent in dodging passing waves, we finally reached the scullery hole where the ship's steward kept the food. We could not find him. Some one told us he had been washed overboard. We found some crackers and raw ham, all more or less soaked with salt water. These after a time we got down to our fellow passengers, who grabbed and ate them like a pack of hungry wolves. Oh, for a drink of pure water! "Water, water everywhere, but not a drop to drink!" We (the two Americans, the German and two other passengers apparently Southerners) returned on deck. We found Captain Gates, like some of his officers and nearly all of the crew, drunk. We found the ship's surgeon and finally persuaded him to go below and try to do something for the injured passenger and those who were sick. The crew was busy in its maudlin way, throwing freight overboard. When they came to a basket of wine or barrel of whiskey they would break the necks off some of the bottles and knock the head of the barrel in and after drinking what they could, would heave the rest overboard with a long, wistful look. The captain was extremely profane and reeled as he walked. I do not see how he and others of his crew escaped going overboard. I heard the captain call over the railing to Chief Engineer Marcus and inquire what show there was to start the pumps, and what was the condition of things in the furnace room. The engineer answered that he was trying his best to fix the pumps and could get them started if he had men to work them; that the ship was leaking; that the boilers were adrift and moved with every motion of the ship; and that the water was up to the fire holes. At this news the captain threw up his hands and exclaimed excitedly, "My God! My God! We are lost!" and immediately gave orders to the second mate, who was about the only sober officer on the vessel, to prepare to launch the boats. I tendered my services, as also did my companions, but the captain answered excitedly that it was every man for himself and yelled the order, "Launch the boats." Not an officer or sailor obeyed the order. There were only five boats, including the captain's gig, not enough to carry all the passengers, to say nothing of the crew, the majority of whom by this time were so dead drunk they were oblivious to danger. The men ignored all the captain's orders and some told him to launch the boats himself. The second mate set us to work making boat pegs, etc., and while getting the boats ready, told the captain that the boats would be dashed to pieces before they could clear the ship. Such was the impression of all sober, intelligent people on board. Even the drunken sailors expressed a determination to stay by the ship as long as she could float. Hawsers had been stretched across the deck to prevent further opening and to hold the ship together. Had this not been done the ship would have been split in two with the pressure of the two thirty-ton boilers and coal in the bunkers sweeping from side to side and pitching endwise with every motion of the vessel.

When the captain gave orders to launch the boats, ending with the remark, "It's every man for himself," many of the passengers who had followed us on deck commenced to seize life preservers. I remember one especially, a minister of the Gospel from the state of Mississippi, who put on several, including one on each leg. If I should ever be called upon to paint or describe a picture of despair, I would have this reverend gentleman in my mind's eye. He appealed to me pitifully to go down in the hold of the ship and get some valuable papers out of a trunk he had there. I respectfully declined, although he offered me big pay. I had lost everything except one leather trunk in which I had some papers, bills of the merchandise I had purchased, some recommendations, letters of introduction, and the suit of clothes for which I paid $175.00 to wear at President Lincoln's funeral. I had made my peace with God and was not afraid to die. But that poor minister—I pitied him. I did not even put on a life preserver. I felt that if I had to go a life preserver would not save me.

Some time about noon the chief engineer signalled that he had the pumps fixed and ready for work but no sailors to man them. I told the captain I could pick out sixteen passengers and I would agree to keep those pumps going every moment if necessary. He told me to select the men and keep the pumps working and that I could promise the men I hired $5.00 per hour for every hour they worked the pumps and that I would receive double that amount for my services. In less than twenty minutes I had the men and the pumps going at full speed. It was anything but a desirable place down in the hold of that ship, standing in over two feet of black water covered with a heavy coat of oil when the ship was still, but when rocking or pitching the water sometimes went over our heads, nearly blinding and suffocating us. The coal in the bunkers, like the boilers, moved with every motion of the ship. Most of the sailors were still occupied with throwing freight overboard except when it came to liquor, when they would save what they could of that by drinking it.

One happy sailor, tired of his duties, sat down in the corner between the ship's sides and the coal bunkers and sang, "By the soft silver light of the moon." At times he would have difficulty in finishing a verse and even a line on account of the pitching and rolling of the vessel that sent the black, inky coal dust and oily water into his mouth, ears, nose and eyes. This would often choke him for a time but we could always depend on his finishing the line or verse after ridding himself of the inky and oily water. Such a comical scene, may have tended to lighten the terrors of the dismal hole in which we were working the pumps. It was not the dirty water in the hold alone that continued to saturate us with every movement of the vessel, but it was also the sea water, which, though salty, was clean, that poured down on our heads from twenty feet above us, that we had to contend with. It was now Thursday afternoon. We had gained on the water a little. The second mate, holding a signal of distress, had lashed himself to the only mast standing.

Friday morning dawned. The sun came out bright. The sea was much calmer. We had lowered the water nearly two inches since starting the pumps. I was working the men in eight-hour spells. While I felt weak from lack of food and thought I would have to give up, yet the thought of saving our lives until some friendly vessel would pick us up gave me and a few others courage to continue the struggle.

About ten o'clock in the morning our mate on the lookout called out, "Ship Ahoy." Some of my pumpers left their positions and climbed on deck to see the ship but it could not be seen with the naked eye and it did not see us. Some wreckage floated by us—one piece of a vessel indicated that it was what was left of the "Jesse Reeves." The warm water and current told us we were in the Gulf of Mexico and in the route of northern bound vessels. Even the drunken sailors began to show themselves when they heard the glad words, "Ship Ahoy." They had defied the captain's commands to launch the boats, declaring they would stay by the "Victor" until it went down. The captain was much put out at this defiance of his authority and threatened to shoot some of the sailors on sight. About two o'clock in the afternoon the man at the mast shouted again "Ship Ahoy." It was nearly an hour later before it could be seen from the deck with the naked eye. It finally saw us and steered toward us. Oh, the relief from the long suspense! The joy of being rescued!

Passengers, captain, officers and sailors all shouted and cheered as the merchantman hove near us. The vessel turned out to be the "Alabama"—not the pirate, but one bearing the same name, loaded with cotton from New Orleans to New York. Our captain, who was getting a little sober, asked the captain of the "Alabama" where we were. This answered, our captain offered the captain of the "Alabama" $35,000.00 to tow us into the nearest port, which was Fortress Monroe. The offer was accepted and before dark many of the "Victor's" passengers had been transferred. The captain, officers, crew, and what passengers there were on the "Alabama" treated us with the greatest kindness, giving us food, water and some change of clothing. It was hard to tell whether we, who had been working the pumps in that frightful hole, were colored or white men, and no wonder. A few people on the "Alabama" did not warm up to us as they did to the other passengers until they found out what we had done. In short, we had saved the "Victor" from going to the bottom of the sea. Captain Gates admitted this and in giving me the order on Livingstone & Fox, the agents of the "Victor" in New York, for payment of the men and myself, he was profuse in his thanks for what we had done.

It was but a short trip from Fortress Monroe to New York, and on presenting the captain's order to the agents they declined to honor it, giving the excuse that in doing what we had we had only tried to save our own lives and property. For a time it looked as though we would be kicked out of the office or put in jail. I told them that for my own part I did not care whether they paid me or not, but that I should insist on the sixteen men being paid the amount stated in the order. I told the agents they could think the matter over and that we would call on them at ten o'clock in the morning, which we did. The agents still thought we were not entitled to the pay, when I plainly told Mr. Livingstone that it was true we were saving our lives and property in working those pumps, that we possibly saved the ship also, that the captain and nearly all the crew were drunk, and that if the order were not paid by noon I would, if possible, prevent them from getting one dollar's worth of insurance. This plain language set them to thinking and thinking hard, for before noon they had called me into their private office, and the amount due each man was paid him and his passage money refunded or he was given another pass on their next steamer. I was treated with the greatest consideration, the amount due me was paid cheerfully and I was offered a first-class cabin passage in the next steamer leaving for New Orleans. This latter I declined. This company's best steamer, the "Atlanta," had been wrecked in a gale on its passage to New Orleans a few weeks before and over one hundred passengers had been drowned on account of lack of boats.

I remained in New York a short time resting from the terrible ordeal I had passed through. Remember, dear reader, I had lost nearly every dollar I had in the world. I had not insured my goods as I ought to have done. I thought if I got through safely the goods would also. But no matter. I was young, unencumbered and willing to try again. I had escaped with my life and I felt confident that I would win in the end, if grit, energy, honesty and perseverance would bring me success. I could have received assistance from home or possibly from friends in Chicago had I appealed to either, but I would not. I determined to make the trip to New Orleans and if possible recuperate my lost, little fortune.

CHAPTER X

Re-embark for New Orleans—Homeless, Starving and no Work—War Prices—Employment at Last

IT was near the 20th of November, 1865, when I stepped aboard the "Morning Star" destined for New Orleans. My belongings consisted of the leather trunk containing the suit of clothes worn at President Lincoln's funeral, a few other things, a few letters of introduction and recommendations, all more or less water logged, a silk umbrella and a plug hat. I had a few dollars left after paying my passage money. I tried to make some plans for the future but had nothing to build on but hope.

After an uneventful trip I arrived at New Orleans. The ravages and effects of civil war were plainly seen in every part of the Crescent City. Hundreds of discharged soldiers from both armies were drifting into the city daily. I saw some business chances if I only had had the money to take advantage of them. I visited many of the stores and business houses, seeking employment, but failed to secure it. A few inquired if I had been in the Southern army. When I answered "no," I was quickly told they could not help me.

I was rooming and boarding at a house on Tchoupitoulas street kept by a widow lady, who reminded me kindly one morning that my board and room rent was due. I gave her all the money I had and my silk umbrella, requested permission to leave my leather trunk with her and stepped out into the cold, cruel world. That day and other succeeding ones I went from place to place trying to secure employment, yes, and something to satisfy hunger, but I met with no success as to getting employment and with but little encouragement in getting something to eat. I was ashamed to beg and would not steal. I was willing to work for my board, but this was denied me. Starvation stared me in the face. I slept wherever I could, sometimes on or between the bales of cotton piled up on the levee. Many nights I slept on the planks forming the paddle wheels of the steamers and vessels lying along the river banks. Sometimes, when on an angle of forty-five degrees, I inwardly hoped that before morning I would unconsciously roll off and thus end my despair in the river, but I could not. Why? Should I write home or to friends to help me? No! A thousand times no!! I knew the comment would be, "I told you so." If I had to die this way, none should know how I had suffered from hunger and starvation in my adopted country. Some days I got one meal, some days more. I came across others suffering similar hardships. Why should I complain?

I was wearing, during my vain search for work, the (dress) suit of clothes I wore at Lincoln's funeral and that plug hat. Neither recommended me as a working man. I determined to change these, and entered a Jew store near the French market, picked out a blue flannel shirt, a pair of pants and soft hat and asked the Jew what he would give me to boot. He said he had no use for that hat and that kind of a suit, but to help me out he would give me $1.50. I accepted the bonus and changed clothes in the rear part of the store. This done I went over to the French market and bought a biscuit and a cup of coffee at an expense of $1.00. I had fifty cents left. After this elaborate meal I went down to the levee, and among the bales of cotton I rubbed some dirt on my hands, neck and face (I had tried to keep clean by frequent washing in the river), to make myself look like a working man. This done I picked up a stick, got on top of a pile of cotton, stood the stick up and let it fall, noting its course. This course, leading up the river, I followed, hoping it would bring me luck. I went aboard every boat. I did not secure employment, but I got a square meal on one of them, and that night I slept on the bales of cotton covered by the canopy of heaven.

I attach here a list of prices that prevailed at this time and you can imagine how far the fifty cents I had left would go. The following is taken from a newspaper clipping:

PRICES DOWN SOUTH DURING WAR

Quinine was $1,700 an Ounce and Flour $300 a Barrel

In 1865 an ounce of quinine could not be purchased for less than $1,700 in the South. Provisions were simply enormous in price. Here are just a few instances: A ham weighing fifty pounds sold for exactly $750, or at the rate of $5 a pound. Flour was $300 a barrel.

Fresh fish retailed all over at $5 a pound and ordinary meal was at $50 a bushel. Those who lived in boarding houses paid from $200 to $300 a month. White beans retailed at $75 a bushel. Tea went for anything from $20 a pound to $60 and coffee in like ratio.

The most ordinary brown sugar was sold for $10 a pound. Ordinary adamantine candles were sold for $10 a pound. In a cafe breakfast was ordinarily $10. In April sugar went to $900 a barrel and articles of wearing apparel sold, coats at $350, trousers at $100 and boots at $250.

Butter was $15 a pound. Potatoes went for $2 a quart. Tomatoes of the size of a walnut sold for $20 a dozen. Chickens varied from $35 to $50 a pair.

The prices on the bill of fare of the Richmond restaurant in January, 1864, were: Soup, $1.50; bread and butter, $1.50; roast beef, a plate, $3; boiled eggs, $2; ham and eggs, $3.50; rock fish, a plate, $5; fried oysters, a plate, $5; raw oysters, $3; fresh milk, a glass, $2; coffee, a cup, $2; tea, a cup, $2. ·

These figures are taken from various sources and have the virtue of accuracy, if nothing else. Always was present the fear of famine, and time and time again did the soldiers donate a portion of their rations, taken from their apportionment in the field, to relieve the pressing necessities.

The shrinkage of the currency was, of course, responsible, and some idea may be gathered from a story that went the rounds at the time. A soldier galloped along the country road and a farmer leaning over a fence admired the animal. He called to the trooper, offering to buy the horse:

"Give you $30,000 for him, Johnny," he said.

"Not much, old man, I just paid $15,000 to have him shod," was the reply.—*Spare Moments.*

What had I done to merit this punishment? Why had God forsaken me—He who cares for the birds? How much longer could I stand this? No home, no shelter, nothing to eat, without friends—no wonder I was becoming discouraged. My usually strong, healthy body had become weak. I almost reeled as I walked. Life was becoming daily and hourly a burden. Often when near the river I would look at it wistfully and murmur to myself that very soon it would be my haven of rest. These sad days had grown into weeks when on Saturday, while passing a saloon on the levee front, I entered it and began looking at some newspapers lying on a table near the door. I picked up one, the New Orleans Picayune, and read over its want columns, where my eyes fell on an advertisement which read: "Wanted:—One thousand men to work on the levee. Apply at No. — — Canal St. next

Wednesday at 9:00 o'clock A. M." I could scarcely believe this good news and read it again. Yes, it was true and no doubt I could get work, but how could I live until Wednesday and would I be able to do this work? That night I went to sleep on the bales of cotton, feeling happier though supperless. I thanked Him who cares for the unfortunate and knew He would not make my burden heavier than I could bear.

I had begged three meals in the interval between Saturday and Wednesday morning when I joined the motley crowd standing around the address given on Canal street. Most of them were laboring men. Some were drunk, some sober, some hard lookers like myself, but none more frail. Some were wearing the blue, but many were wearing the gray, and some were genuine levee men. All seemed to pass the good-natured Irish foreman at the window who looked them over, asked their names, which he wrote down, and told them to be at a certain levee at seven o'clock the next Saturday morning. One good-natured, broad-shouldered fellow, pointing to me, asked some comrades what they thought I wanted to do. "Oh, I suppose he wants to work on the levee," was an answer. Another remarked that it would not take much ice to keep me from spoiling if I died. While waiting my turn at the window I heard many other remarks referring to my physical condition, which caused me to lag back and lose my turn, preferring to wait until the last, when I mustered up courage to present myself at the window and ask whether he could not give me something to do; that I was willing to do anything at any price he might want to pay; that I had been unfortunate, having lost everything I had by a late shipwreck in the Gulf of Mexico, and that I was actually starving. With tears rolling down my cheeks I begged him to help me by giving me a chance. After looking at me carefully a few moments he asked my name and told me I could go along if I got to the boat in time but thought I would not be of much use. I need not say that I was on that boat early Saturday morning and was not ashamed to visit the cook-house where the cook gave me a large plateful of food and when I went back for another he asked me if I had thrown it overboard. I told him I had not and that I might come back for a third, as the food tasted so good.

After satisfying my poor, hungry stomach I lay down on the deck near the boilers and did not wake up until dark when I found the boat was being rushed up the Mississippi as fast as steam could send her. Our captain was racing with another boat, which at times would be almost alongside our craft, when our stokers would throw chunks of tar, bacon and rosin in the fire boxes and the old boat would almost heave itself out of the water in breasting the swift, heavy current. This was kept up the greater part of the night or until we left our competitor a long distance behind. At daylight it could not be seen.

We finally arrived at our destination, Morganzie, in the bend at the mouth of the Red River, where we disembarked to build a levee five miles long, one hundred feet base, thirty feet high and twelve feet at the top. The work was undertaken by the State of Louisiana.

CHAPTER XI

ARRIVING at Morganzie we found many shacks north of the Red River and south of the Mississippi River that General Banks had built for his negro troops on his Red River expedition. These were very convenient for our men, who numbered nearly seven hundred. I did not secure a shanty. I had no bedding; why did I need a shanty? There might have been others like me but I did not see them. I walked back to the point on the river where we landed, but the boat had returned to New Orleans. Finding no place to sleep, I followed the river bank north a quarter of a mile or more, where I was stopped by a bayou jutting out from the river. Here I lay down and slept the sleep of the just.

This had been my resting place for several nights when one evening, shortly after supper, I fell into conversation with a young man named Hunter, from Ohio. Like myself, he had seen better days. We talked on various subjects and when it came time to part he asked me where I slept. I told him a short distance up the river; that if he had no objections he could go with me and I would show him and it might be we could share the quarters together. I thought I had nothing to lose on the proposition. It was getting dark by the time we arrived at the bayou. Hunter had already asked where I was taking him, when I stopped and told him that the wallow in the ground at our feet was my bed and my pillow a small stick of wood which I had covered with moss and grass. This wallow, scraped down the better to fit the projecting bones of my emaciated body, made it not the worst kind of a bed. One thing, I was out of reach of drunken, foul-mouthed companions, many of whom, especially the Southerners, did not know that the war was ended and went around with a chip on each shoulder, daring any Yankee to knock it off. When I told Hunter that this had been my sleeping place, he could hardly believe it and remarked it was a wonder I was living.

As yet I had felt no bad effects, except that my clothes failed to dry on me on cloudy days. Some mornings I could wring the water out of them, owing to heavy dews that fell during the nights. This was probably the latter part of December, 1865. I had seen happier Christmas days than this one. One night as I lay there, shivering with cold, a large alligator struck the side of my head with his tail, making me dizzy for a time and spoiled my rest for the balance of the night. Until this happened I had slept peacefully in the open. The thought had flashed through my mind, "What if one of these ugly monsters should take a notion to bite off a leg or an arm?" But this could not happen. God was my protector and would keep me from harm. It did not take much coaxing by my new found friend, Hunter, to persuade me to accompany him to his fairly decent shanty, through the roof of which we could see daylight and the stars at night, and share his bunk, which was supplied with two pairs of blankets. It is unnecessary to state that I had a good refreshing sleep that night, feeling as though I were in a palatial residence instead of in a clapboard shanty eight by ten.

It was some ten days after our arrival that the wheelbarrows, planks, spades and shovels arrived for the work of building the levee. During this time I had learned much about my fellow workers, both the whites (termed Yanks and Rebs) and some one hundred or more negroes who had come more to be fed and cared for than to work. The Yanks and Rebs, as the soldiers of the North and the South were designated, were continually fighting. They were about evenly matched in numbers. The Yanks would constantly remind the Rebs that they had been whipped. This the Rebs would deny, when both sides would go at it again. The negroes would, as a rule, take sides with the strongest in number if the fight were easy. If the fight were fierce the colored men would take to the brush. We would often be called upon to bury one or more after these fights and send a few to the hospital.

A "jigger" of whiskey was rationed out four to six times a day to those who would drink it—one before breakfast, one about ten o'clock in the morning, one before dinner, one about three o'clock in the afternoon and another before supper—and an old "soak" could get one before he turned into his bunk. Very often these "sots" would get three drinks before breakfast by fooling the "jigger" boy. It was amusing to watch these men where they slept in the large bunk house. I watched one roll out of his bunk and go to the "jigger" boy in his undershirt and drawers. A few seconds later he came again, after having added his hat to his costume. He came next with his hat off but with his pants and overshirt on. Shortly he came back, completely dressed, and drank his fourth "jigger," but did not appear very drunk. By the time he sat down to breakfast he became noisy and wanted to lick somebody. He was accommodated and could not work that day.

It was a common thing to see cups of hot coffee and plates of soup flying through the air at different heads. Nearly every man carried a dirk, if not a revolver. The dirk knife was the most popular. A thrust and a groan and all was over in almost an instant. The soul went to its Maker.

I well remember the day the work commenced, when we started out with our wheelbarrows and shovels from camp, the planks having been taken out ahead by team. By the time I arrived at the work I could keep my barrow going straight ahead instead of in a zigzag direction as when starting. The planks were laid in lines fifteen to twenty feet apart and fifty to seventy-five feet in length. An expert at loading wheelbarrows was at the lead of the fifteen to twenty men with barrows behind him. This lead man was paid extra and when he said, "All aboard," we were all supposed to be ready with loaded wheelbarrows to follow him. Well do I remember my hard efforts to fill and navigate that wheelbarrow on that plank. I was unaccustomed to the work. I fell off more than once. I had not noticed that I was wheeling much more dirt than many of the others. I would bat my shovelful down while the expert leveeman would pile his up edgewise and with eight shovelfuls would fill his barrow. I would put in twelve. No wonder I felt faint before ten o'clock. Large drops of sweat were running down my face. Big water blisters were on my hands. When the "jigger" boy approached me with a small tin cupful of whiskey I declined it, but Hunter, who was behind me, insisted that I drink it. After some hesitation I drank it. I soon felt its effects and the only wonder in my mind was why the contractors wanted to work such a large force of men on a small job like this. Why, it seemed that I could build that levee myself in a short time. Such were my thoughts while under the influence of the liquor. This buoyant feeling, however, soon vanished.

It was nearly noon when Mr. O'Hay, one of the contractors (the Southerner), came along examining the work we were doing. He had stood watching the gang of men on our plank. I was conscious that he was watching me. Coming up near where I was filling my wheelbarrow, a rather pleasant, kindly voice remarked that the work seemed to be a little hard for me and asked if I had ever done such work before. I told him I had not but that I either had to do it or starve; that I had been shipwrecked in the Gulf of Mexico and lost all I had except a few letters of recommendation. He asked what I had been accustomed to do. I told him, intimating that I could do clerical work but was anxious to do anything. He told me to bring my recommendations to his office after dinner and he would look them over. I did so and that afternoon I was made purchasing agent for the camp.

CHAPTER XII

*Experiences as Purchasing Agent—Frazell Kills O'Hay—Floods
Break the Levee—Freight Checker on a River Boat*

I WAS fast resuming my normal condition and although
my position was an improvement on what I had been
doing and the dark clouds that had hung around me were
beginning to disappear, yet I made up my mind to get away
from this work and these demoralizing associations as soon
as I could. Mr. O'Hay gave me full instructions as to my
new duties. I was to purchase certain lines of provisions at
the lowest possible prices, either at New Orleans or from
nearby planters, and to take proper bills for everything I
purchased, these to be receipted when I paid for them. A
sum of money was placed to my credit in one of the
New Orleans banks for this purpose. I was getting along
nicely and giving satisfaction to my employers and, with the
exception of the daily fights at the camp as to "whether the
war was over," the work was progressing as well as could be
expected. It was no unusual thing to see the cooks cleaned
out of the kitchen, the waiters on the tables and bosses off the
dumps two or three times a week. This was tolerated. The
only question was to keep the work moving, as the river was
rising rapidly and levees about us were reported to be weakening. Before the first of February it was reported that some
levees had gone out. One some twenty miles above us, it
was claimed, might go out at any time.

One morning the sad news reached camp that Frazell had
killed O'Hay in a quarrel in the St. Charles Hotel saloon
in New Orleans. On receipt of this news our camp became
a scene of bloodshed. All work stopped. The men demanded their pay. The bosses could not control them. The
Southerners swore they would kill every Yankee in camp,
threatened to burn all the buildings and throw the wheelbarrows, planks and shovels into the Mississippi. Provisions
were getting low and it nearly cost me my life because I

gave the men soup for breakfast instead of coffee. I re-member riding several miles one night to a planter's house to get coffee, sugar, syrup and beef from him. I told him if he did not help me I would have to abandon the work. The Governor of the state sent up the Attorney General, who made a speech to the men, telling them that the state would see them paid and that ample provisions would be sent us. Frazell was liberated under bond, but his presence in camp made the Southerners sulky and mean. More than one tried to kill him until they heard that the coroner's jury had justified Frazell's action in killing O'Hay.

News reached us that the levee a number of miles above our camp had burst in several places and that it would be only a question of a short time before we would be surrounded by water. Many men were sent up by first boat to repair these breaks. Thousands of sacks of sand, trees, etc., were thrown into these breaks but without effect. One might as well try to stop an ocean. The country around us was flooded for twenty miles and it became a serious question as to whether we could save ourselves, let alone any of the camp equipment. Every boat, going up or down the river, was signalled and the men and their belongings were either taken up or down the river, the majority of the men returning to New Orleans.

Mr. Frazell had treated me with the greatest kindness and begged me to go to Natchez with him. He even offered me a partnership with him, but I had been reading about the Placer gold mines in the Gallatin valley in Montana and I had made up my mind to go there. He left me standing on a knoll about two hundred yards square above the rushing waters around me, he going on a boat to New Orleans and promising to have the first boat he met call for me. One, the "Olive Branch," did so before dark. Had it not done so, the mound and this writer would have dis-appeared before morning in the "Father of Waters."

I went to St. Louis, arriving there about April 1, 1866. I found that overland trains of horses, mules and oxen would not leave Fort Leavenworth, St. Joseph or Nebraska City, the three principal outfitting points, before the middle of May. Having no money to burn and anxious to keep busy I hired out to the captain of the "Olive Branch" as freight checker for a trip to New Orleans. I did this for the purpose of bringing up the leather trunk I had left with my former landlady on Tchoupitoulas street. This trunk I secured, brought it up to St. Louis, took it across the plains with me, and kept it for many years, when finally I gave it to an old employee named Coleman.

This trip to New Orleans on a river steamer gave me a chance to observe life on a first-class steamboat on the Mississippi. Though the luxuries were nothing like they were before the war, yet it was a pleasant trip. The boat was crowded with passengers and freight. It carried its own band. I had plenty to do in keeping account of the freight received and discharged. At the same time I was always ready and willing to take the lead of a tow line when we had to make a landing. I did this at Cairo on our return and jumped into the river, holding the head of the line, thinking the river was about six feet deep. Instead it was about three feet deep, with two feet of very soft mud in which I stuck, with the boat fast coming onto me. The pilot saw my danger of being smoothed down under the boat and though he signalled the engineer to reverse the engine, this alone would not have saved me. However several stout deck hands lay down on the edge of the boat, grabbed me under the arms and pulled and dragged me on to the boat as it reached me. I did not do this fool trick any more.

We finally arrived at St. Louis where, after discharging our cargo, I resigned my position as freight checker. I remained in St. Louis several days and became acquainted with a Mr. Swank, formerly a lieutenant in an Ohio regiment. He had been shot in the face with a bullet and badly disfigured. I found him a good sort of a fellow who, like myself, had the Gallatin valley gold fever on the brain. We decided to double up and go there together. He had made one trip as bullwhacker over the Smoky Hill trail and this experience on his part proved quite a help to me later on.

CHAPTER XIII

Gallatin Valley Gold Fever—Destination Fourth Company Post
(Ft. Phil Kearny)—Nebraska City in the Early Days—
My Five Resolutions—Life as a Bullwhacker—
An Enemy—Mr. Bass

AFTER gathering all the information possible Swank and I concluded to take passage on boat to Nebraska City where it was said that some ox, mule and horse trains were to leave shortly with government freight for Fourth Company Post east of Fort C. F. Smith and northwest of Fort Reno. Our little "stern wheeler" got stuck several times en route up the Missouri River from St. Louis to Nebraska City. An old German inland sailor was taking the soundings on the bow of the boat and calling them out very regularly, when all at once he shouted, "Not very much vater here," and when our boat ground on a hidden sandbar, the old sailor yelled out, "Didn't I told you so?"

We arrived at Nebraska City, which had not yet given up the thought of becoming the terminal of the Union Pacific Railroad. Many horse, mule and ox teams were there, all busy getting their outfits together. Swank and the writer had no trouble in finding work. We hired out to a Mr. Bass, a big, rough, six-foot Missourian, a nephew of the owner of the twenty-eight six-yoke ox teams. Our pay was to be $45.00 per month and board and we were to take our discharge out at Fourth Company Post, our destination point. Mr. Bass agreed to arm each bullwhacker with gun and ammunition when we arrived at old Fort Kearny, better known as "Dobytown."

Nebraska City at this time was not a large place. There were a number of well-stocked stores on Main street, several forwarding warehouses, many saloons, dance houses and gambling dens. Everything was wide open, free and easy, like the bullwhackers, mule skinners and horse team drivers—

quite a different class of men to my late companions on the levee, these being more frank and generous. At the same time each carried a chip on his shoulder and perchance it were knocked off, an account for it would be called for very quickly. Nearly every man carried one or two revolvers on the well-filled belt of cartridges around his waist, besides a bowie knife sometimes stuck in his belt and sometimes stuck in the top of his high-legged boot.

The city marshal, a man of nerve, tried to keep order; but at times, toward midnight, crazed by drink, the men and sometimes the women would get too boisterous and too many for him and would run the town to suit themselves. At these times camp would be the best and safest place, since the fun would usually end in a killing. It was these wild scenes in the West and others that I had witnessed on the levee that caused me to adopt for my future guidance some resolutions: one that I would not drink; another that I would not gamble; a third that I would avoid swearing; a fourth that I would not smoke or use tobacco; fifth that I would try to be a good, moral man. I noticed many young men going down the road to destruction at a rapid rate and I determined to avoid this if possible.

I had rigged myself up in bullwhacker's garb—blue flannel shirt, pair of pants, belt, cartridges, revolver, bowie knife, pair of heavy boots, broad-brimmed hat, and an up-to-date bullwhacker's whip—three feet stock and twelve feet lash, with extra buckskin to repair the whip lash and make new poppers at the end of lash. With two pairs of blankets, a war sack (an empty seamless sack) and an old army over-coat, I was ready to accompany Swank and join the outfit, which was camped some three miles west of the city.

We arrived at camp shortly before noon and I was ordered by the assistant wagon boss to go out to the herd and relieve the herder. The herd was a mile or so west of camp. This herding was new to me and being afraid that some steers might stray away, I made it an unnecessarily hard task. But the work was not without interest. While tramp-

ing around the steers I imagined I could pick out friends
and enemies. These work cattle! Some had never seen a
yoke, let alone been worked. Part were native cattle, others
Cherokee and some Texas. When the two mounted night
herders came out about dusk to relieve me I thought I had
put in a faithful half day. I returned to camp but found it
deserted. Even my friend Swank had gone to the city. I
went through the cook wagon and tent, thinking I could find
something to eat but did not, so I spread my blankets under

Life as a Bullwhacker

the wagon, lay down and was soon fast asleep. The bullwhackers continued to come into camp until towards morning,
when one of the night herders rode in to wake the cook to
get breakfast. It consisted of coffee, syrup, fried bacon
between a thick pancake or thin pone of bread baked in a
covered skillet. The bread was made from flour and common
baking soda. The cook said the sugar had not come yet.

In the morning I was set to work with Swank making ox-
bow keys and fitting bows to yokes. I began to get acquainted
with my fellow bullwhackers. A few were good, some
medium and others very bad. Lack of enforcement of law
and order seemed to add to their meanness. The men ranged

in years from twenty to forty-five and as I seemed to be the only one in this crowd of about thirty-three men who did not drink, swear, play cards, smoke or chew tobacco, I was soon put down for a "goody-goody" or a fool for lacking these accomplishments. One remarked that my early education had been sadly neglected. I took these jokes good-naturedly.

On or about May 15, 1866, we broke camp and started on our perilous trip. We could not pick up a newspaper that did not have something in it about Indian depredations. Road ranches, stage stations, emigrant and freight trains, stage coaches and pony express riders were being attacked daily on the California and other trails. Red Cloud and other noted chiefs of the Sioux nation had been invited to a conference at Fort Laramie by the Indian commission. The Sioux nation at this time was not, as a nation, at war with the whites but the depredations were being committed by roving bands of Indians belonging to different tribes.

Each teamster, with a sixty-hundred loaded wagon, consisting of coffee, sugar, beans, flour, bacon, salt, crackers, condensed milk, syrup, desiccated vegetables, boots and shoes, etc., etc., was given six yoke of cattle. The wheelers and lead cattle were somewhat gentle but the four yoke of swing cattle were more or less wild, as this was the first time they had been yoked up. It took sometimes a dozen men— teamsters, wagon bosses and night herders—to get one team started. At times the wild swing cattle would start on a run or stampede, getting ahead of the leaders, when all we could do was to keep them in the trail. We upset two wagons and by the time night came we had made probably a mile. We dropped the chains from the yokes of the swing or wild cattle and unyoked the gentle cattle only. It took about ten to fifteen days before we controlled our wild cattle, but once broken they did good work.

I think we had made nearly sixty miles on our journey without my swearing, much to the disgust of my fellow bull-whackers, who often scolded me for not doing so, when one morning between three and four o'clock, while engaged in yoking up my team, one of my steers stepped on my foot and I am sorry to say I said "Damn you." It went through the camp in an instant and many of the men cheered and commended me highly for the start I had made and hoped I would keep it up. While my comrades were doing this and showering me with bouquets on this mild beginning, I was just as busy in the opposite direction, quietly asking God to forgive me and asking Him to keep me from it in the future.

The daily routine of a bullwhacker's life on the trail, while a hard one, was not all clouds. It had its sunshine. Each day's travel presented something new, as there always is in going through a new country. Each day's experience would make an interesting chapter if written. We would be awakened by the night herders about three to three-thirty A. M. with the call, "Cattle in the corral!" This meant for all to roll out and the night herders to turn in. It usually took from one-half to three-fourths of an hour to yoke up and commence moving on the trail, which we would follow about eight miles before breakfast, much depending on water and feed for the cattle. Our wagon boss or assistant usually would go ahead and locate these camping places which had to be selected with care, usually on high ground not too close to timber, brush, river or creeks, sudden hills or depressions in adjoining ground—all with a view to avoid being ambushed by Indians. We would try to make these morning camps between eight and nine-thirty, forming our wagons into a circle, the lead team to right forming left wing of corral —second team bowing out in forming right wing of corral, bringing the tongues of the two wagons within twenty feet of each other. The wagons would follow in their places— first to left, next to right and thus alternately, the off front wheel coming close to the nigh hind wheel of the wagon ahead and vice versa on the right hand wing of the train. After a little practice we could make these corrals almost perfect and by chaining the front and rear entrance, and any wagon wheels that did not come together snugly, we would have a solid corral in which to put our cattle and the night herders' and wagon bosses' horses in case of an Indian attack. The gaps all chained, the yokes belonging to each wagon were then put on the inside of the corral ready for the next yoke-up. The cattle were unyoked and taken by two herders—bullwhackers, in their proper term—to graze and water in the daytime, usually resting until about one to two P. M., when the steers were brought back into the corral and yoked up and another drive of about eight miles made before dark, two other bullwhackers taking charge of the work steers until the

Cattle and Wagon Corral

night herders had their supper, when they would take charge of the cattle until time to corral again the next morning.

The bullwhackers in camp, when there were no wheels to fix, tires to tighten, boxes to wedge, oxen to shoe, or clothes to wash or mend, could sleep, play cards, write letters or tell stories. The stories of one old bullwhacker who had seen much of frontier life were quite interesting. He would tell about the noted stage company boss, Jack Slade, who caught one of his stage tenders listening at a door and who whipped out his bowie knife and cut the listener's ear off, telling him if he ever caught him doing it again, he would cut his heart out—and hundreds of other such bloodthirsty stories. We had one bullwhacker in our train who had been scalped by the Indians near Fort Larnard. The Indians scalped him, stripped all his clothes off him, and to see whether he was dead, stuck sharp pointed arrows between his toes. We had another bullwhacker who carried several scars made by Indian arrows. But no matter—this is old. Maybe I will be given a chance to tell what we saw, which I expect to chronicle in this book, without coloring, just as it occurred.

All our men were strong and healthy, good shots and ready for any emergency, even to a fight with Indians. At this time had the writer been killed, it would have taken more ice to preserve his body than it would had he died in New Orleans about the time he hired out to work on the levee.

Some of the stage coaches we would meet coming from the West would show the hard knocks received—some with bullet holes in them and some with arrow heads broken off. Often the driver would come tearing along with four instead of six horses. Some coaches, beside having trunks and mail sacks piled high on the hind boot, would have six to ten passengers aboard, all well armed as well as the driver.

By the time we reached "Dobytown" (old Fort Kearny), even our wild cattle were becoming gentle so we could unyoke and give them a better chance to feed and rest.

In spite of all my sincere resolutions not to swear, I am sorry to say that sometimes when I got stuck in a mud hole or in heavy sand, I would find myself saying curse words before I realized it, when I would resolve again to stop it.

Arriving at "Dobytown" we learned much about Indian depredations. It was said that the Indians had burned every ranch between "Dobytown" and Fort McPherson and that all stage coaches, and emigrant and freight trains, coming or going, were being attacked. The troops at both posts were kept hot on the trail of the Indians in trying to protect people from being massacred on the trail over which we also had to go. Many of these depredations were being committed by the Sioux, but it was claimed that other tribes, Cheyennes especially, were aiding in these butcheries.

As stated, our wagon boss, before leaving Nebraska City, had agreed to furnish us guns and ammunition on arrival at

"Dobytown" but none had arrived. Five of us bullwhackers objected to proceeding farther without them. This made Mr. Bass very angry and he gave us to understand that he could get along without us and that we would receive no pay for work done. He said we were leaving because we could get more pay here at "Dobytown." True, we could get more pay but we all wanted to go to Fourth Company Post or farther. A firm by the name of Lydell & Brown kept a store at the place and Mr Lydell was Justice of the Peace, a very important officer on the frontier. To him I stated my case in the presence of Mr Bass and he told Mr Bass that if he did not furnish us each with a gun and ammunition as agreed at Nebraska City, we need not go with him and he would have to pay us for work done. This decision enraged him. He wired for guns and ammunition, which reached us in a few days, when, after coupling up with three other ox trains loaded with government freight and with Mr. Bass as captain, we pulled out for the west. Mr Bass gave it out cold that he would get even with us, especially with the writer.

I attach a brief history, taken from a newspaper, of this old Fort Kearny, formerly called Fort Childs.

Among the western forts established by the national government for the protection of settlers and travelers to the gold fields of the West, none had a more romantic history than did old Fort Kearny, which members of the Nebraska delegation are asking to have converted into a national park. Located near the geographical center of the country on the second bottom lands of the Platte river, on the direct route of the great caravan of gold-seekers for the Oregon country, the fort was the center of numerous encounters with the Indians as well as the rendezvous of hunters and scouts and other picturesque citizens of the west.

Fort Kearny was established under orders of Secretary of War Marcy, in 1848, by Captain Childs of the Missouri volunteers. He intended to establish the fort near the present city of Aurora, in Hamilton County, but decided on the Kearny location because of the advantage of Carson's Crossing of the Platte river, the fording of the Platte farther to the east being dangerous. Buildings at the fort were commenced on June 17, 1848, but on July 8, the Platte rose rapidly and swept away the buildings partially constructed. The troops then moved farther away from the river and continued the construction of the fort. Here the fort was eventually completed and its ruins lie there to-day with the trenches and embankments plainly showing on the prairie. The fort was named from its builder, Fort Childs.

In February, 1849, Childs was succeeded in command by Major Ruff of the Mounted Rifles, U. S. A., and soon after the name of the post was changed to Fort Kearny, Oregon Route. In 1854 the name was again changed to Fort Kearny, Nebraska Territory. It was named in honor of General Phil Kearny and was known as "New Fort Kearny" on account of the old fort at Nebraska City bearing the same name.

In 1849 Major Ruff was sent to establish Fort Laramie and was relieved of his command at Fort Kearny by Colonel Crittenden. He was succeeded by General Phil Kearny and, later, General Harney took command of the post.

Trees were set out and preparations were made to make the fort a permanent fixture on the prairies. Gradually the fortifications were strengthened and the fort was made one of great strength. During all the years of overland travel, the fort was the point at which travelers stopped to recruit. For years the Indians were peaceful but in 1864 the Sioux and Cheyenne Indians became hostile. The trouble arose because some owners of strayed oxen refused to pay a reward to the Indians who returned them. Receiving no reward, the Indians withdrew, taking the oxen with them. A detachment of soldiers was sent after them and a fight ensued in which many soldiers were killed. The Indians began in earnest to drive the whites back and they successfully carried out several massacres. Settlers became frightened and the fort was thronged with families fleeing from the redskins. For a short time all travel to the West was stopped at Fort Kearny. Then the travelers were organized into bands of from fifty to one hundred families, a captain being chosen for each, before they would be permitted to proceed.

Before proceeding on the trail I happened to be in the sutler's store where I picked up a "Harper's Monthly," which I asked Mr. Bass to purchase for me. He declined, remarking that he would give me something else to do besides reading that damned Yankee book. There was a gentleman in the store (I think it was Dr. Miller, later publisher of the Omaha Herald) who heard the talk between us. He asked if I wanted that "Harper's." I told him I did very much and he gave it to me. This kind act on Dr. Miller's part added fuel to the flame between Mr. Bass and myself. Some years later I met Dr. George L. Miller in Omaha and thanked him for this kindness, which he seemed to remember.

CHAPTER XIV

On the Overland Trail—Fort McPherson in 1866—The Morrow Ranch—Other Noted Road Ranches

EACH day's drive was a repetition of the previous one except that it unfolded a new and undeveloped country, presenting new and ever changing scenes as we followed the trail along the south bank of the Platte River, on which grew more or less brush and timber, the latter mostly cottonwood and elm. Some days we would camp on the river bank and sometimes a mile or so distant. Our train had one cook and mess outfit. Each driver was supposed to do his best to supply fuel, either in wood, buffalo or cow chips. The latter made good cooking fuel, if dry, but when wet and no dry wood accessible we could drink water and eat crackers and molasses.

Before arriving at the Midway ranch, which had been fired by the Indians and was still burning, I discovered that Mr. Bass was making his word good about getting even with me. I often noticed a little favoritism practiced by him. He seemed to take especial delight in keeping me busy while many of my fellow bullwhackers were allowed to rest. His frequent order was, "Now, Bratt, you do this." We were supposed to supply the camp with water in five-gallon kegs in our turns but I was often asked to do this before my turn came. In case of sickness of one of the night herders or drivers I would be requested to take his place or to drive two teams. If another driver's wagon wheel needed fixing, I would be requested to help him. If some of the steers strayed away from the night herders, I would be sent out to find them. If some driver's steer became lame, I would be requested to exchange one of mine for his. Sometimes my best wheel or lead steer would be taken from me and an outlaw would be given me in place of him. These and many other outrages were heaped upon me. Even some of my

bullwhacker companions would speak to me about these im-
positions and advise me to protest against Mr. Bass's treatment, promising to stand by me no matter what happened.
I took all good-naturedly and without protest for a long time,
thinking that after a while he would exhaust his hatred or
become ashamed of his actions toward me. But no! The
farther we went and the more I did for him, the worse he
became.

We again began to meet east-bound coaches that had
been savagely attacked by Indians. Sometimes one or more
horses had been killed and one passed us in which there was
a dead passenger and another in which a passenger had been
fatally wounded. So far, owing, no doubt, to precautions
taken, our trains had escaped attack. Extra day and night
herders were sent out with the cattle, keeping scouts ahead
of our trains which we kept well closed up and guarded,
especially through the hilly country.

We arrived at Fort McPherson, after having passed
several road ranches that had been abandoned or burned to the
ground. Among these may be mentioned those of Peniston &
Miller, the Gilman Bros., and others, who had taken refuge
at Fort McPherson; also John Burke and family, Sam Fitchie,
E. E. Ericksson and others who barely escaped with their
lives. Fort McPherson was a large post built principally of
cedar logs. Officers' quarters were frame buildings located at
the mouth of Cottonwood canon, accommodating ten or more
companies of cavalry and infantry, who were kept busy trying
to keep the Indians off the overland trains, stage coaches
and settlers. Here we were halted, arms and ammunition
carefully examined and our force strengthened by two additional ox trains loaded with government supplies for Fort
Laramie, when we were allowed to proceed, with our big
Mr. Bass still acting as captain and meaner than ever to me.

The Platte River, at this point said to be a mile wide, at
this time was bank full of yellowish, muddy water. Much
driftwood was going down in the current. Some of this we
caught and slung under our wagons, expecting it to dry out in

Lincoln's Funeral Car. It Formerly Served as His Private Traveling Car

Fort McPherson in 1866

the course of a few days. We caught some fish. This with the deer, antelope and buffalo that we occasionally secured, gave us some variety with our beans, coffee, bacon, syrup and Dutch-oven bread.

Some miles west of Fort McPherson we passed what was left of the Burke ranch. Like others, they grabbed what little they could and fled to Fort McPherson to escape being killed by the Indians, who, out of vengeance, because they could not overtake the fleeing family, took everything of value and then set fire to the buildings. Little did I dream at that time that the little blue-eyed daughter, who came so near being captured, would one day become my wife.

A wagon bridge had been constructed by John Burke a year or so before this over the South Platte River, about the point where it flows into the North Platte River, for the accommodation of freight and passengers coming and going by Platte City, now known as North Platte, a place at that time of 300 to 500 people.

When we were opposite the junction of the North and the South Platte rivers we ran against the Jack Morrow dike that the noted ranchman had dug to prevent any freighting or emigrant wagons from traveling north of his road ranch, which at this time was located at the foot of the hills north of the Jack Morrow cañon about one mile south of Bratt's old ranch, now the Turpie ranch. We stayed an hour or so trading at the Morrow ranch and I had the privilege of meeting that noted ranchman, who wore a diamond (said to be valued at $1000.00) in his yellow and badly soiled shirt bosom. There were several hundred Sioux Indians, squaws and papooses camped near the ranch, besides numerous squaw-men and others, among whom can be named Jack Sharp, Bob Rowland, Tod Randall, Turgeon and some other noted frontiersmen who could talk the Sioux language fluently. This noted ranch had a hard name among emigrants on account of its record of Indian thefts. Scarcely a train passed it but that lost stock and when the owner of the stolen stock would appeal to Morrow, that gentleman would be truly sympathetic

and offer to sell him others at a big figure. Morrow or some
of his crooks would usually have a bunch of work cattle,
work horses or mules under herd in the hills. This herd was
kept replenished from emigrants' stolen stock, which he would
sell "just to help them out." The ranch was well stocked
with provisions, clothing, firearms, whiskey, tobacco, etc.,
which were sold at very high prices. A squaw offered me a
little Indian boy, naked save for a string of beads around his
neck, for a plug of tobacco. I did not make the exchange.
While here I caught a glimpse of Mrs. Morrow, wife of this

On the Overland Trail

noted ranchman. She seemed to be a modest, refined, rather
neatly-dressed woman and much out of place at this frontier
road ranch. Had any one told me then that my four
daughters would be born within a mile of this notorious
ranch, I would not have believed it.

Our trading done, we resumed our journey northwes*
toward the south bend of Fremont Creek (now known as
Fremont Slough) and so named in honor of General Fremont
when he made his overland trip many years before. Here
we camped for the night, using every precaution against theft
by the Morrow Indian raiders. It was probably this doubling
of guards and night herders that saved us from loss. We

next passed the Bishop ranch, later known as the Beers ranch, next the well-known Lou Baker road ranch and stage station, dreaded on account of its frequent Indian attacks. Mr. and Mrs. Lou Baker seemed to be out of place here. They were both so good and homelike. The best was never too good for any one who stayed at this ranch. It was known as the O'Fallon road ranch. Often they had to flee to save themselves from capture by the marauding bands of Indians (both Cheyenne and Sioux) whose excuse was to hunt buffalo but in reality to hunt scalps and live stock. The daredevil stage driver, pony express rider, the freighter and emigrant, if living to-day, could tell of some narrow escapes. The California Trail between Fort McPherson and Fort Sedgwick, if its history could be written between the years 1849 and 1868, would reveal the tragic death of many a brave man, both civilian and soldier.

Our next stopping place before fording the South Platte River was just east of Fort Sedgwick, at which place several companies of soldiers, both cavalry and infantry, were stationed under command of Major O'Brien.

CHAPTER XV

ALTHOUGH it was nearly 4:00 P. M. when we (the lead team) arrived at the crossing, our Mr. Bass, now called captain, as head of all the trains traveling with us, gave orders to commence crossing. The river was nearly one-half mile wide at this point and bank full of dirty, reddish colored water. The clouds were dark and low and distant rumbling of thunder could be heard, streaks of sharp lightning shot across the sky and the wind blew in short, strong gusts. Mr. Bass had not neglected me one moment since we left "Dobytown"; I was thinking that now perhaps he might overlook me, when a sharp voice yelled to me to go in with the first team, twelve yoke of cattle hitched to a wagon, loaded heavily with bacon, flour, sugar, coffee, salt, crackers, etc. Our captain, two assistant wagon bosses and four bullwhackers, two on either side (I had the lower side), started the team in the river where we progressed for nearly two hundred yards, when, owing to the pelting rain which had commenced to fall, our team stopped and tried to turn their backs to the rain. We succeeded in getting another pull but the cattle could not move the wagon which was fast settling in the quicksand. Four more yoke of cattle were added and another pull made, when some of the chains parted. We then doubled the chains and the next pull they got tangled in their chains, fell down and would have drowned had we not unhooked the chains and cut the ox-bows. Two of the yokes were lost at this time. (Two years ago they were found in the river when it was low; the iron rusted and wood rotted, as would naturally be expected during a period of fifty years. The writer presented these to The Nebraska Historical So-

ciety and they may be seen there in Lincoln, Nebraska.)
Darkness overtook us; some of the yokes of cattle went across
the river dragging their chains and some came back to the
main herd south of the river. When we left the wagon in
the river the current was running over the top of the end gate
and it looked as if it might disappear entirely before daylight.

Nearly all the bullwhackers went up to the Post that night
and many got drunk. I turned into my blankets wet to the
skin and supperless. About three o'clock the next morning
Captain Bass came and wakened me and said he wished I
would get on the mule tied to the wagon, cross the river and
bring back all the yoked cattle that had strayed away the night
before. This order, with some misgivings as to results, I
obeyed. It was hardly daylight yet and I could not see the
getting-out place on the opposite side of the river. It was my
first experience in water on mule-back. I had been told many
times that a mule, especially if he could not touch bottom
with his feet and keep the top of his back dry, became the
greatest of cowards in water and would prefer drowning to
swimming. I had not proceeded far when I had the time of
my life to get him past what was to be seen of the top of the
wagon we left in the river and then my mule went down and
tried to roll over me and seemed determined to commit suicide
by drowning. He got his ears full of water and hesitated
some time as to whether he would proceed or go back to camp.
The only way I could coax him was to lead him. The water
most of the way across was up to my breast, but in a few
places I had to swim. We both often went down in quicksand. Two-thirds of the way across the water became shallower, averaging about three feet deep, when I again mounted
and soon got out. I found five yoke of cattle grazing peacefully. After rounding them up and fastening the chains to
the yokes I soon had a five-yoke team crossing the river, which
I crossed safely without dismounting, my mule going under
only once on the return trip.

Having found the ford in the river, by ten o'clock in the
morning we had begun in earnest to cross our wagons; and

our captain, aided by the good common sense of the different wagon bosses and assistants, had learned to send his lightest wagons over first, putting perishable goods, such as sugar, flour, salt, beans and crackers, on top of canned or wet goods. Captain Bass kept me in the river all day. I and three other bullwhackers brought seven wagons across—making fourteen times that we crossed the river that day. We usually rode on the backs of our steers on the return trip. We were not through crossing all the wagons in our different trains until the night of the third day.

Out of sympathy for a Mormon family (a poor woman and her son) pulling a cart, I allowed the woman to ride across the river and hitched the cart behind the wagon, the son fording the river with me. For this humane act I received a severe cursing from Captain Bass.

For several days after crossing the South Platte River I suffered greatly. The skin on my neck, arms and body was so badly sunburned, blistered and irritated by my heavy woolen shirt that I was in misery both night and day. Had my flesh been seared by a hot iron I could not have suffered more.

We crossed the twenty-eight mile ridge between the South and the North valleys, making a dry camp one night. We passed Mud Springs, a telegraph and small stage station. We also passed Chimney Rock and Court House Rock, pictures of which are here given. Nature seems to have done her work well. Court House Rock has quite a history. It is claimed that a band of outlaws were followed from the Gallatin valley mines by Captain Bailey's company of mountaineers, were overtaken, tried and found guilty and twelve of them shot to death on the top of this Court House Rock, hence its name. Could a true history of it be written it would make very interesting reading. The storms of many years have beaten upon it and worn much of it away but there is yet much left of interest for the traveler, especially if he succeeds in climbing to its top.

We passed "Brown's Road Ranch" west of Scott's Bluff. This ranch was kept by "Stuttering Brown," to whom I may refer later in this book. We finally wended our way, through a crooked, narrow pass, through Scott's Bluff.

Two miles west of these bluffs, standing on the south bank of the North Platte River, was Fort Mitchell, a two-company adobe post. Directly south of this, across the overland trail, stood the Mitchell Road ranch and stage station kept at this time by John Sibson. This will also be referred to later. Twelve miles west of this we passed Horse Creek ranch kept by Charles Blunt. Between Blunt's and Antone Reynolds' ranch, I remember making a drive late in the night. Some of our teams got scared at either a herd of buffalo, a pack of wolves or sneaking Indians while we were doubling teams, pulling over sand hills at the west end of the Mitchell bottom. Never before did I see six-yoke ox-teams stampede on a run with loaded wagons containing sixty to seventy hundred pounds of dead freight. Some fifteen teams did this for nearly half a mile, going faster than their drivers could run. I don't see how we escaped being run over. I was sitting in my wagon half dozing when my team started with others in front and in rear of it. Hanging on to the wagon bow saved me from being thrown out of the wagon, from which at the first chance I jumped, just clearing the wheels of my own wagon and causing the team of the next wagon to shy from me as I struck the ground and commenced to scramble to my feet to get out of the way. The noise made by this little stampede was not unlike the passing of a vigorous cyclone. The only damage done was the upsetting of one wagon and the crippling of a steer.

We passed the Reynolds' and the Jules Coffee road ranches and many stage coaches that the Indians had chased and in some cases attacked. We crossed the Laramie River at Fort Laramie. Here the two ox-trains owned by Majors Russell and Waddell, that had joined us at Fort McPherson, remained. They were loaded with general merchandise and provisions—a rush order intended for Red Cloud's band of Sioux Indians said to number 2500 warriors who had left Fort Laramie a few days before we arrived, swearing vengeance against the whites; and incoming freight trains, stage coaches and pony express riders testified to the fact that they were making their word good. Red Cloud's great speech on that occasion before the Indian Commission closed with these words: "We have given you the buffalo land of the Shallow River (the Platte) for your iron horse road and will keep our people back and protect you. You have promised to save our hunting lands to the north of us but by sending these soldiers now on the march into our hunting grounds you are acting the lie. I will take my people back. We will fight you every mile of the way to the Big Horn. We will let your milestones be the graves of your dead. You have lied to us and have now nothing to expect of us but war! war! war!!" Red Cloud then assembled his people of about 2500 to 3000 and left Fort Laramie that same day. How well he kept his promise in giving war is a matter of history. The war began immediately and did not end until the white troops were driven out of the country. He and many of his followers were in active hostilities from the latter part of June, 1866, until the fall of 1871. The following is a truthful sketch of his career.

RED CLOUD, THE MAN OF 200 BATTLES

A young Oglala chief of the Sioux nation dashed across the Dakota prairie, followed by a band of youthful braves who had chosen him as their leader. From the chief's shoulders waved a scarlet blanket. Some poetic onlooker, observing the foremost rider's fiery-colored shoulder covering, said: "He looks like a flying red cloud."

The speech pleased the young chief. From that time he was known as Maq-pelu-ta—Red Cloud.

Red Cloud was born in 1818. He was of obscure birth; but by sheer genius for warfare and leadership soon made himself a sub-chief. His early wars were waged against the Pawnees, Crows and other tribes, who hated the fierce Sioux. Then, in 1848,—already a noted warrior—he began a conflict with the white men that raged off and on for more than thirty years. During much of that period Red Cloud was practically the war lord of Nebraska, Dakota, Kansas and large parts of Iowa, Wyoming, Montana and Minnesota.

Pioneers began to invade his realm. Many of them were white men of the most daring, lawless sort and some did not scruple to cheat, rob or even kill any Indian who crossed their path. Red Cloud regarded these newcomers as a hostile tribe and treated them as such. The white man slaughtered the buffaloes and other game and trampled on their ancient customs. Red Cloud and his braves retaliated by slaying some of these "undesirable citizens" and declaring death-war upon the rest.

Chimney Rock

Court House and Jail Rocks

Sitting Bull

Red Cloud

FIGHTS AGAINST FEARFUL ODDS

The government rushed to the protection of its settlers. Red Cloud now found himself opposed to trained soldiers instead of lawless frontiersmen. But he fought on as fearlessly as ever against these greater odds.

A body of regulars was sent to garrison Fort Phil Kearny in Wyoming. On December 22, 1866, Red Cloud, with a band of Sioux, attacked a foraging party from the fort. Captain Fetterman, with one hundred soldiers and citizens, was sent out to the party's rescue. Red Cloud's savages, in a terrific battle, killed Fetterman and every one of his men.

Encouraged by this feat, Red Cloud next attacked a detachment of soldiers under Major Powell, who were crossing the prairies with a consignment of metal wagon bodies. Using these wagon bodies for bullet-proof fortification, the troops defended themselves so gallantly that Red Cloud could make no headway against them. Again and again he led his warriors across the open ground in a wild charge against the wagon fort. And every time the soldiers' quick, unerring volleys emptied dozens of saddles and sent the Indians reeling back. Red Cloud lost more than 300 men in this fight before he would consent to withdraw out of reach of the deadly hail of bullets.

Some of the older Sioux chiefs wanted to yield to the government and to sign a peace treaty. Red Cloud was asked to join them. He replied furiously: "No! I want war!" The more valiant young warriors echoed his defiant shout. And war they had for years thereafter. Red Cloud kept the frontier ablaze with excitement.

Among the famous soldiers who fought against him from time to time were Generals Miles, Sheridan, Crook, Terry and Custer. More than once he proved too wily for the best of them. But one leader, be he ever so inspired, cannot with 6000 savages defy a whole country forever. So, in course of time, Red Cloud and his braves were cooped up on a reservation. But again and again they broke out, committing fearful ravages among the settlements, and were brought back to the agency only to burst forth again at the first chance.

GIVES UP UNEQUAL STRIFE

When Sitting Bull, in 1876, in the campaign which cost Custer's life, went on the warpath, Red Cloud prepared to join the renowned Medicine Man; but General Crook swooped down upon his band just as they were making ready to start, took away their ponies and made Red Cloud a prisoner. Later the government offered to pay $28,000.00 for these ponies and for other confiscated weapons if Red Cloud would sign a treaty.

This was in 1880. Red Cloud was 62 years old. His long, tireless years of warfare had resulted in the thinning out of his warrior band and the loss of thousands of miles of his territory. Whereas, the white men in the West were every year more numerous. He saw the bitter hopelessness of it all and consented to sign what he called a "peace paper".

The old savage had been in 200 pitched battles during his stormy career. Now—penniless, old, helpless—he laid down his weapons. Nor did he, outwardly at least, ever break the treaty he had so reluctantly made. In more than one subsequent Indian outbreak he was suspected of having stirred up the local braves to revolt; but nothing could be proven against him.

And so he lived on, at government expense, without a shadow of his former greatness, becoming at last blind, deaf and almost childish.—*Albert Payson Terhune.*

On leaving Fort Laramie strict orders were issued to every member of each train to be eternally on the watch against sudden attacks and never to fire a shot night or day unless attacked by Indians and that the moment a shot was fired, every man must be ready for any emergency. Guards were doubled as well as night herders around the cattle.

While these precautions kept the captain, wagon bosses and assistants and every man in camp busy, the captain did not relax his supervision over me, making life very uncomfortable. Several times my better nature rebelled against carrying out his profane orders. Why not stop it and assert my manhood? Better die than lead such a dog's life. I was called on in every emergency, no matter whether it was my proper turn or not.

The day after passing Fort Laramie I was called upon to find several steers that had strayed from the herd and was given the same contrary, stubborn, old mule and told by Captain Bass to go and find them and not to come back without them. After riding down the river a couple of miles I came to a quaking asp grove in a bend of the river. Thinking the missing steers might be in there, I dismounted and tied the mule to a tree on the edge of the grove, with difficulty working my way in afoot through the heavy underbrush. I had proceeded some two hundred yards when I heard breaking of branches which assured me that I was on the trail of the steers. I proceeded farther, when I came face to face with a big, black bear. It did not take me long to reach my mule and I had scarcely mounted when the bear appeared. I can still see that mule trying to get away. I could neither guide nor hold him for nearly a mile down the river. About an hour later I passed this place with the missing steers but "Mr. Mule" had lost all confidence in me and must have thought I was putting up a job on him in taking him back to where we left the bear. I had great trouble in getting him past the spot without going nearly a quarter of a mile to the right of it. I finally arrived at camp just as it was getting ready to move.

In crossing the bad lands west of Fort Laramie we broke several wagon wheels and I was hurried back to Fort Laramie with a yoke of cattle, hitched to a light wagon containing the broken wheels, with strict orders to get the wheels repaired as quickly as possible or buy new ones. Being loaded with government freight I had no trouble in getting an order from General Palmer, the commanding officer, to the blacksmith to work all night fixing the wheels, which were ready for me by daylight the next morning.

By sunrise I was passing the cemetery where Shen-tag-a-lisk's (Spotted Tail's) daughter, Ah-ho-op-pa, (the Sioux name for wheaten flour), had recently been buried. I have read several stories of the life and death of this beautiful and sensible Indian maiden, who, it is said, died, on the Powder River, of consumption but in reality of a broken heart. Having fallen in love with a young officer who did not return her affection, Ah-ho-op-pa had become so attached to the whites that while on her deathbed she exacted a promise from her father, Shen-tag-a-lisk, that he would never go to war with the whites again.

I could write an interesting story of this love affair but space will not permit.

Shen-tag-a-lisk, or Spotted Tail, kept this promise and some years later, in 1879, saved the writer's life at Rosebud Agency, where Spotted Tail later died and where an imposing shaft marks this great chief's grave in the Rosebud cemetery at that agency.

Anxious to see where Spotted Tail's daughter was buried, I stopped my team in passing the cemetery. I had no trouble in finding the grave, which was marked by four posts about seven feet high above the ground. A platform was nailed to the posts and upon this rested the coffin covered with a red blanket. On the blanket were laid many Indian trinkets— beads, paints, moccasins, looking glasses, shawls and leggings. To the two north posts were nailed the heads of her two white ponies and their tails to the south posts.

While viewing this I was suddenly surrounded by a dozen or more Sioux warriors, who angrily asked what I was doing there. I told them I was looking at Spotted Tail's daughter's grave. I had picked up a few stones and pebbles lying on the ground under the remains and an Indian snatched them out of my hands and struck me over the head with his bow. I told them as best I could that I meant and had done no harm, when several of them commenced to beat me with their quirts, bows and arrows. I could not defend myself from the blows of so many and jumped into my wagon and started my yoke of cattle on a run. They nearly frightened the cattle to death, sticking arrows in their sides to see them twist and run. At the same time they continued to whip me over the head, back and shoulders, tearing my shirt off me. They chased me thus over two miles and I believe they would have killed me had I not taken refuge in a Mormon train that was on its way to Salt Lake City. I meant no disrespect but I could not make the Indians see it that way. My fellow bullwhackers hardly knew me when I got to camp and the most pleased man I ever saw was my constant caretaker, Captain Bass. He would have liked to have sent me back on a second trip.

I could write a big chapter of this Captain Bass's mean, brutish ways, which I had made up my mind to tolerate no longer.

A couple of nights after my whipping by the Indians we had just formed corrals for the night. I had unyoked my team. Many of the other teamsters had not commenced to unyoke theirs. The captain rode up to me and ordered that I take the cattle to water before I picked up my yokes and chains. I mildly remonstrated and asked him how I could do so when many of the teams were not unyoked. He answered with an oath and told me to do what he said. I made no reply but walked to where my lead yoke lay on the ground, unhooked the chain and proceeded to pick it up. He was watching me and immediately rode up, whipped out his revolver, leveled it at my head and with a bad oath accompanied by an expression still common in some parts of the West, tried his best to push the end of his revolver into my mouth and commanded me to drop that yoke. I threw the yoke to the ground and told the captain what I thought of him; that, although I had done everything in my power to please him, there were many things I ought not to have done; that he had imposed on me ever since we left old Fort Kearny; that although he was captain of the entire outfit, and his uncle owned the train, yet—even though he was big enough to whip me—I was not afraid of him and was willing to fight him any way he chose, with guns, revolvers, knives or in a fair fist fight. By this time many of the bullwhackers had gathered around us and were urging me on by yelling: "Go for him, Bratt! Go for him, Bratt!! We'll stay by you." All the outfit, including the wagon masters and assistants, hated him. Some of these men pulled him off his mule and took his revolvers and knife from him. This done, I threw my revolvers and bowie knife on the ground and in a few seconds we were both fighting in "dead earnest" and I was soon getting the worst of it. He not only punished me with his fists but jabbed his spurs in my neck. He was a giant compared to me. The men pulled him off me once but I went at him again and finally got the lobe of his left ear between my teeth and, though I am sorry to tell it, I did not let go until I spit a part of his ear on the ground. He finally got up amid the taunts and jeers of the crowd of bullwhackers, picked up his revolvers and knife, put a dirty, old, red handkerchief to his bleeding ear and started for his wagon, swearing he would fix me yet. I came out of the fight badly used up, my face covered with blood, some teeth missing, but with many congratulations from my fellow bullwhackers who promised to stand by me should he tackle me again. This, I think, prevented him from carrying out his threat later, since he saw the sympathy of nearly all the men was with me, and instead of abusing me, he became more considerate and let me alone the rest of the trip. Whether this was caused by shame or fear of the further ill will of the men in the different outfits, I don't know. For the present I shall leave him to heal up his notched left ear. Enough to say that I picked up my yokes and chains before taking the steers to water.

CHAPTER XVI

*Cheyenne Indians Visit our Camp—Dull Knife and his Band become
Enraged—The Peace Pipe is Smoked—A Quart of Whiskey
Poured down Tenderfoot—A Herd of Five
Thousand Buffalo—Attacked by the
Arapahoes*

A FTER crossing the North Platte River at Fort Casper, we met some returning horse and mule trains and one stage coach, the driver of which and remaining two passengers turned over to us for burial the body of one dead passenger who had been instantly killed that morning while fighting a band of Indians who were chasing the coach. We dug a hole on a sandy knoll near the trail, wrapped the remains in a blanket and laid them gently to rest, marking the head of the mound with part of a cracker box lid, on which was written in pencil: "John Harrison. Killed by Indians August 2, 1866, while en route by stage coach to St. Joseph, Missouri."

We had come this far without being attacked by Indians except for the whipping the writer received east of Fort Laramie when curiosity got the better of judgment. We were still very watchful, both night and day. We might have thought this double guard duty unnecessary had it not been for what we saw and heard from travelers returning in the stage coaches and freighters.

It was near here that, after breaking camp one morning and traveling some three miles, we noticed grazing in the hills about a mile distant on the left a bunch of ponies. We were ordered to halt, while wagon bosses and assistants, all mounted, and some twelve or fourteen of us bullwhackers afoot, all well armed, started towards the ponies. The hill was not a high one but was bare of sagebrush and greasewood and sloped gently toward the trail on which our wagons were standing, which caused me to wonder how we afoot could defend ourselves in case of an Indian attack. The mounted men were far in the lead of us and it was not very long before we saw them reach the top of the hill and return as fast as their horses could run. This caused us to beat a hasty retreat toward our wagons. On catching up with us the mounted men informed us that there were several hundred ponies grazing on the other side of the hill and a valley full of Indian tepees and Indians, who, as yet, apparently had not discovered us. With this knowledge, all in the different outfits, even to our friend, the captain, were willing and anxious to resume our morning drive, not a few of us frequently casting a watchful eye back toward the hill where the same bunch of ponies continued grazing.

We had proceeded some two miles over a rather level country when we came to a deep canon (said to be a dry branch of the Cheyenne River), and here the recent high water had almost obliterated the trail and left it practically impassable. There was nothing to do but go into camp and commence fixing the crossing. About the time dinner was called two mounted, fine-looking Indians came within shouting distance of the camp and in pigeon English and their native language told us they were good Cheyennes; Sioux and Arapahoes were bad, but they—throwing back their blankets and placing their hands over their hearts—were "heap good." A short consultation was held between Captain Bass and the different wagon bosses. The former favored inviting them into camp, while all the latter opposed it. Notwithstanding this, Captain Bass went out and shook hands with the two Indians and brought them into camp, where they were soon surrounded by the bullwhackers who asked them many questions as to their camp, tribe, number, where they came from, where they were going, whether they had any squaws and papooses, ponies, buckskins or moccasins. They said they were Cheyennes, were going south to hunt buffaloes and visit their people, had their squaws and papooses, heaps of ponies, buckskins, robes and moccasins, and pointed toward the bluff or hills where we had seen the ponies grazing. On looking through the field glasses in that direction, we noticed many objects on the hillsides. These objects were neither ponies, sagebrush, greasewood nor rocks and when Captain Bass told the two Indians to bring their Indians into our camp, one of the Indians went some distance from our wagons, obviously to get an unobstructed view. Upon waving his blanket three times the objects on the hillside sprang to their feet and scattered, some going from us over the hill, presumably for their ponies, others coming afoot to our camp into which they came stringing in all manner of fashion—some mounted, some afoot, and others, squaws and papooses lying or sitting on tepee poles dragged by their ponies, until there were about eight hundred or more bucks, squaws and papooses. The total number of whites in our camp was less than two hundred, but all were pretty well armed with revolvers, guns and bowie or butcher knives.

It is seldom one meets a similar bunch of men of this class and character without having one or more bad men among them. Nearly all drank when they could get liquor, used profane language, smoked or chewed tobacco, and gambled. I regret to say that I, too, had commenced to swear and this, together with my fight with Captain Bass, gave me better standing and more respect in the eyes of my bullwhacker comrades; still I was looked upon as a tenderfoot because I had not adopted their other vices. When invited to join in their games or listen to their obscene stories I would beg to be excused and steal away to my wagon where I would read again and again the "Harper's Monthly" given me at "Dobytown" by good Dr. Miller.

The Indians were enjoying their friendly visit with us, after having filled their stomachs with our boiled beans, bacon, pone bread and coffee, which the cooks of the different outfits had provided in plenty. Much swapping and trading had been done in the purchase of buffalo robes, elk and deer skins, moccasins, etc., for money and other considerations. Everything was going along nicely. By giving him my plate of dinner in addition to what he had already eaten at other outfits, I became well acquainted with Dull Knife, the head chief of this band of Cheyennes. Suddenly the old chief dashed his plate and what little there was on it to the ground, mounted his pony, and commenced to talk to his people in his own language, the substance of his words was that one of these whites had stolen a buckskin from one of the squaws and he not only asked the return of the skin but wanted the man also. Our brave captain suggested that this request be granted, but some others suggested we give up the captain, who soon disappeared, to be found later after considerable search, pretending to be busy writing in his wagon, with cracker boxes piled up in front and rear, thus hiding him from view.

I, like some others, had commenced to yoke my cattle but our assistant wagon boss, Green, ordered us to stop and prepare to fight. All was excitement and commotion. It took but a short time for the Indians to prepare for us. The squaws, papooses and old men were sent to the rear while the bucks, nearly all mounted,—some in the corrals, others outside—a number with guns and revolvers but the majority with bows and arrows (some arrows poisoned), all strung and ready for action—were all eagerly awaiting the word to attack. Dull Knife and his sub-chiefs insisted that the man who stole the skin be given up and had we not hid him under some cracker boxes in one of the wagons, the Indians would have killed him quickly and the squaws, young and old, standing directly behind the mounted bucks with their knives all sharp, would have quickly finished the work of scalping and mutilating the body.

A hasty consultation of the different wagon bosses and assistants was held and it was determined to find Mr. Bass and make him settle the trouble since he had brought the Indians into camp without the consent of the others. After pulling away the cracker boxes Captain Bass was soon located in his wagon, and ordered to come out and settle the matter.

Old Dull Knife, who had six scalps dangling from his belt— one of them a woman's—poked his head into Captain Bass's wagon and called that gentleman the meanest name he could think of, which was "Heap Squaw, big white chief." Bass thought his time had come and shook like an aspen leaf in a breeze. The captain finally came out of the wagon and appealed to the different bosses as to the best way to settle the trouble. They frankly told him to settle it himself, seeing there was no way out of it, or fight. He suggested giving the Indians some provisions, but the other bosses did not concur in this, perhaps fearing later complications. The buckskin was returned and Bass ordered some of his men to throw out a sack of coffee, a sack of sugar, a sack of beans, a sack of bacon, a sack of salt and six boxes of crackers. When Dull Knife saw him hesitate about throwing out more the old chief called out, "Heap more! Heap more!" and Bass told the men to throw out more. They doubled the quantity, but this did not satisfy the Indians. They wanted many sacks of flour and boxes of canned goods. Bass checked the men up several times, but Dull Knife, a good judge of human nature, had him scared and occasionally would talk to his warriors, who would crowd up closer and put on a bolder front. It was not until the Indians had nearly a wagonload of provisions—all government property—lying on the ground that they were satisfied.

This incident demonstrated how easy it was for a boss, using bad judgment, to get his employers into trouble and jeopardize the lives of his men. Had Bass followed the advice of the other wagon bosses and the majority of the men who had crossed the plains and dealt with Indians before, he would not have gotten us into this scrape, but he was the nephew of the man who owned the train and *knew it all*. He was now letting his hair grow long. The large notch in his left ear could be seen when the wind blew his hair back, but he was kinder to me.

After the return of the buckskin and present of the provisions to the Indians, they lighted and passed around to any one who would smoke it, the pipe of peace and everything was again peaceful and harmonious. I shook hands with old Dull Knife, who, taking off my hat, gave me to understand that after three nights' sleep we would be in the Arapahoes' country and must look out for our "Zip," meaning our scalps. Two of our steers died at this camp, which gave the Indians an additional feast.

It was late in the afternoon when we pulled out. The crossing of the gulch had been fixed and after letting the first few wagons down by hand and ropes we did not have much trouble, except for the breaking of two wagon wheels. It must have been midnight when we got all the wagons across. It started to rain shortly after and at daylight the gully was a raging torrent, full from bank to bank. It drizzled all next day and we remained in camp repairing our broken wheels and exchanging visits with the Cheyennes. Some of our men went to the Indian camp on special invitation to dine with them. At this banquet some of the fattest and choicest dogs were killed, cooked and served a la mode.

The next morning we continued our journey, taking a northwest course, leaving Pumpkin Butte to our right. For three days we had been following a rather indistinct trail. We had had three sleeps since leaving the dry fork of the Cheyenne and were crossing the dry bed of what, at certain seasons of the year, might have been a river very wide and extremely sandy, so sandy that we had to double teams to cross it. We had all but eight of the wagons across when a small party of Indians (maybe twenty), mounted and carrying spears in addition to the customary bows and arrows, came charging at breakneck speed out of the adjacent hills and with a war whoop rode close up to the eight teams and commenced to shoot arrows at the teamsters and the cattle, sending some of their arrows into the flanks and sides of the cattle. This lasted for a few minutes until the men with the teams retaliated with guns and revolvers, when the Indians, whom we took to be Arapahoes, judging from what Dull Knife told us, went back to the hills as fast as they came and were out of range of the guns of the wagon bosses, assistants and quite a lot of bullwhackers who had crossed with the other wagons and had come back on a run to the aid of the eight teamsters and their wagons.

This little scare served to make us more vigilant. Failing to get water for our stock, we drove the greater part of the night. This was hard on our cattle and caused us to lose several by death. We remained in camp next day, digging quite a few rifle pits for protection against Indian attacks, since we saw a number of Indians watching us from nearby hills. Extra herders went out with the cattle and night guards around the camps were doubled, all having strict orders not to fire a gun or revolver except in an Indian attack.

We finally crossed the Powder River at old Fort Reno, which place I shall always remember. I had often expressed my disapproval of the gambling and drinking indulged in by my fellow bullwhackers and made the remark that I had taken two drinks of whiskey in my life—one prescribed for me by a physician at Elizabeth Port, New Jersey, the other on the levee plank at Morganzie in the bend at the mouth of the Red River in Louisiana—and that they would be my last. Some of the bullwhackers said they would see that I got a third, and they did. Half a dozen bullwhackers seized me that night, threw me down and forced down my throat between a pint and a quart of the worst old road ranch whiskey that I ever smelled. The result was that I had to be hauled in the wagon for over a week. For several days it was a serious question as to whether I would live or die. The men who did this (I knew them all) became alarmed, and were greatly relieved when after the sixth day I showed some signs of rallying. In many ways they manifested their regrets at their action and I forgave them. Talk about Keeley Cure! If the worst drunkard ever got a dose like I did, he would never taste another drop.

At one point, after crossing the Powder River, we had to cut one of our ox-trains in two to allow a large herd of buffalo, headed southwest, to pass us. I think this herd was fully a quarter of a mile wide. We killed several and had a feast of buffalo meat for several days. It was interesting to observe this herd of buffalo on the march. There were fully five thousand in the band which traveled in a flatiron shape. They were led by a large male, the cows, calves and yearlings on the inside, protected on the flanks by dry cows, heifers and males of two years and over, thus displaying a wonderful instinct in protecting their young.

Our trail took us through bad and good country, smooth and rough. A good quality of soft coal cropped out of the banks in many places and there were many indications of other minerals and oil.

The Indians now began to show themselves in larger numbers and some continued to follow us in the rear and on both flanks. No chances were taken. The cattle were herded in separate bunches during the day but thrown into one big herd at night with a big force of men around them, both mounted and afoot. A strong night and day guard all well armed was kept around each outfit camp. Every precaution was taken to avoid an ambush or surprise by the Red Skins, especially if traveling through a rough or broken country. Some of our cattle became footsore and had to be shod.

We had passed Smeed Lake and were nearing Crazy Woman's fork, the valley of which was covered with thick brush and considerable timber. The actions of the Indians caused us to expect an attack when we attempted to cross the Crazy Woman's creek. We camped some distance from the creek that night and kept all cattle and horses in the different corrals formed by the wagons. As soon as it was dusk a great number of bullwhackers in charge of wagon bosses and assistants went to certain strategic points around the different trains and dug rifle pits and threw up breastworks for defense in case of Indian attacks. Every man in the different camps was on guard duty some part of the night. No fires were kept lighted after dark and every man was ready to shoot at command, and although this was a long, sleepless night, our vigilance probably saved us from attack and maybe a bad slaughter.

The different wagon bosses, while working in harmony, had to some extent deposed Captain Bass, whose actions at the Cheyenne Dry Fork had shaken their confidence in him as a chief.

It was proposed to cross the Crazy Woman's fork the next day. A heavy guard was thrown out along the creek bottom to protect the teams and teamsters and we had pulled many large stones out of the creek on one side or the other so that our wagons would not be impeded while crossing. We had crossed probably forty wagons when the Indians began to close in on us. Our guards did good work and more than one Indian was sent to the "Happy Hunting Ground" while attempting to steal his way through the brush to pick some of us off. Having some mounted men to help us bullwhackers keep the cattle moving briskly, we finally commenced to send the teams on a trot through the bottom, and even through the creek which was two to three and one-half feet deep. By four o'clock in the afternoon we had crossed all teams safely except for the breaking of two wheels and were out in the open where we spent another watchful night. Our casualties were several head of cattle wounded and three men struck by arrows. Luckily, the arrows were not poisoned. The cattle got well but one of the men died from blood poison after three days. We did everything possible to save him. His remains were carefully wrapped in a blanket and tenderly laid in a deep grave by the side of the trail and another piece of box lid had written on it: "James Edison. Killed by Indians while crossing Crazy Woman's Fork in Jackson Ox-train September 4, 1866."

After a few other exciting events, with no more loss of

life, we arrived at our destination "Fourth Company Post," at this time being rapidly changed into Fort Phil Kearny, by which name it was later better known.

The poisoned arrow was usually poisoned as follows for war purposes: The Indians would take a fresh deer liver, fasten it to a long pole, and then go to certain places where they knew they would find rattlesnakes in abundance.

About midday the rattlers are all out of their dens and coiled up in the sunshine. The bucks would poke the first rattler with the liver. A rattler, unlike common snakes, always shows fight in preference to escaping.

The snake would thus repeatedly strike at the liver with its fangs until its poison was all used up, whereupon it would quit striking and try slowly to move on. The bucks would then hunt up another rattler and repeat the performance, keeping up the work until the liver was well soaked with snake poison.

The pole was carried home and fastened somewhere in an upright position until the liver became as dry as a bone. The liver was then pounded to a fine powder and placed in a buckskin bag, to be used as needed for their arrows. This powder would stick like glue to any moistened surface.

CHAPTER XVII

AFTER reporting the arrival of the different trains in our outfit to the Commander of the Fort, Colonel Carrington, that officer ordered us into camp at a certain point on Piney Creek near the fort. All was bustle and excitement. Hay, wood and log teams, drawn by horses, mules and oxen, came and went, but all under proper cavalry escort, since Red Cloud, joined by other hostile Indians, was making his threat good. The stockade, built out of pine logs twelve feet long, set endwise in the ground about four feet and enclosing about forty acres, together with the officers' and men's quarters and stables for the horses and mules, was being rushed to completion as fast as possible in the face of hostile Indians who raided the contractors' teams and camps daily and kept the mechanics and carpenters continually in hot water, guessing when and where the next attack would be made. Men were scarce and commanded big wages.

The second day after our arrival we commenced to unload our train. Mr. Bass's position as captain gave him some prestige over the others. By the end of the third day our train of supplies was unloaded and my Missouri friend, the captain—the nephew of his uncle—with his disfigured ear now almost completely hidden by his long hair, informed the five of us who had hired to take our discharge here that he was ready to settle with us. He left me until the last when I was called up to his wagon and upon being informed the amount due me he said he would write out an order, or what he called a due bill, for the amount.

He had already settled with the other four men in this way. I told him that although he had settled that way with the others, I could not accept his due bill; that I wanted and must have the cash. I considered that a due bill on Mr.

Keith of Lexington, Missouri, over one thousand miles distant and much of it through a country infested with hostile Indians—unless I could cash it there—was worthless to me. He said he could not pay me the money. I told him that my contract with him called for the money at destination point and not an order to pay. He said he could not help that and would give me cattle. These I also declined. He then told me that was all he could and would do. I reminded him that I had already had a mix-up with him and that I did not want others. At this remark I could not help looking at his left ear. On leaving him I told him I would expect my money by ten o'clock in the morning.

During the evening he requested the men he had settled with to try to get me to accept a due bill like theirs. Accordingly, Swank, as spokesman for himself and the others, approached me and said he had made several bullwhacking trips over the Smoky Hill trail, that he had always been paid this way and never lost a dollar by it. I replied that that might all be true and asked him to take his due bill into the sutler's store and ask what they would give him for it. He did so and they told him they could not use it at any price but would take it for collection without assuming any responsibility. I had sized up the matter rightly and was more determined than ever not to accept one of those due bills for my pay.

All this time Mr. Bass was rushing around and getting ready to pull out the following morning. Ten o'clock came. He seemed to be busy at the sutler's store and appeared to avoid me.

Determined to stand on my rights I started for Colonel Carrington's tent. Before reaching it I heard some one call me. Turning around I saw it was Mr. Bass, who had evidently been watching my movements. He asked me to wait for him and on joining me, asked what I had decided to do about accepting the due bill. I told him that I was going to lay my case before Colonel Carrington but he asked me to go to the sutler's store with him and told me he would do his best to get me my money, even if he had to sell the train. He said if I would promise to work for Mr. Carter in the hay camp that gentleman would advance the money on his freight bill to pay me. I would promise nothing except to make him pay in cash what he owed me. In less than half an hour I had my money. The four men he had paid in due bills demanded their money but he refused to pay them as he had settled with them and held their receipts. This made them angry.

It seems that Mr. Bass had reported to the quartermaster that a band of Cheyenne Indians had attacked our train and that to make peace with them and save what he had, he had given them the provisions and stuff he was short on his bill of lading; and this on his statement was allowed by the quartermaster on his freight bill and a voucher was issued accordingly for about nineteen hundred dollars' worth of provisions. Some one told a quartermaster sergeant the facts. It might have been one of the four men who had been paid off in due bills. At any rate, in a very short time Mr. Bass was under arrest and the camp placed under guard. A thorough investigation was made, resulting in charging to the outfit all shortage on goods, together with eleven cents per pound freight on same from the Missouri River to Fourth Company Post.

The last seen of my big Missouri friend, he was on his favorite mule, the faces of both turned toward the rising sun. He might have been a sadder but no doubt he was a wiser man.

"Good-bye! Take care of yourself, Mr. Bass."

CHAPTER XVIII

*Perilous Times—Employed by Mr. Carter—Indians! Indians!
Indians!—More Gallatin Valley Gold Enthusiasm—
My Guardian Angel*

MY stay at Fort Phil Kearny from the middle of September to the early part of November, 1866,—nearly two months—was the most exciting time I ever experienced.

The firm of Coe & Carter had the contracts for getting out logs, wood and several hundred tons of hay, the former to build houses for officers and men, and stables for horses and stockade purposes. The logs cost $1.00 to $3.00 each, depending on size. The wood was $10.00 per load and the hay as high as $126.00 or more per ton. The latter was mostly cut on Goose Creek three to five miles distant. The wood was cut and hauled from the Piney Creek bottom one to two miles distant and the logs from patches of timber at the foothills six to eight miles distant. Horse and mule teams would usually make one trip a day for logs, cattle two to three trips a day for wood and one trip a day (usually a long day) with loose hay hauled in racks.

Learning from Colonel Carrington and others that there was no possible chance for a few men to make their way to the Gallatin Valley mines that fall unless some troops were going to that point, I concluded to hire out to Mr. Carter at $60.00 per month to help haul hay, logs and wood.

The job was anything but a pleasant one. The sutlers, namely, Judge Kinney, Messrs. Weston, McCrary, Coe and Carter, who ran the store and had interest in the hay, wood and log contracts, had had several wood choppers, hay makers and teamsters killed and wounded by the Indians and had suffered serious financial loss in capture, by stampede or theft, of horses, mules, oxen and harness. Wagons, hay, tents, wood, logs and camp equipage had been burned in raids by hostile bands of Indians headed by the noted chiefs, Man Afraid Of His Horse, Red Ribs and Red Cloud.

These Indians scarcely allowed a day or a night to pass without hurling their warriors against what they considered to be our weak points at and near this fort with a view to destroying it and exterminating all "pale faces" connected with it.   They had made up their minds to wipe out this particular link in the chain of forts across their hunting grounds.   Runners were sent to the different Sioux tribes and many responded.   The result was that this post was attacked oftener and more fiercely during its existence than any post ever built on the frontier.   One month it was attacked fifteen times, another twenty times.   For three years, or until 1869, it was in a constant state of siege.   In the six months ending January 31, 1867, the Indians killed in this vicinity one hundred fifty-four persons and wounded more than two hundred others.   Hundreds of oxen, work horses and mules were taken and several trains of wagons loaded with hay, logs, and wood, also wagons loaded with freight for Fort C. F. Smith and the Bozeman trail, were captured and destroyed.

It was about eight o'clock at night before the hay wagons on which I was to go to the hay camp were unloaded.   It was late when we arrived at camp over a somewhat crooked trail that was, unknown to me, guarded by mountaineers at different points.   The camp was on a high flat overlooking the Goose Creek Valley.   There were a few tents and some wagons loaded with hay, under one of which I spread my two pairs of blankets and turned in with my boots on.   I was cautioned by one of the camp guards to place my revolvers where I could get at them quickly but not to fire a shot unless I was ordered.   Supperless and tired I slept soundly until I was awakened by one of the night herders a little before daylight, calling: "Breakfast ready!"   After breakfast, consisting of bear meat, beans, skillet bread and coffee, I was given a pitchfork and told to go with Kellogg who had charge of loading the hay wagons.

On the way down the hill to the hayfield I soon became acquainted with Kellogg, who was a typical frontiersman. He feared neither God nor devil, let alone a man. He was an old miner who had been to the Gallatin Valley and other mining camps and he and another miner had come down with Captain Bailey's company to get a grub stake with which, when made, they expected to return to those placer diggings. He told me these were very rich and easily worked. I told him I was on my way to those mines and should be glad to go with him at any time. Kellogg said they would like to return that fall but the Indians were making things so hot for them that they might have to winter at the post unless some troops should be going up there or to Fort C. F. Smith, when they would accompany them that distance if possible.

The miner, who was nearly sixty years old, warmed up to me considerably when I told him I would like to go with him. He told me confidentially that he could take me to a place where all I would need would be a shovel and a sack. He said the Indians had run him and a party of forty men out of these mines the previous May. He was so earnest and frank that I believed him.

Before parting he gave certain instructions as to my duties in helping load the wagons and then pointed out to me a certain dark object near the middle of the hayfield. The point indicated was some breastworks thrown up and to this hurried all the haymakers, mowers, rakers and teamsters, with their teams in case the Indians swooped down on them, which was often three or four times a day.

We had loaded two wagons and started them for that point when there came a yell from the men: "Indians! Indians! Indians!!!" Not having much hay on the wagons we dropped the gooseneck in the tongue from the ring in the yoke and started the oxen on a trot towards the place designated by Kellogg. Other teams, some with mowers, rakes and wagons attached, were coming from different parts of the valley to the same place.

About this time I noticed a large band of horses coming

tearing down the hill that we (Kellogg and I) had come down that morning, and I started on a run, revolver in each hand, intending to stop them. I passed near Kellogg and he yelled: "Come back, you d—d fool, or you'll get killed." I continued my gait and finally stopped the horses at the creek crossing, expecting every moment to be surrounded by Indians. I had picked up the trailing lariat of some of the best horses, intending to jump on one should the Indians try to surround me. After a few anxious moments I was most agreeably surprised to see a lot of mounted white men gathered around the band of horses. One of these men rode up to me, and was soon joined by others, who began to ask me questions as to what I was doing there. I explained that while running towards Kellogg's camp in the field I had noticed this band of horses coming over the hills and that I succeeded in stopping them.

I had by this time picked up the ropes of several and made the remark that I had made a killing in securing such a nice bunch, thinking all the time they were Indian horses. I was soon given to understand that the band belonged to the men, who continued to gather around them. Noticing my ignorance they asked when I had come to the camp. I told them late the night before. I further told them that if I had done them any good in stopping the horses I was glad of it. They made me a present of a nice young horse and from that day on, while these fifty mountaineers remained in our camps to guard us, I was "the white-headed boy."

Kellogg cautioned me not to take any more chances like that as I might take one too many.

Mr. Carter paid these fifty mounted men $5.00 per day each for themselves and ponies to protect the camps and teams from Indian raids. These men, the bravest I ever met, were kept busy under the charge of Captain Bailey. Not a day and scarcely a night passed without Indians attacking us either in the hayfield, or on the road to and from the post. Captain Bailey maintained strict discipline over the mountaineers. His word was law as is shown by the following incident:

One of the men stole a watch from another. The case

was called with Captain Bailey as judge and the other men as the jury. The sentence imposed was "To be shot."

After the sentence was pronounced the unlucky fellow gave his horse, saddle, bridle, blankets, gun and revolvers to his best friend, bade them all good-bye, pinned a piece of buckskin over his heart, and walking ten steps out of camp, stood with hands behind him, and without a tremor told the five men detailed to shoot him, that he was ready and for them "not to miss the buckskin."

He fell dead without a murmur. No tears were shed. One comrade made the remark as he looked at his dead body, "Poor Bill."

A crumpled letter was found in poor Bill's saddle pocket. The letter was dated Chicago, March 3, 1865. It was from poor Bill's mother, asking him to come back home.

"Poor Mother! Bill will never come back." Perhaps he committed a crime in taking the watch but he died a hero worthy of a better cause.

I could fill many pages describing the character and habits of these brave, generous men. They did not know what fear was and were always ready to fight Indians day or night. They were divided into squads for night and day. Part would escort the hay, wood and log teams hauling to the fort, and part would be guarding the haymakers, log and woodcutters and the camp. I came across only one who did not drink, chew tobacco and swear. His comrades said "he was off and batty," and treated him as such.

Those guarding the haymakers and hay camps would usually go in pairs, never more than three, to some high hill overlooking the surrounding country, keeping in sight of some of their comrades and the haymakers in the valley below, to whom they would signal if they saw signs of an intended Indian attack, when all would hasten to the weakest point. On the contrary, if everything was quiet and no Indians in sight, they would dismount, throw the bridle reins over the horses' heads and untie the lariats from the saddles, allowing the horses to graze a certain distance around them. Guns were within easy reach should they be needed, and after looking over the country with a view to avoid any sudden attack, they would sit down by their guns and indulge in a little game of poker. They would always play for money and sometimes for heavy stakes.

Once while thus engaged, a band of Indians stole up on two mountaineers and took their horses without being discovered until nearly a quarter of a mile distant, when one of the scouts grabbed his gun and sent one Indian to the "Happy Hunting Grounds." Other Indians carried the dead one away and escaped with the two horses. The two mountaineers came back angry and swearing. One had a canteen of whiskey and $5000.00 in gold coin and nuggets in his saddle pockets. He never mentioned the money and nuggets but how he did swear at the loss of his whiskey. Whiskey, any kind of bitters, alcohol and Jamaica ginger brought any price asked for it from $3.00 to $10.00 per bottle.

Attacks came so thick and fast from the redskins that we began to wonder which of us would be the next to go under a little mound. One or more were killed every day, besides others who were wounded and taken to the Fort hospital. If the Indians could not see a favorable chance to steal in on the haymakers through the line of guards, they would set fire to the long grass and this, fanned by a favorable breeze, would cause us to flee for our lives, when they would swoop down upon us and stampede our horses, mules and cattle, while we were trying to save ourselves and camp outfits. Assisted by the mountaineers and often by one or two companies of cavalry from the fort, we would make the Reds pay dearly for these raids.

I remember one afternoon the Indians had made several attacks on us. They killed three of our men and wounded some others, captured nearly all our mowing and rake teams and had us all corralled on a high hill where we spent the evening and the greater part of the night in digging rifle pits and in defending ourselves and the stock we had left. Mr. Carter was with us and paid our old stuttering blacksmith,

Jose, $500.00 to go to the fort five miles distant to get relief. I thought it strange Mr. Carter did not call on some of the mountaineers for this hazardous trip; but perhaps it was because we needed them with us, since every time they fired a shot, down would go an Indian to join others sent to the Hunting Grounds. Mr. Carter knew Jose and knew he would execute the order or die in the attempt, even if Jose was a stuttering German. We estimated that more than one thousand Indians had us surrounded and judging from the many signal fires being built around us other Indians were being told to come and help finish us. Unless we got relief before daylight we knew that our chance to escape would be slim.

It must have been nine o'clock in the evening when Jose mounted the best horse we had in camp and started for the fort. A few stars were out but the night was rather dark. Thin clouds of smoke from the prairie fire the Indians had started in the afternoon hung over our camp. The fire was still burning in spots.

Jose, armed with two revolvers and a sharp butcher knife in his belt, had been gone some ten minutes. The sound of his horse's hoofs had died away on the gravel ridge road leading to the fort and we were congratulating ourselves that he had gotten safely through the line of redskins, when to our surprise he came at breakneck speed into camp followed by a bunch of Indians, some of whom we tumbled off their horses before they escaped. Mr. Carter and others were soon at Jose's side asking him what he proposed to do next when Jose answered, "I most believe I will try it another way," and in less than ten minutes he disappeared in the darkness in an opposite direction as though he were going to the Tongue River or Big Horn Mountain.

It is not necessary to say we spent an anxious night. Not an eye was closed. Every man who was able was either lying in a trench or on the rise of some hill or behind some object, with gun or revolver in hand. A detail of men was taking the best care possible of the wounded.

Just about the peep of day we saw the Indians scattering to right and left of a large body of mounted men. It proved to be two companies of cavalry with old Jose in the lead. I have talked with many of the Indians, even with Red Cloud himself, and all assured me that they had enough Indians to kill us all and had planned to do this at sunrise had not the cavalry come to our rescue when it did. We gathered what was left of our camp equipage, horses, mules and cattle that were tied, and with our dead and wounded men, came to the fort.

This finished our haymaking. A wagon trail had been cut around a steep hillside, thus saving us nearly three miles between our hay camp and the fort. To follow this trail with an ox-team with a load of hay took the most careful driving to avoid upsetting and rolling down several hundred feet. Several wagons and teams had gone over this bluff and lay in a heap at the bottom with the oxen dead under the wreck. The teamsters escaped this cruel fate.

A few days later E. C. Miller, an old wagon master of Mr. Carter's, was sent with some horse and mule teams, men and an escort of cavalry to bring in what he could of this wreck that was of any worth. While working at this, Miller's party was attacked by Indians. A couple of teamsters were killed and some wounded, the others escaping with their lives under the protection of the escort of cavalry. An Indian shot at Mr. Miller, the ball striking his watch, which was smashed to pieces, thus probably saving his life. Mr. Miller was cut off from the rest of his men. He hid in the hills that night and returned to the post about noon the next day.

After finishing the hay contract, on which the firm must have lost much money, even if they did receive $125.00 to $128.00 per ton, part of the outfit set to work hauling in wood from the bottoms on Piney Creek and part were sent for logs, principally the horse and mule teams. I was detailed with the ox-teams to haul firewood although good coal cropped out in many places. We made, as a rule, two trips per day for wood when the Indians would not molest us for two or three hours a day. We received $10.00 a load for the wood. About one-third of the mountaineers guarded us and the others guarded the log choppers and haulers.

At sunrise every morning Colonel Carrington, commander of the fort, would send a mounted squad to the top of the high hill overlooking the fort with a view to guarding against Indian raids and surprises. When this guard would see Indians approaching they would make certain signals to the guard in the fort below and this would be communicated to the officer of the day. These signals would give the approximate number of Indians in the party and from what direction they were coming. This guard would sometimes stay at their post until the Indians came very close, when the men would come tearing down the steep hill at a breakneck speed. Then the Indians would take the places of the guard and with a buckskin fastened to their bows, would imitate the guard, much to the disgust of Colonel Carrington and fellow officers. The mountain howitzer would fail to reach them.

Our camp at this time was near the stockade. Wagon beds, each by a little crowding, affording sleeping quarters for from two to four men, were set on pine logs raised one to two feet off the ground, thus making a circle or corral in which the work cattle were driven to be yoked. At night huge camp fires would be lighted in the corrals, by which those inclined to indulge in card games, usually poker, could get all light needed.

These camp fires were also a temptation to the Indians to steal through the cordon of guards stationed around the outside of the corrals and spot the card players as they sat on the ground deeply interested in the game.

I have seen as much as $5000.00 in gold and gold dust change hands in one night. The men, especially the mountaineers, would stake their money on anything—on the race of a worm or bug and very often on the race of vermin. They would chalk a small ring on a warmed tin plate and another outside of this near the rim of the plate, when bets ranging from \$10.00 to \$100.00 would be made on the different worms, bugs or vermin that would get outside the outer ring first. The winner would sometimes clean up \$500.00 on one race.

We had a very talkative boy in our camp named Brown who was frequently giving advice to some of these mountaineer gamblers about playing cards. One of them resented this by picking Brown up gently and setting him on top of a hot camp fire. The boy was more scared than burned but he never gave any more advice to that mountaineer about cards.

I had no interest in these games and would usually, when not on guard duty, retire to my wagon and if I could not obtain a lantern, which was a great luxury, I would read and re-read my "Harper's Monthly" or write letters by the light of a tallow candle or a light from a rag saturated with oil or dirty grease on some old tin plate.

I was occupied this way one evening, probably about nine o'clock, when three shots were fired between my wagon bed and another where several men were playing cards. I blew out the light as quickly as possible, grabbed both revolvers and aimed at the rear end of the wagon bed. At first I thought I had been shot.

The card players in the next wagon scrambled out of it quickly. I recognized my bunkey's (only known name Dick) voice, appealing to the others to get their guns quickly as three mountaineers out of a party of six, playing cards by the camp fire in the corral, had been killed. Dick pushed his head in my wagon and grabbed his gun which stood with mine in the rear end corner. I challenged him. He answered, "It's Dick," and told me to get out quickly as three men had been killed and the country around the fort was on fire.

We found that some Indians had crawled inside our guard line without being discovered and shot the three mountaineers as they sat playing cards by the camp fire inside the corral. Two were dead and the other was taken to the

Indian War Dance

hospital with a bullet hole through him. This man recovered later and made many "good Indians."

Instead of the country around us and the fort being on fire, the Indians had built several signal fires around the fort and could be seen dancing naked around them and were heard yelling their war songs.

The excitement in the post was intense. Every man was called to arms. The women and children were gathered together and put in the powder magazine with a good, trusty officer, who was told to blow it up if the Indians entered the stockade and tried to capture them. Of course, our camp was outside the stockade, hence the Indians would have to wipe us out before entering the stockade on our side of the fort.

Captain Bailey took charge of the bullwhackers, wood choppers, mule skinners, etc., as well as his company of mountaineers. Every man had his place and many were lying flat in the grass on their stomachs. All had positive orders not to fire a shot until ordered. Colonel Carrington concluded to try his mountain howitzers on the Indian dancers. After a few shots the gunners got range on some of the Indian fires, and many fires were extinguished and some dancers' lives went out with them.

Our work cattle were being night herded by two Germans, one, Fred W. Kracht, who was living at No. 724 North Thirtieth street, Omaha, Nebraska, when he called on me in April, 1909. Though it was forty-three years after this exciting night, we knew each other and had a very pleasant visit, reciting our experiences at Fort Phil Kearny during those exciting days.

One night volunteers were called for to go and rescue Fred and the other German, who was known by the name of Charley, and bring in the work cattle. I was one of the fourteen men who responded. Jose and Kellogg were with us. We crawled on our hands and knees for over a mile through the brush along Piney Creek. Several times Indians rode uncomfortably close to us and it seemed that they had discovered us. Their ponies shied from us and one Indian remarked that "Tagaleska warsiches" were in the brush. What Indians we saw were naked. The cattle were grazing quietly in the open along the stream until we or some of the Indians frightened them.

On our way up the creek, when we thought no Indians were near, Kellogg, who was in charge, would halloo: "Fred!" "Charley!" but receiving no response for some time, we continued working our way up the creek through the brush. Finally we discovered several Indians trying to set the brush on fire. Had they succeeded they would have made it warm for us, but the Indian method of starting a fire at this time was very slow, especially when the grass and brush were damp from the dew and light fog. We heard the Indians say the herders were in the brush. They guessed rightly.

After failure to set the grass and brush on fire the Indians fired several shots and arrows into the thickest of the brush, hoping, no doubt, to kill the herders. Some of these shots and arrows came near us. Later we heard a pretended wolf howl. A few seconds later the two herders dashed out of the brush and shouted, "Hurrah for camp," for which they started as fast as their horses could go, chased by fully one hundred Indians. We arrived at camp just as the company of mountaineers and two companies of cavalry were leaving to bring in the cattle, which they finally did about two hours later, leaving them between the stockade and our camp where we held them the balance of the night, expecting the Indians to close in on us before sunrise.

About four o'clock in the morning a soldier, standing guard on the raised platform at the corner of the stockade, yelled for the corporal of the guard to come quickly as Indians were trying to lariat him. This was all imagination, as we had fully twenty-five well-armed men around the cattle and fully seventy-five outside of these guarding camp. The picket refused to remain and was marched to the guard house and two other guards took his place. As stated, the cattle were being held close to the stockade and it would have been impossible for Indians to get between the stockade and the cattle without stampeding them.

Some one in our camp disobeyed the order not to fire a shot until ordered and cruelly shot and killed our old pet mule "Lize." She made a rule of coming to the cook wagon and bread box every night for a few scraps which the cook would usually set aside for her. No doubt some of the night guards thought her an Indian.

The Indians kept up a few signal fires all night but out of reach of Colonel Carrington's guns.

I have talked with many Indians who were at Fort Phil Kearny at the time I was there and all told me that the night Colonel Carrington used his mountain howitzers on them the Indians had planned to destroy the fort and kill every white man, woman and child in and near it. This intention was changed when that grape and cannister shot from those mountain howitzers came down among them. Several Indians were killed and more wounded and they concluded that the Great Father was angry with them in thus dropping fire upon them. A council of the head chiefs was held and it was concluded to wait until a more favorable time and thus the intended massacre was postponed. At this time the redskins had no knowledge that such a murderous fire could be discharged from a gun. They evidently had not met General Harney or Colonel Chivington, otherwise they would have known better.

All were pleased when daylight came. The Indians had disappeared and carried off their dead and wounded, and after we had buried our two mountaineers who had been killed the night previous we went to work again hauling logs and wood for the fort, which the Indians were determined that we should not.

I pause here to say one word of praise for Colonel Carrington, his brave officers, their wives, and soldiers under his command. None knew what fear was. Always ready for any call to duty night or day, they would rush out any time to save us, often when they knew they were going to certain death. Be all honor and glory to American soldiers such as Colonel Carrington, his officers and men, and many other like heroes, whom I have met and known on the frontier; the Fettermans, Browns, Crooks, Carrs, Palmers, Hayes, Walkers, Miles, Emerys, and scores of others, not forgetting their brave wives who went through severe hardships at these frontier posts. These men helped blaze the way for the opening of the Western Empire where untold wealth in gold, silver, copper, coal, iron, and many other rich minerals cropped out freely here and there from Nature's bosom, begging and coaxing the brave and hard pioneer to come and help himself.

Yes, many of us might have claimed our share of this wealth had it not been for the pressure of the noble Red Man who claimed the earth and counted his wealth in the number of buffalo, elk, deer, and other game that he considered his to be captured and killed at will. He had fully determined to keep all the pale faces out of his country. The Great Sioux Chiefs who were at the Fort Laramie Council and many others who had joined them since were making that threat of Red Cloud good.

Kellogg, his chum and I had nearly finished our little log shack on Piney Creek near the fort. My last thought on going to sleep and first thought on awakening was: "Don't stay!" "Don't stay!" "Don't stay here but return with the train to Fort Mitchell!" Mr. Carter had often urged me to do this, intimating that he had special work for me at that fort, but I could not do so without breaking faith with Kellogg and his partner. I had purchased one-third of the provisions to last us through the winter. Flour was $16.00 per sack, sugar $1.00 per pound, and other provisions in proportion.

The work was about done. Snow had begun to fall on the high hills around the fort and the nights were getting cold and many miles had to be covered by the rather thin work cattle, horses and mules before reaching Fort Mitchell. I was not superstitious and I would try to banish the thought "don't stay" from my mind but could not.

Our train was starting and as my wagon passed our little log house I rushed in, rolled up my bed and told Kellogg and his partner that some impending disaster, that I could not explain, was causing me to return with the train to Fort Mitchell.   I told them they were welcome to all I had in the shack, that I hated to leave them, especially Kellogg, who had been so kind to me, but I could not resist the unknown power that had continued to tell me for some weeks past not to remain.   Kellogg intimated that I was a fool to notice such things when he knew that, once in the Gallatin Valley mines, we would all be rich.

To my Guardian Angel alone I attribute this timely warning.

I bade Kellogg and his partner an affectionate farewell. Tears came into the old miner's eyes as I shook hands and said good-bye.   This was the last I saw of these two brave men.

CHAPTER XIX

Experience at Fort Mitchell—Phil Kearny Massacre—Sibson's Road
Ranch—A Ride for Life—Big Mouth's Threat and
Deception—A Stranger Crosses my Path—
Indian's Revenge on an Outlaw

I HAD lost track of Swank and the three other bull-whackers who came to Fort Phil Kearny with me. I think they must have returned to the Missouri River with some earlier train or have been killed.

Though disappointed by not being able to go to the mines in the Gallatin Valley, I congratulated myself on leaving Fort Phil Kearny alive. I could count quite a few chums who were not going back. Their bodies were lying in some unmarked graves. Citizens living in this part of the Great American Republic one hundred years hence will have no conception of the hardships experienced by the men who blazed this Northwestern trail, which hundreds of times has been sprinkled with the blood of the bravest of both men and women. If a detailed history of the many murders committed by Indians on this trail from 1866 to the Custer Massacre could be written, it would blacken all Indian history on the American continent; but while condemning their cruel mode of warfare, we must not forget the fact that they were savages fighting for home and country—yes, for very existence as they understood it.

Part of our wagons were loaded with buffalo hides, elk, deer and other skins, besides bales of furs. We worked the best and strongest of our ox, horse and mule teams and drove the others loose, keeping together as far as Fort Laramie, where we arrived the latter part of December, 1866, without any serious accidents except for the loss of a few work cattle, horses and mules on account of lack of feed. Here that part of the train consisting of horse and mule teams, which was going to the Missouri River, left us, taking all the bales of buffalo robes, skins and furs. The ox teams, now with empty wagons, followed in easy drives to their destination, Fort Mitchell, fifty-five miles east of Fort Laramie.

Before our arrival at Fort Mitchell we heard of the Phil Kearny Massacre. Out of seventy-eight men and officers who went into that fight not one escaped alive. Poor Kellogg, Wheatley, our mining chum, and other civilians who went with the troops, shared a similar fate. If I had remained at the fort, the fate of these men would have been mine. Like some of the officers who went with this company, the civilians were scalped, cut and butchered to pieces and their hearts and tongues cut out. Some of the hearts were eaten by the savages to make them brave. Nearly every bone in the bodies of the whites was laid bare by the cruel knife. Large piles of empty cartridge shells lay near many of the bodies, especially near Major Brown's, Wheatley's and Kellogg's. The Indians had led the troops into ambush where they closed in on them, allowing none to escape.

Such was the Phil Kearny Massacre on December 21, 1866. It was well I obeyed that warning or I would not be here writing this autobiography. It makes me sad to think how these brave men died. They sold their lives dearly. It is said that after killing all the Indians they could and seeing their comrades mowed down beside them by a force of nearly twenty to one, with no possible chance to escape, some of the officers and men shot themselves rather than be captured alive by the savages. Long before this I had determined to do so rather than be captured by Indians. For some months I had carried a sharp dirk, intending to send its keen blade into my heart rather than submit to capture by them. I knew well the kind of death I would die if my red brothers had the management, since I have seen many of the frightfully muti· lated bodies of their white victims.

On one trip from Fort Laramie to Fort Mitchell we saw some small bands of Indians between Reynolds' ranch and Horse Creek, but the extreme cold weather prevailing had apparently congealed their energies, since they made only a weak attempt to harass us. They proved tame compared to the Indians around Phil Kearny.

On arrival at Fort Mitchell, which was then a two company adobe fort beside Jack Sibson's stage station and road ranch, we overtook the mules and horse teams that left us at Fort Laramie. They had been resting and waiting for the melting of the snow that had almost blocked the deep and narrow trail through Scott's Bluff. The second day after our arrival the stage coach from the East and a twelve-wagon mule train came through the bluffs and opened the trail so our horse and mule trains, with all extra bullwhackers we could spare, pulled out for Nebraska City. The wagons were formed in a circle near the corral, stripped of bows and sheets, and the ox yokes and chains all stored under cover at the Sibson road ranch, with the exception of one covered wagon with necessary provisions, two yoke of cattle and three horses in charge of three men, including Al Hale, the wagon boss, who went out to Robideaux Springs with the cattle where we intended to winter them.

After assisting in taking the steers to the winter camp, which lay some miles south of Scott's Bluff, Mr. Carter instructed me to remain at the ranch and make myself useful in any capacity required by Mr. Jack Sibson, who for a time seemed to look on me as an intruder. Confidentially, Mr. Carter told me that he and General Coe had sold the ranch and considerable stock, of which he gave me a list, to Captain Childs and Jack Sibson, partly on time, and that Mr. Childs had sold his interest in the ranch and stock to Mr. Sibson, who was in default in payments of both interest and principal, and I was to remain at the ranch to keep tab on the stock and merchandise. With these instructions Mr. Carter left on the first coach going east for the Missouri River.

This was not an enviable job and I would like to have gotten out of it, but Mr. Carter, whom I learned to like, insisted that I remain. I do not think that Mr. Carter had told Mr. Sibson why he wanted me to remain but, no doubt, Mr. Sibson suspected the reason. I had dropped in as a bullwhacker out of a winter's job and had been recommended by Mr. Carter as a good, reliable man. Mr. Sibson agreed to pay me $40.00 per month and I was to make myself useful at anything.

One thing I disliked about the road ranch was that Jack Sibson kept a Sioux squaw ostensibly to do the cooking, with which Mr. Sibson, the stage tenders and I often helped, especially when the stage coaches came in filled with passengers, some of whom were very prominent people, who had, however, left their frills at home. The road ranch was large, built of cedar logs and had seven fair-sized rooms besides the store. It had dirt floors and roof. It had a large corral built out of cedar logs set closely together, some three or four feet in the ground and standing eight feet high above the ground, with port holes on all sides. The large log stables were built to accommodate the stage stock and emigrant travel and were located inside the log corral or stockade. We milked a number of cows, butter selling readily from fifty cents to seventy-five cents per pound. There was also a good-sized bunch of ponies and some work cattle and horses. These were kept for trading purposes.

There were several Indian tepees pitched outside but near the corrals. A large one was occupied by John Hunter, a white man who had married General Garner's squaw wife, by whom Mr. Hunter had several half-breed children. The other tepees were occupied by relatives and friends of Mr. Hunter's Indian family. The fort across the road was garrisoned by two companies of the Eighteenth Infantry under Captain Hughes. One company had been mounted. His garrison was kept busy protecting the stage coaches, road-ranches between Fort Laramie and Pole Creek, and freight and emigrant trains, and keeping up the overland telegraph line built by Edward Creighton and others.

During pleasant days the stock was allowed to graze outside in charge of a herder and was corralled at nights. The store carried the usual stock of a road ranch—clothing, provisions, including canned goods, and plenty of whiskey, much of which was adulterated behind closed doors by Mr. Sibson. He would never let me into this secret but I think, from observation, much of the adulteration was tobacco juice. We also sold buffalo robes, elk and deer skins, harness, saddles, guns, revolvers, ammunition, and many other articles too numerous to mention.

I was pleased one day when Mr. Sibson told me he had taken a one hundred-cord wood contract to be delivered at the fort, and I, another bullwhacker and John Duval, a colored man, were set to work filling it. As a rule we made two trips a day with horse teams. The wood in dead tree lengths was easily obtained and had it not been for the bitter cold weather, the work would have been a picnic except for the poor food given us.

Mr. Sibson, without exception, was the stingiest man I ever met. For a time the officers at the fort took their meals at our ranch, but the food and cooking became so bad they had to quit. For transient guests, going through by stage coach or otherwise, who desired meals and lodging, the quality was some better, canned goods being used more or less. Deer, elk, buffalo and bear meat and bacon would be fried, and salt, cream of tartar and soda would be used in the biscuits. The beds, made on the dirt floors, consisted of buffalo, elk and bear skins, with whatever could be found for a pillow. Ladies did not mind in the least if their bed covering adjoined that of another bed occupied by some strange man, especially if their husbands or relatives were along.

I remember Brigham Young's sharing my bed for two nights. He was on his way to Salt Lake by stage coach and awaited the arrival at our ranch of a Mormon train that he had passed on the other side of Chimney Rock. He was one of the nicest and most sociable men I have ever met. No one could know him and not like him.

When the telegraph wires were not working between Fort Laramie, our ranch, Mud Springs or Pole Creek, and stage coaches were not making their usual trips, I was often called upon to carry dispatches to these different points. My trip to Fort Laramie, fifty-five miles distant, was usually made in eight or nine hours, either day or night, the latter being preferable. To make these sometimes dangerous rides I selected the best horses in our bunch. I could tell of some exciting trips that I was called upon to make in this work. On the night Mr. Gilman and Mr. Kountz lost their twenty-eight four-mule teams while camped within a quarter of a mile of our ranch and Fort Mitchell, the stage coach coming from Laramie or Reynolds' stage station was chased the last five miles of the road up to the door of the ranch by a large

Stage Coach Chased by Indians

bunch of Indians, said to be Big Mouth's band of Sioux. One dead passenger was in this coach.

The wires were down and I was called upon to make the trip to Fort Laramie that night with a rush message. I arrived at Antone Reynolds' Ranch between one and two o'clock in the morning. The dogs at the ranch were barking loudly. I commenced to whistle, which probably saved my life, since on nearing the ranch Mr. Reynolds with gun in hand halted me, shouting, "Stop!" I answered, telling him who I was, when I was allowed to approach. He wondered how I got there, asking whether I had been attacked by Indians. He said a bunch had been bothering him all night and had finally ridden away, driving away all his stock after trying their best to burn his ranch. He begged me to stay with him until daylight, saying that I would run into the Indians and get killed, but I could not remain. I had positive orders to get to Laramie by six o'clock that morning and I had twenty-eight miles yet to go. A little light was peeping out of the eastern horizon as I galloped past Jule Coffee's ranch, six miles east of Laramie, and I arrived at the latter place and delivered my message to General Palmer about forty minutes later.

On this trip I passed within a quarter of a mile of several hundred warriors and was right behind the thieving band who cleaned out Mr. Reynolds' ranch. But I missed them all, thanks again to my "Guardian Angel."

Another trip I tried to make to Fort Laramie in June, 1867, in which I was not so fortunate. Mr. Sibson had sold twelve head of work cattle to Ben Mills, clerk of Seth Bullock, the sutler, arranging that I should drive them up as soon as possible. I was hoping that some ox-train would be coming along soon in which I could take the steers but there was none reported on the trail between our ranch and Mud Springs, hence in order to keep faith with Mr. Mills, there was nothing to do but take them.

The Indians, encouraged by their successes at Fort Phil Kearny and other points, began to make it hotter for the whites all along the Phil Kearny trail, north and east as far down as old Fort Kearny and even on the trail to Denver. Unfortunately I had incurred the ill will of Big Mouth and a few other Indians living around the Mitchell ranch because I would not give them whiskey. Big Mouth was a sub-chief under Spotted Tail of the Oglala band. When I refused Big Mouth the liquor he became very angry, pulled his tomahawk out of his belt and struck at my head. My dodging backwards saved my life. He missed my head about an inch. He rushed out of the store, saying, "Sichie wa sichie," meaning that I was a bad white man and punctuated that remark by shouting he would kill me the first chance he had and I knew he would do so if he ever got the drop on me.

I tried to keep it quiet that I was going to take twelve steers to Fort Laramie and thought I had done so but it proved otherwise.   About nine o'clock at night I was all ready and had one of the stage tenders open the corral gate. I was well mounted and armed with a Sharp's carbine, two revolvers, a belt full of cartridges, and my usual sharp knife stuck in my boot leg.   I had a soldier's overcoat tied on the back of my saddle.   I had some trouble in getting the steers to leave the ranch but finally got them on the trail.   The night was rather warm and somewhat dark.   The quarter moon was hidden by clouds.   On the distant horizon in the northwest could be seen an occasional flash of lightning.   The wind began to rise and before I had traveled five miles the clouds became black, and muffled sounds of distant thunder could be heard; the wind blew in gusts and the lightning became more vivid. The steers were hard to keep on the trail. At times they would stop, raise their noses and sniff the rain-laden breeze.

I had probably gone ten miles when the lightning increased in vividness and the thunder became louder. The wind blew so hard it was difficult to face it. The rain fell in great drops and from a distance could be heard the approaching storm, which the steers refused to face, but turned their backs and commenced to drift slowly with it. Though in front of them and doing my best to hold them, it took hard riding to keep the steers close to the trail, which I could only see by the flashes of lightning.   The driver of the stage coach, that arrived at the ranch about two hours before I started, had warned me of seeing several Indian tepees near the south bank of the North Platte River about where the storm struck me; this made me cautious in hallooing at the steers while driving them.   The rain fell in sheets and many streams of storm water came rolling down the draws to the left of the trail and across it. The rain finally ceased. Although I had put on my overcoat, I was wet to the skin and my long-legged boots were full of water. I got cold and dismounted, walking to warm me. The little moon began to show itself as the clearing clouds swiftly rolled past it.

I had walked about a mile, when in a small depression of the trail, much like the bottom of a saucer, my horse suddenly stopped, wheeled around, and with head and ears erect, faced to the east and commenced to prance around. His actions told me quickly that something was wrong. I soothed him all I could and tightened the cinch of my saddle. I tried my two revolvers, that were loaded with paper cartridges—all wet and worthless. I knew I would have to depend on my carbine with its metallic cartridges and my bowie knife. During this short interval my horse became more excited and came very near breaking away from me. He was an Indian war horse. The Cheyennes and Arapahoes had owned him and Mr. Sibson had bought him from the Sioux. He had been in many a battle between Indians and between Indians and whites. Though he was nervous, he was gentle and I could guide him with my knees without a bridle. The steers were tired and stood resting, but with ears pricked and faces towards the east, like the horse. I could see nothing and hear only an occasional howl of wolves.

I finally put my ear to the ground and after listening a few moments, I heard a faint noise not unlike the jingling of bells, and other Indian trappings, and on rising to my feet and looking towards the horizon, I faintly saw the outlines of one, two, three and other mounted objects, apparently approaching between hill and sky. In an instant I was on my horse, attempting to stampede the cattle, but being tired they merely stood and looked at me. The next moment I was brought to my sense of danger by hearing the war-whoop yell. I imagine I can hear that yell as I sit penning these lines. It was given in earnest and with vigor. Had I been a black-haired man I think my hair would have turned white as they came galloping toward me. Fortunately I had tightened the cinch on my saddle. I heard one voice, that I recognized as Big Mouth's, yell in Sioux: "Stop, Yellow Hair. We have you now!" I had sent my spurs into my horse's flanks and was going as fast as I could, lying almost flat on my horse's back to avoid the arrows that were dropping around me.

I intended, if possible, to reach the Charley Blunt ranch, which a few months previous had been abandoned by Mr. Blunt on account of frequent Indian raids. Mr. Blunt's road ranch, rather a small one, was built near the mouth of a draw at the foot hills and had an outlet up the draw by underground passage. My intention was to get to this and, if possible, fight off my pursuers. Before I realized it, my horse plunged into Horse Creek, which was bank full and rushing its storm water into the North Platte River less than one-half mile distant. I came very near being dismounted. The strong current threw my horse on his side, forcing me out of the saddle for a moment. The Indians, some twelve or more in number, were gaining on me. I had fired one shot out of my carbine at the Indians, which, if it did not hit, checked them for a few moments. While I was struggling to get up the bank on the west side of the creek, some of the Indians were floundering in the water on the east bank. I saw it would be impossible to reach the Blunt ranch, so turned my horse's head down the creek on the west side, thinking I could get into the brush and maybe save myself. The continued yells and flying arrows served to make me urge my horse faster and before realizing my danger, I was carried over the six-foot bank into the rushing waters of the North Platte River. The plunge over the bank into the river, which at this point was nearly two-thirds of a mile wide, was a surprise to the Indians as well as myself and horse. One of the Indians came near following on top of me. Throwing his pony on his haunches saved both. The Indians had sent one arrow into my horse's left cushion, which I knew pained him, judging from the way he favored that leg. On striking the water I was instantly lifted out of my saddle as my horse went under. I lost my carbine and hat and for a time my horse, who came up several yards from me down stream. Though weighted down with two revolvers, a belt full of cartridges and a heavy, wet overcoat, it was but a short time before I caught hold of my horse's tail and worked my way swimming to the stirrups and bridle rein, which, fortunately, dropped over the saddle horn. I immediately commenced to slacken my cinch, when my horse commenced to swim better. It had been about all he could do to keep his head above water. Aided by the current, I was carried from the bank toward the middle of the river and very soon out of reach of the arrows of the Indians, who seemed to be still walking their ponies on the bank down stream. They called me to come back, saying they would get me yet.

I had continued swimming along the side of my horse until I reached what I thought to be about the middle of the river, when the water became shallower. Several times I felt like giving up, I became so tired and exhausted. The water was now about up to my waist. I took off my overcoat, revolvers, belt of cartridges and threw them in the river and pulled the arrow out of the horse's cushion, then mounted and headed the best I could for the north bank of the river. It was not long before I was in swimming water and the steep river bank ahead of me began to show itself. I floated down stream for a quarter of a mile before I could find a place to get out, but my horse could not climb the steep bank and fell backwards into the river, pulling me in after him where I swam along by his side. My faithful horse seemed to realize, like myself, that it was a fight for life for both of us. He was willing at all times to obey my slightest wish.

After swimming for some distance along the north bank of the river I came to the mouth of Small Creek, where, thank God, I got out. The arrow wound in my horse's cushion was yet bleeding slightly and I got a handful of wet soil and pressed it over the wound. I took the bit out of his mouth and held him by the lariat, allowing him to graze while I stood holding him, chilled with cold.

Do not wonder, kind reader, if I offered up to Him who

controls the destinies of nations as well as of men a short prayer, thanking Him and that same Guardian Angel for bringing me through in safety.

The last sound from the Indians indicated that they had followed down the river. I learned afterwards that some of them did this, expecting that I would recross, when they would intercept me. Others, I was informed, took the twelve steers west to some Indian camp on the La Bonta.

I began to hear dogs barking and concluded I could not be far from the Raw Hide Agency or some band of Indians camped close to there. It must have been between one and two o'clock and I knew that if I remained there until daybreak I would be captured by some of the Raw Hide band. I finally decided to walk up the river, leading my horse in order to keep warm. I had gone nearly two miles without finding an inlet into the river. The barking of the dogs became louder and made me more anxious to cross the river and to hurry matters. I mounted my horse and struck a trot. I think I had gone about two and one-half miles when I found a sand bar at the mouth of a draw that led into the river, which I felt confident I could cross. I was soon in swimming water, then shallower. My horse went down in the quicksand several times but giving him the rein and his time, he wallowed out of it. I began to see the bank which was too steep to climb. Later I found a place where the bank had caved in more or less and by getting off my horse I succeeded in getting him up the bank and was once more on terra firma, not very far west of the mouth of Horse Creek where the Indians ran me into the river. When I crossed the creek, one-half mile south of the trail, it had gone down and resumed its normal size.

I was numb with cold with not a dry thread on me and had not had any food for nearly six hours.

Day was peeping as I got fairly into the hills one-half mile or more south of the trail. My horse was getting quite lame and did not look like the same animal I started out on a few hours before. His slow gait told the hardship he had gone through. To ease him and keep myself warm I walked, hugging the south tips of the bluffs with a view to looking over the Platte Valley for Indians, especially for Big Mouth and his band of outlaws. I failed to see any or anything of the twelve head of work steers. They had, I presumed, been driven off. The sun came up bright and warm, which I appreciated very much as my clothes were yet wet.

I reached the ranch about ten o'clock in the morning and the first Indian to greet me was Big Mouth. He, like the many soldiers that soon surrounded me, wanted to know what had happened to me and the cattle. I told them Big Mouth well knew what had happened and knew where the cattle had been taken. A few days later he told me that I had escaped this time but he would fix me yet.

A short time after this one of the Indians who was in the party with Big Mouth told me that Big Mouth led the twelve Indians to kill me and capture the cattle, which four of the Indians had taken to Black Dog's camp on La Bonta Creek. Big Mouth having learned that I had been told that he led the attack and knew where the steers had been taken, to save himself from arrest, came and told me that it was a joke they played on me and that I would find the steers all right at Black Dog's camp if I would go and get them, and if the steers were not there, I would find them at Jim Bellamy's ranch west of Fort Laramie.

A few days after learning where the steers were I started to get them, riding to Fort Laramie the first night and the next day to Bellamy's road ranch about fourteen miles west of the fort.

Between the fort and Bellamy's ranch I overtook a very interesting specimen of a degenerate white man. He was rather short and heavy set, dark complexioned and with long, matted hair and beard. His clothes were a combination of soldier's clothes, canvas and buckskin. He wore moccasins and had two revolvers and a knife fastened to his belt of cartridges. Upon overtaking him he wanted to know where I was from, where I was going, and many other pertinent

questions which I answered evasively. He said I was riding
a good horse, asked what I would take for her and whether
I would not let him try her a little ways. I told him I did not
care to part with her. This horse was a seven-eighths thoroughbred Kentucky mare that I had borrowed from Bob
Mason, who remained at the Mitchell ranch courting "Puss,"
John Hunter's half-breed stepdaughter, while I went to get
and turn the steers over to Ben Miles, the sutler's clerk at Fort
Laramie. I kept my new friend in the best humor I could

A Degenerate White Man

and he seemed to appreciate my company by pulling from his
inside shirt pocket a bottle of whiskey which he offered and insisted I should drink. I told him I could not drink it as the
smell of it made me sick. He then asked me what day of
the week it was, the date and year, which I thought I answered correctly but he denied it, saying it was a damned lie.
I eased him up by saying he might be right. He then wanted
to know if I smoked. I told him I did not. Did I chew?
I said "no." Did I play cards? I answered that I did not.
He then asked me, "What kind of a damned man are you
anyway?"

While carrying on this conversation we walked along the

trail, when shortly, to my relief, we met an old Indian and his squaw and the three commenced talking in Sioux language. I finally broke away from this trio. When I left, the Indian had the bottle and my white friend was making eyes at the squaw and the squaw was casting one eye at her white friend. The other eye was blind.

I left under protest and was glad to get away. Had I continued my journey with him I have every reason to believe that he would have killed me and taken the horse. While walking with him he tried to keep on my right, while I worked every scheme to keep him on my left near the muzzle of the gun I carried in front of me.

I arrived at Bellamy's ranch before dark and received information as to where the twelve steers were. Mr. Bellamy kept a large ranch made out of logs and sod. He had two squaws and a large family of papooses, some of them in their teens. He had a young man working for him who had come from the East some two months before. I think he was an outlaw. He told me confidentially that he had bought a squaw that day and was celebrating the event by trying his best to get drunk and was succeeding to a great extent. I saw the young squaw—rather a nice-looking girl, whom I could not help but pity. The young man said he had given her parents two ponies for her. Her parents came back in the evening and wanted some additional presents, but the young man refused to give them, when the parents left very angry, swearing vengeance against him.

Mr. Bellamy had shown me a place to spread my buffalo robe for the night near the bed of the young man and his bride. Mr. Bellamy, his squaws and family slept in the other end of the large log room. I had fallen asleep on a pile of buffalo robes in the store when I was awakened by the crying of the girl whom I heard that brute of a man striking and cursing. I waited until all was quiet when I stole into the room and lay down on my robe and was soon asleep, only to be awakened again by the cursing of that drunken brute who again commenced to strike the girl lying beside him. I finally told him what I thought of him and appealed to Mr. Bellamy to make him desist. The young man became very angry at me, telling me it was none of my business; that he had bought that squaw and he was going to do what he pleased with her. The girl rose from her bed and ran out of the ranch. He tried to follow but was too drunk. Mr. Bellamy finally told him if he struck that squaw again or abused her in any way, he would fix him. After that the night passed in quietness.

When I went to get my horse the next morning I came across the, poor girl. Her face was swollen and covered with blood, and one eye was swollen shut from his heavy blows. I did not see him.

After breakfast I saddled up and started to find the steers, Mr. Bellamy giving me directions where he thought I would find them. It was nearly an all-day trip but I got them. When I returned to Mr. Bellamy's ranch, part of it was in ashes and that young man was never seen or heard of afterward. It was learned that the girl, known as a "trading squaw," had gone back to her people that morning and they, with the help of other Indians, came to the Bellamy ranch and caught and killed the young man. Mr. Bellamy and family barely escaped with their lives, the Indians blaming him for not protecting the young squaw.

I drove the steers to Fort Laramie before daylight and later turned them over to Ben Miles, Seth Bullock's clerk, as per agreement except as to time. The next day I returned to Fort Mitchell with further reasons to thank that "Guardian Angel." I was beginning to think an Indian could not harm me.

CHAPTER XX

Frontier Justice—Hunter Tries to Bribe the Wrong Man—A Forced Confession—Negro John in Love with Puss—Grandma Antelope is Active—A White Woman Appears on the Scene

AMONG other incidents that occurred at Fort Mitchell during my stay at this road ranch and stage station was one that called for frontier justice as usually administered in those lawless days.

As previously stated, John Hunter lived with his Indian half-breed family in one of the tepees near the ranch corral. John was cross-eyed, but could shoot straight. He could also drink bad whiskey, play poker, swear, and was treacherous and cold-blooded as an Indian, yet with all this he had a winning, persuasive way about him that usually succeeded in taking the last dollar from the soldiers, and sometimes the officers, the stage-tenders, freighters, bullwhackers and mule skinners, whom he would often accompany a day or so on the trail. He made friends with the officers and soldiers and it was not long before I began to notice that Mr. Sibson's friendship with them was on the wane, principally owing to his narrowness and stingy ways in doing business and dealing with them.

It happened one day that the Indians had raided a freight train between Pole Creek and Mitchell and the commander of the Fort, Captain Hughes, had taken what mounted men he could scare up of his command and gone in pursuit of this thieving band. The morning after the departure of the mounted troops, two soldiers came over to the ranch, claiming to be sick and begged Mr. Sibson to give them each a drink of whiskey, which he did, his sympathy in this case getting the better of his judgment. This feigned sickness was a job put up on Mr. Sibson by Mr. Hunter and Sergeant H—. In about half an hour Sergeant H— came over and handed to Mr. Sibson a telegram the contents of which read as follows:

Fort Laramie,

John Sibson,
    Fort Mitchell.
        You are hereby notified to leave the Fort Mitchell Military Reservation immediately.

(Signed) GENERAL PALMER.

Sergeant H— gave Mr. Sibson ten minutes in which to leave. Mr. Sibson gave me a bill of sale of all his personal property and delivered to me a power of attorney to act as his agent in all matters, and bidding me a hurried good-bye, started west on horseback. I never saw or heard of him afterwards. I had heard from some source other than Mr. Sibson, that Mr. Hunter and Captain Childs had had some dealings which were not settled satisfactorily to Mr. Hunter.

In the afternoon of the day Mr. Sibson was ordered to leave Fort Mitchell, little Billy Garner, a step-son of John Hunter, came over to the ranch and informed me that some of the soldiers had our milk cows in the fort stables and were milking them. I went over to the stables and found they had saddled some of our horses and mules and that a soldier was milking one of our ten cows. I made the soldier stop milking the cow, unsaddled the animals and turning them and the cows outside, returned to the ranch by way of Sergeant H—'s quarters but found that gentleman asleep. I had scarcely entered the ranch before the sergeant was at my heels reproving me severely for what I had done in standing on my rights. Luckily, I had a friend in Operator Bundy and immediately sent a wire to General Palmer at Fort Laramie, informing him what Sergeant H— had done and asking him by whose authority he was acting. I signed my name as John Sibson's agent. In a short time I received a reply from General Palmer stating that Sergeant H— had acted without authority and had been instructed to turn all of Mr. Sibson's stock over to me and not to interfere in civil matters again without orders. Sergeant H— received a wire from General Palmer that brought him to his senses. I had established my rights as agent to Mr. Sibson's property but had incurred the deadly enmity of the sergeant and some of the soldiers, especially the one I knocked off his seat on the milking stool while he was milking one of our cows.

That night John Hunter came over to the ranch and had a long, confidential talk with me. Its substance was that Mr. Sibson owed him considerable money on contracts and other transactions and if I would quietly go away, he would pay me $3000.00 in gold. I told him that the proposition had come so unexpectedly that I would want some time to consider it. He said that was all right if I would not be too long about it and intimated that it would be but a short job to put me out of the way. I told Operator Bundy what had occurred and that night began sending messages to Mr. Carter at Nebraska City, Denver and other points and to General Coe, whom I had never seen, at Salt Lake City and other Western points, telling both that they had better send some one to take charge of Mr. Sibson's property as John Hunter with his Indians was liable to take it by force. I could get no word from either. Mr. Hunter had asked me twice what I had decided to do. I told him I was still thinking over his proposition. Yes, I was thinking what a deep-dyed, unprincipled scoundrel he was to offer me $3000.00 to betray my trust and become a thief. "No! John Hunter, never, never!"

A few days after this, Billy Garner, referred to before and who has since filled the position of Government Inspector at Pine Ridge Indian Agency, came to the ranch and stated that John Hunter was mean to his mother, brothers and sisters, his grandmother and himself; that he often whipped them with a quirt; that he had done this last night and that he would not put up with it another minute. Billy was then about twelve years old and a manly little boy. He wanted to know whether I would not loan him a couple of revolvers and some ammunition. I told him I would and gave him two revolvers and fifty rounds of cartridges. About 1:30 the next morning John Hunter came to the ranch and commenced kicking on the door and rapping on the window. I inquired what he wanted and he replied that he wanted me to open the door and turn out his family or he would fix me. I informed him that his family was not in the ranch and that I knew nothing about them. After making many threats and uttering a basketful of curses, he at last staggered to his tepee. The next morning early I heard him prowling around the ranch and soon saw him carry a black leather satchel to the fort and in a few minutes return without it. I guessed what all this meant. Shortly afterward he mounted his favorite horse and started up the trail and judging from the way he watched the trail, first on one side of his horse and then on the other, I knew he was looking for tracks. He soon put his horse at a fast pace. He had evidently found their tracks and was now determined to overtake them. Horse and rider were quickly lost in the distance and nothing indicated his course except the little cloud of dust, which finally disappeared on the trail. On the third evening after his departure he returned, armed with the same old trusty carbine, two revolvers and bowie knife in his right bootleg, but without his family. One of the stage drivers told me that he had overtaken his family at Antone Reynolds' ranch but they refused to return with him. He was angry.

The next morning after his return and a visit to the fort, he came into the ranch and in an appealing way intimated that he was in trouble. I inquired what was wrong. He said before going after his family he had taken his satchel containing $900.00 to $1000.00 and left it in the safe keeping of Sergeant H— and that, unknown to the sergeant, some one had gone through the satchel and taken all the money. He said both he and the sergeant suspected Sanders, who had just deserted the day he left to hunt his family. I asked him what caused him to think that Sanders had taken the money. He answered because the sergeant and some of the soldiers thought so and his desertion at this particular time seemed to confirm it. I told him I did not believe Sanders, whom I knew well, had done anything of the kind. Sanders had often called on me to write letters to his widowed mother and sisters, who seemed to be very good, honest people, and since they had told him they would like to have him come home and work the little farm, he had requested me to write them that he would do so as soon as his time was out in the army. He had about one year yet to serve. I told Hunter that I was satisfied that Sanders had not taken a cent of his money but that Bundy and I would do all in our power to arrest him and bring him back and that I thought I could find his stolen money. Bundy, the operator, gladly joined me in the proposed plan to arrest Sanders. Wires were quickly working to Mud Springs, Pole Creek and Laramie, authorizing the arrest of Sanders, a recent deserter and accused of robbery of nearly $1000.00 at Fort Mitchell. I then determined to test Sergeant H—'s nerve and honesty in the matter. Mr. Bundy thought the plan I proposed somewhat severe but consented to it. Mr. Hunter was in for anything that would give him back his money, even to killing the sergeant, to which both Mr. Bundy and the writer objected. My idea was to scare him and get him to confess that he took the money himself.

We went out to the log stable and fixed a hangman's noose over one of the roof logs and set a box under the noose. This done and a gun prepared for an emergency, it was arranged that I should go over to the sergeant's quarters at the fort and invite him to the ranch, where it was proposed to question him closely about the money and if possible, get his acknowledgment of the theft—even if we had to put the rope around his neck and see some daylight between his feet and the box under the noose. Everything arranged and understood, I went to get the sergeant, who hesitated at first about coming but I told him he ought to try to help us recover Mr. Hunter's money. He did not know we had had the wires busy and that Sanders had wired us from Mud Springs that he would be up on the first coach.

Once inside the ranch, I locked the door and put the key in my pocket and picking up a revolver, I joined Hunter and

Bundy who were seated at a table in the dining room, inviting the sergeant to a vacant chair in front of us. As soon as seated I accused the sergeant of stealing Mr. Hunter's money and said that everything pointed to him as the thief. He became very excited and said he had never seen or touched a dollar of the money and did not know what had become of it, but was satisfied that Sanders, the deserter, had taken it. We told him that Sanders had wired that he would be up on the first coach and that we were satisfied that Sanders had not taken the money. This information caused him to become more excited, and he said he could take an oath on a stack of Bibles as big as the bluff (meaning Scott's Bluff) that he was innocent of the charge and thought we were doing him a great injustice in accusing him of the theft. We insisted that he make a clean breast of it and give it up, or we were prepared to take extreme measures with him. We gave him a severe examination, at the end of which all were satisfied that he was the guilty party. Hunter threatened to kill him right there, if he did not give him that money, and I believe he would have done so had not Bundy and I prevented it. This hurried me to open the rear door of the ranch leading to the stable and I asked him to follow, which he did, Hunter and Bundy bringing up the rear with revolvers leveled on the sergeant should he make a break. It was but a moment before we had him standing on the box, his arms and legs tied and the noose adjusted around his neck. I told him we were sorry to have to take such extreme measures with him and asked him whether he had any word to say or send to his friends before we hung him. He said he had not, and if we carried out our plan, we would hang an innocent man, but he was prepared to die. With this remark we pulled him up and for a few seconds had him swinging with the box out from under his feet. He was getting black in the face, his eyes bulging out, and apparently strangling, when we concluded to let him down. We laid him on the ground and it was some time before he revived. As soon as he did we asked him if he wanted to pray or send word to his folks. He answered "No" and tears rolled down his cheeks. *He was weakening.* We told him he had better pray before we finished him. He said he would not and we could finish the job. In an instant we had him up again. I had intentionally placed a handkerchief around his neck to ease the tightening of the rope, especially where the knot was under his ear. It seemed for a moment that we had finished him. His face, blacker than at first, eyes protruding and tongue out, he struggled hard and at last gave us a sign to let him down. It was about half an hour before he revived so he could talk, when he told us that he had taken the money and that Sanders was innocent. He finally took us over to where he had hidden the money in a manure pile. It was all there but about $15.00 that he had given to some of his soldiers. He was placed under arrest.

The next day Sanders came in on the eastern coach and told us that the sergeant came to him and told him to desert, giving him a gun, ammunition and a good lunch, and told him not to let him see which way he went. The sergeant acknowledged this story to be true.

The last I saw of Sergeant H— was at Fort Laramie. He was wearing a ball and chain and was later sent to Fort Leavenworth military prison to serve out a well-deserved sentence.

After this, John Hunter was my best friend and I did not turn the ranch or any of its property over to him or receive or accept his $3000.00 or any part of it. His family later returned to him on his promise to be good and on the strength of some presents he distributed among them.

Bob Mason had been gone for some time on one of the coaches, bound for the Missouri River, from where he intimated he was going to Texas with General Coe to buy Texas cattle. He had not married Puss Garner, the beautiful half-breed stepdaughter of Mr. Hunter, but Bob was very much in love with her and promised to come back some day and make her his squaw wife. It would have pleased Hunter to have me take Mason's place, but I preferred to have something to say about that. I had made no advances or encouraged Puss to come to the ranch but she often hung around the store with her little brothers and sisters. Imagine my surprise when one day our colored man, John Duval, came to me and confidentially informed me that he was in love with Puss and would like to make her his wife, take her back with him to old Missouri and show his old master Duval what a nice girl he had for a wife. I frankly told John that she would not marry him because the Sioux had no love for the colored people and if any were captured the Sioux made slaves of them. John remarked that he did not care what the Indians did with him if he could buy Puss. He finally asked me to see what I could do towards getting her for his wife. I told him I disliked very much to have anything to do with it, and that he might spend all his money in trying to get her and then she might not accept him, when he would blame me. He had $600.00 and would give it all to get her and begged me to see what I could do. I promised to speak to her folks about it and I did. They ridiculed the idea of Puss marrying a negro. When they spoke to Puss about it she became very angry and her old grandmother threatened to kill him if he ever came near Puss, and from that time on she carried a sharp butcher knife for John Duval. The old lady was a full-blooded Oglala Sioux, small of stature, deeply wrinkled, thin, wiry, had a violent temper, and though I judged her to be over seventy years old, she was as fleet of foot as a deer. Once she had chased me nearly a quarter of a mile with a knife because I had dumped the carcass of a steer into the river instead of allowing her to take the sinews out of it, and it had taken some time to regain her good opinion.

John was persistent and bothered me considerably with his love affairs. I told him he might give her and her relatives every dollar he had and then not get her, but he did not care and wanted me to go ahead. I told him he would have to present her with two white or spotted ponies, a nice saddle, two red blankets, several dollars' worth of presents—looking glasses, beads, paints, moccasins and shawls, and numerous presents for her friends and relatives; besides he would have to pay for a big feast which might take all his money and then not secure her. He did not care if it did and said for me to go ahead. He bought the ponies, one white and one spotted, a nice saddle, bridle, blanket and lariat, and many other presents, as previously enumerated, for Puss and all her relatives and friends. Puss hesitated a long time before consenting to even a mock marriage and old Grandma Antelope invested in another whetstone to make her knife doubly sharp for John.

I had a hard time to get all matters satisfactorily arranged. The officers of the Post were taken into the secret and entered into it with much zeal. Dr. Cunningham, the Post Surgeon, was to perform the ceremony. The ponies,— one bearing the saddle, bridle and blanket, were tied to a post opposite Puss's tepee and after a time that Indian half-breed maiden came out, unsaddled the ponies, carried the saddle, blanket and bridle into her tepee and staked both the ponies out, which meant she accepted John's good intentions and the proposed marriage and festivities were set with the understanding that Puss need not live with John or go to Missouri with him unless she felt like it, since it was only a mock marriage, as Duval was given to understand before the ceremony took place.

We put old Fort Mitchell ranch in a blaze of light that night. We had no lamps in those days but made the twenty-pound candle box look pretty empty before we got through lighting up. We also borrowed several lanterns from the fort and increased this flood of light by setting fire to rags saturated with bacon grease. The ranch presented a lively appearance.

Officers, soldiers, stage drivers and tenders, Indians and half-breed, bullwhackers and mule skinners were there, and among the noted guests who came in on the coach that evening was the famous stage coach owner, Ben Holladay, who delayed the departure of the west bound coach an hour to witness the ceremony.

Puss was rigged up in all her finery and looked very pretty. Her coal-black eyes looked like bright diamonds. She wore a beaded buckskin jacket, short skirt, leggings and moccasins, with a new red blanket thrown around her shoulders. Her long black hair was plaited in one long braid which hung down her back. She had several strings of different colored beads hanging around her neck and rather large, well-polished brass earrings in her ears. Her features were regular, her teeth white and even. She stood between her mother and Grandmother Antelope. The latter occasionally, to show her disapproval of what she thought was to be a real marriage, flourished a large, new butcher knife that Duval had given her and which she would have been glad to use in taking the sinews out of John's body should she get a chance.

Duval had scared up what was once a white shirt but now the color of chrome yellow. This, with some clothes loaned him for the auspicious occasion, made him present a rather respectable appearance. He was somewhat nervous and excited, especially when old Grandmother Antelope made a lunge at his yellow shirt bosom with her big knife, hissing between the few teeth she had left the words "Sichie! Sichie! Sichie!" I finally had to leave John to go to Grandma who was getting worked up to fever heat as the time to perform the ceremony approached.

At last, all being ready, the ceremony proceeded. The doctor read some lines from one of Shakespeare's plays, made John jump several times backwards and forwards over a long stick, made him stand on his head, crawl on his knees, walk on his hands and feet, bark like a dog, meow like a cat, bawl like a cow, howl like a wolf, yell like an Indian, give the war whoop, and do many stunts that created much merriment, but John took for granted it was all a part of the ceremony. After the ceremony came the marriage feast, which all relished, except the whites when it came to dog soup and dog meat which the Indians present enjoyed very much.

The feast over, John insisted on sending a telegram to his old "Massa Duval" in Missouri, stating that he had married Princess Antelope of the Oglala Sioux nation. Puss was anything but sad, but seemed not quite as happy as John.

It was two o'clock in the morning before the guests began to leave the ranch. Puss had slipped quietly away without saying one word to John, who became very sad. He told me Puss had gone and wanted to know what he should

Grandma Antelope Becomes Active

do. Someone suggested that he go to her tepee and if she decided to let him enter, they, her folks, would soon inform him. John wanted to know if that old grandma did not live in that tepee. We told him she did, but that perhaps she might not hurt him since he was married to Puss. It was a long time before John mustered up courage to raise the tepee lid. When he did, Grandma Antelope poked her head outside and then took after John with her large knife, yelling at the top of her voice the loudest of Indian yells. John took to the prairie as fast as a deer, followed by the old Indian woman and a bunch of barking dogs. Had she caught him there certainly would have been one colored man less. He came sneaking up a draw to the ranch a little before daylight, almost scared to death. He never had the courage to go back to the tepee to claim his bride. Neither did the bride Princess ever try to claim the colored, would-be husband. We succeeded in getting back some of the presents but not all. The last seen of John was when he returned to the Missouri River with a freight train a few days later, a "sadder and a wiser man." He said he did not care and thought he was lucky not to have to take a dog-eating Sioux Indian squaw for a wife, and that his old Master Duval would have discarded him had he done so.

The Sioux at this time did not take kindly to the negro. Any captured ones were made to do all the hard, dirty work of the band of Indians that captured them.

It was while here at Fort Mitchell that I spent nearly six months without seeing a white woman. I had nothing to read but an almanac and that was for the preceding year. I could read it backwards and upside down. I had been riding around the stock one day when I was told that a fourteen wagon mule and horse train had passed sometime that morning en route for Montana and that they had a white woman with them. I determined to have a look at that white woman. Without waiting for lunch I saddled another horse and started in pursuit of that emigrant train and after about a seven-mile ride caught up with it.

I rode along the side of the last wagon, and the driver, apparently surprised and somewhat excited when he saw me, stopped his team, when I asked him if they had a white woman in their train. After looking me over and sizing me up, he answered hesitatingly, "We have." I told him I meant no harm nor disrespect; that I lived at the Fort Mitchell ranch they had just passed and that it had been nearly six months since I had seen a white woman and had come to take a look at her to see what my mother looked like. Convinced that I meant no harm outside of gratifying an idle curiosity, he told me she was in the sixth wagon ahead.

As I passed the drivers of the wagons they eyed me suspiciously, but when I hallooed "Howdy" they let me pass although I think some of them grabbed their guns. I was armed with two revolvers, Sharp's carbine, bowie knife and carried a field glass.

Catching up with the driver of the seventh wagon, an old man probably sixty years of age, I told him that I heard the train had a white woman in it, that I had lived several months at the ranch they had just passed and had not seen one and if he had no objection, if she was his wife, I should like to take a look at her to remind me of what my mother looked like. He commenced to laugh and called back in the wagon, "Ma, here's a young fellow wants to see you." "Ma" crawled up toward her husband. She wore a sunbonnet, and after hearing my story, threw it back on her neck, revealing her gray hair and a very kindly face. I thought her handsome as I talked with her and her husband riding along beside their team a couple of miles, when they went into camp and insisted that I take dinner with them. I enjoyed my visit with these people, who came from eastern Iowa.

When I was ready to leave and bade them good-bye, a feeling of sadness came over me as I turned my horse's head toward the Fort Mitchell ranch with its responsibilities and strenuous life. I thought of home and the loved ones there.

It was not many days after this that two bullwhackers came to the ranch one night and requested supper, lodging and breakfast. They had walked from Fort Laramie without being attacked by Indians. They had due bills given them for service by some freighter they had worked for but had no money. I gave them supper, lodging and breakfast and told them they could stay at the ranch until some coach or train came along, but they declined, saying they were anxious to get to the Missouri River. I told them they were running a great risk and were liable to be killed or captured by Indians, but they thought not and would risk it. Taking a lunch they bade me good-bye and started up the trail toward Scott's Bluff Gap. Two days later I had some business to transact at Brown's ranch about fourteen miles east of the bluff and en route about eight miles east of the bluffs I came to a pack of wolves feasting on the dead bodies of these two men. They had evidently been killed by Indians. They had been scalped, ears, nose and other members of the body cut off, tongues cut out, hearts laid bare and nearly every bone in their bodies exposed—partly by the wolves and partly by Indians. I returned to the ranch and went back the next day with half a dozen mounted infantry. We gathered up what little was left of their bodies, placed them in a blanket, buried them in a hole dug by the side of the trail and drove down a stake to mark their nameless grave.

These two men, like many others, took desperate chances and paid for it with their lives. Many venturesome frontiersmen have met a similar fate. The loved ones at home, no doubt, have often wondered why the boys did not write or come home. I should have been glad to have told them had I known their names, but there was nothing left to identify them, not a scrap of paper nor even a stitch of clothing on their mutilated bodies. Those two lives were wiped out. They were only a short link in the chain of progress and civilization in the opening and development of our great Western Empire with its billions of hidden wealth. Our downeast friend and kind philanthropist thinks the Child of the Forest, the untutored savage, is justified in these acts of cruelty in the loss of country. Banish the thought.

Before closing this already long chapter I cannot pass unnoticed a very comical incident, that occurred on a trip I was making from Fort Mitchell to Fort Laramie between Stuttering Brown, proprietor of Brown's ranch located between Mitchell and Mud Springs, and Stuttering Bill Smith, corral boss at Fort Laramie. Both had killed their man, knew no fear and would shoot on the least provocation.

Brown came to our ranch one evening intending to go to Fort Laramie and as I had some despatches to carry to General Palmer at that Fort, it was arranged that we go together, starting early the next morning. During my ride with him to Reynolds' ranch we became well acquainted. He told me of many strange things that had occurred during his life, some of which were of no credit to him in my estimation. We had scarcely dismounted at the Reynolds' ranch before a great, big fine-looking man, weighing nearly two hundred pounds, stepped to the ranch door, walked up to Brown, pushed the end of a big revolver into Brown's mouth and commenced to work the trigger. I expected to see Brown's head blown to pieces. Brown tried to talk but could not, owing to the end of Bill Smith's (such being the name of the good-looking man) revolver being in his mouth. Brown kept backing away but Smith followed him, saying loud and earnestly: "P-p-p-p-pa-pay me n-n-n-now." Brown tried to pull his revolver but Smith took it from him. I appealed to Smith to give Brown a chance to explain but Smith told me not to "b-bu-butt" in or he would "f-f-fix" me, too. Brown did the only thing he could do—put his hand down in his pants' pocket and after a few tugs, pulled out a large roll of greenbacks, probably $1000.00, pushed it into Smith's hands and in less than five minutes both were drinking large drinks of Antone Reynolds' road ranch whiskey out of the same tin cup. Brown finally explained to Smith that he had come up on purpose to pay him this money, which I think was for mules furnished by Smith through Brown to graders on the Union Pacific Railroad, at that time between Columbus and Grand Island.

I parted with them, leaving them the best of friends. Smith said he would join me on my trip to Fort Laramie if I would wait until morning, but I could not wait.

Smith had come down to Reynolds' ranch for a double purpose. One may have been to pay Brown the money due him for mules but another, and principal object, was to make love to Antone Reynolds' half-breed daughter, a very comely Indian girl, whom he afterwards married. Both Smith and Brown later died with their boots on, the latter at Cheyenne and the former near Elk Mountain.

I could recite many other incidents of interest to the reader that transpired while at this noted road ranch and stage station, but time and space forbid.

Shortly after making this trip, when I had almost given up all hope of being relieved, I received a telegram from Mr. Carter, sent from Mud Springs, stating that he was on his way to Fort Mitchell and expected to arrive on the first coach. He arrived the next day. Of course, I had much news to tell him, especially about Hunter and how he had offered me $3000.00 to turn the ranch over to him, his strategy in getting Sibson away and of my efforts in helping Hunter to get his money back, which had probably been the means of saving the ranch and my own life. Mr. Carter kept me awake the greater part of the night, asking questions about matters connected with the ranch. I had kept a strict account of all money I had taken in and of stock bought and sold, which Mr. Carter checked up and finding everything correct was loud in his praises for the showing I made. Even John Hunter said many good words about me to Mr. Carter.

The two finally agreed on the sale and purchase of the ranch, stock and goods, and in less than a week I bade my friend Hunter and others at the ranch and fort, good-bye, and under instructions from Mr. Carter, who went on to Fort Laramie, I started across the country, headed for Pine Bluffs, riding the Bob Mason thoroughbred mare and leading a pack horse, on which I had all my belongings. I was carrying a letter from Mr. Carter to Mr. Sinclair, manager of Gilman & Carter's tie and wood camp at that point, which the Union Pacific Railroad had passed with its track-laying gangs.

It took me two days to make the trip of about seventy-five miles from Fort Mitchell to Pine Bluffs. It was a lonesome ride and rather a long, lonesome night. I saw no Indians, but some fresh tracks. I also saw a few buffalo, elk, deer, one lone bear, and quite a few wolves and coyotes. I was not sorry when I crossed the Union Pacific Railroad track at Pine Bluffs station (consisting of a box car), about the middle of September, 1867.

Few men as young as I, being only in my twenty-fifth year, had ever gone through the severe, soul-trying experiences that I had while at Fort Mitchell. They were bad enough at times to make a devil out of an angel. It took courage to do right. I think I was justified in my treatment of Sergeant H. It was the means of recovering Hunter's money and the just punishment of Sergeant H. for his crime.

I will leave the verdict to my readers.

CHAPTER XXI

I REPORTED to Mr. Sinclair, manager of the tie and wood camp, but that gentleman did not give me a cordial welcome. I found there were two bitter factions in the camp—one representing Gilman Bros., the other Coe & Carter. Mr. Sinclair belonged to the former faction, hence had no use for me, coming as I did from the service of Coe & Carter, even though carrying a letter of introduction from Mr. Carter, who suggested that I assist in the camp store. Mr. Sinclair said he did not need any one. I told him I preferred outside work, teaming or anything to make myself useful. So I was given a six-yoke ox-team and put under E. C. Miller who had seen service with me at Fort Phil Kearny. He was wagon boss of about twenty six-yoke ox-teams, part of those we had at Phil Kearny. We made a trip a day, five to seven miles, hauling wood or ties from the timber to the station. The company had about thirty four-mule and horse teams. These would haul ties and wood from two to four miles farther in the timber than the ox-teams. There was a large force of tie and wood choppers at work keeping the teams supplied. Many were French Canadians and all made big money at this work.

After being here about a month a telegram was received from General Coe at Fort Sanders, requesting that eight five-yoke teams, the culls of the cattle outfit, be loaded with corn and sent as soon as possible to Fort Sanders under my charge. I was soon on the road with this cull outfit of eighty head of very undesirable work steers, some setters, wild, lame and footsore that I had to shoe before reaching Cheyenne. I also had eight of the oldest wagons, yokes, bows, chains and wagon sheets, and nine of the worst, disreputable bull-whackers in the Pine Bluffs camps, including one extra to act as night herder. To get along with these men, all older than I, and get this cull outfit over the Sherman Hill was no picnic. I had several breakdowns but finally arrived at the Fort Sanders camp about two and one-half miles northeast of Laramie City, which was just in its infancy.

At this Fort Sanders camp, located about a mile northeast of the fort, I first met General Isaac Coe, Mr. Carter's partner. He asked me many questions about Fort Phil Kearny and Fort Mitchell. Mr. Carter had evidently kept him fully advised. He also questioned me closely about the John Hunter matter at Mitchell, more than once commending my action in dealing with him and thanked me for guarding Coe & Carter's interests, saying he would try to show his appreciation of the service I had rendered.

He told me he had sent for these eight ox-teams with a view to selling them to parties who wished to pay for them by getting out three thousand cords of wood on a contract Gilman & Carter had taken to deliver at Fort Sanders, and by filling a large tie contract which the same company had taken from Credit Mobilier, a sub-company of the Union Pacific Railroad Co. Dr. Durant was president of the Credit Mobilier at this time.

After unloading the eight loads of corn at Fort Sanders, the General instructed me to take off the wagon boxes, lengthen out the reaches and prepare to start for eight large loads of dead wood the next morning. He was anxious to show the would-be buyers of these eight teams just what could be done. It was about eight miles to this dead quaking asp wood, which lay piled in every conceivable shape, three to seven feet deep. We camped for the night on the edge of this timber and had no trouble in loading our wagons that evening, thus giving us an early start next morning. We arrived safely with our load at the fort before noon. This trip was the means of selling this cull outfit at a good figure and ridding the firm of Gilman & Carter of several undesirable bullwhackers, who were offered good wages to remain with it.

Relieved of my position, General Coe requested me to accept a clerkship in the camp store but I declined. I had found on arrival at the Fort Sanders camp the same old feud among employees that existed at the Pine Bluffs camp. In addition to this General Coe's selection of the writer to bring up the eight-team cull outfit from the Pine Bluffs camp had created some jealousy among old wagon bosses. The Gilman Brothers older wagon bosses and assistants did not like it and showed their spleen at every opportunity. I was classed as a Coe & Carter "pet" by the Gilman Brothers "pets." The latter usually did what they pleased without regard to results. I had been approached and questioned as to what part of the firm I was working for and had told them for Gilman & Carter, which was the abbreviated name of the company. I frankly told General Coe that the work at this camp would not proceed harmoniously or with profit until both he and John Gilman got rid of their respective pets and that since I was classed as a Coe & Carter man I should be allowed to go with others. But the General would not listen to this and insisted on my going in and taking charge of the store. I told him I might consent to take charge of it on certain conditions; one, that the request must come from Mr. Gilman; the other, that every drop of liquor must go out of the store. The General thought he had something to say as well as Mr. Gilman about who should manage the store. The whiskey part of it I could manage as I pleased, but he asked what I would do with the old wagon bosses and assistants who came in every morning and drank a tin cupful of whiskey before sitting down to breakfast. I answered that they would sit down to breakfast without any store whiskey if I ran it.

I hardly knew Mr. Gilman but he said he knew me and one day asked if I was the John Bratt who was at Fort Mitchell at the time Gilman & Kountz's mules were run off by the Indians. I told him I was. He said he had heard of the service rendered by me in loaning his men all our horses and mules and accompanying the mule skinners across the North Platte River in an effort to recover the stock from the Indians. General Coe must have mentioned this and other incidents of my doings at Fort Mitchell, judging from the intelligent way in which he talked of matters that occurred there.

The Pine Bluffs tie and wood camp was closed shortly after I left and everything was transferred to the Fort Sanders camp and later to a camp two and one-half miles north of Sherman Station and known as Sherman Station camp. Other ox, mule and horse teams had been purchased and the work of getting out ties and wood and telegraph poles was started in earnest. We had several hundred men at work getting out these ties, wood, logs and poles. I was given charge of an ox-train hauling ties to the siding near Fort Sanders and was doing what I thought good work. One morning, on starting out, Mr. Gilman handed me a gallon keg, telling me to sling it on the end of the reach of the lead wagon. Later becoming thirsty and thinking the keg contained water, I took a good swallow out of it before discovering it was whiskey. Mr. Gilman joined me before we got to the timber. I told him I had taken a drink out of his water keg and that it nearly choked me. It amused him greatly to think that a drink of whiskey would upset anyone. He said he usually took about twenty drinks a day and several in the night. His face looked like it, red, blotched and bloated. I told him I had had my last drink of whiskey at old Fort Reno, nearly a quart, and that poured down my throat. He said that was not the way to drink it, to which I agreed. He became talkative, especially after he had taken a big drink from the keg.

He requested me to tell him the facts in regard to the Indians running off one hundred twenty-eight head of his and Mr. Kountz's mules at Fort Mitchell. This I did and told also of our efforts to recover them, how we loaned his wagon bosses, assistants and mule skinners our herd of ranch horses and mules, and how in the chase I rode a barebacked mule that nearly drowned me while crossing the North Platte River. He asked me many questions, riding by my side on our return trip with our loads. Mr. Gilman treated me very kindly and finally asked me whether I would not like to take charge of the camp store. He said it would be easier work than what I was doing and more money in it.   I told him I preferred the work I was doing, provided I was giving satisfaction. He said my work was satisfactory but that he thought I could do good work for them in the store and wished I would take that position. Mr. Sinclair had come up from Pine Bluffs and had full charge of the store at this time but Mr. Gilman said the Company was about to open a tie camp at Rock Creek and needed Mr. Sinclair there. I told him my method of running a camp would be different from Mr. Sinclair's and that it might not suit him, that all old pets, both his and Coe & Carter's, would have to go, also that the store must be rid of every drop of liquor.

He stared at me a moment and asked why, and I frankly told him that these old men had been with the two outfits so long and so much jealousy existed among them, that the Company's interests were suffering and no camp could be run in this way on business principles. Bosses and their favorite teamsters could go to the store any hour of the day and night and help themselves to a tin cupful of whiskey, even without paying anything for it. Mr. Gilman remarked that I was demanding a great deal but believed I was right and if I would, I could try it. I am satisfied that he thought I could not carry out the plan. No one knew the men I had to deal with better than I. Some of them had killed their man and looked upon me as a kid.

Not wishing to force myself I took a few days to decide whether I should take the position or not. Both General Coe and Mr. Gilman came to me again and I finally consented to try it. Some of the old "soak" wagon bosses had heard that I was to take charge of the store and that I intended to abolish the whiskey part of it and had warned me that I had better not do that or I might follow the whiskey, which they had heard I was going to empty on the prairie, so I had notice of what I was going to be up against.

I never saw a worse managed store. The stock consisted of groceries, clothing, blankets, boots, shoes, and everything necessary at a wood and tie camp, including some seven or eight barrels of whiskey—a place for nothing and nothing in its place. Sacks of greasy bacon were piled on stacks of clothing—no cost mark on anything—all valued at probably $25,000.00. Mr. Sinclair was still manager of the store but left soon after I took charge to open a tie camp at Medicine Bow or Rock Creek.

One day I called Mr. Gilman's attention to the whiskey and asked him what I should do with it. He said, "Roll the barrels out and knock the heads in but save a five-gallon keg for me." I never saw him drunk but I have seen him take twenty big drinks of whiskey a day and get up several times in the night to take some. He said it made him sleep better.

The next day I had a four-mule team brought to the store door and loaded all the barrels of whiskey we had, reserving the five-gallon keg as requested by Mr. Gilman, and went with the driver to Wanlen Brothers' sutler store at Fort Sanders, where I sold it.

While clerking at this store I met and became acquainted with Joseph Michael, who later became county clerk of Lincoln County, Nebraska. His estimable and respected wife, later known as Mrs. Neary, resided in North Platte until the time of her death.

Though not unexpected, it would make very interesting reading had all the comments on my act and the many cursings I received from the old wagon bosses, assistants and some of our employees been written. All threatened vengeance on me for thus depriving them of their liquor. Some appealed to Mr. Gilman and General Coe, who frankly told them it was my doings, not theirs; that I was running the camp.

It was not long before General Coe had some Coe & Carter pets en route for Texas to assist him in bringing up a herd of cattle. It was proposed to buy the cattle north of San Antonio. The General insisted that I take a certain interest in this and offered to finance it for what share I wanted to the extent of one-fifth, I to take charge of the books and inside work. I saw there was big money in the venture provided the cattle could be brought safely through the Indian Territory. The largest kind of four and six year old cattle could be purchased for $5.00 in gold and on arrival on the Laramie Plains could be sold for $35.00 to $40.00 each if in fair flesh. The General planned that, while he and his pets, Bob Mason, John Knox and Matt Brooks, were gone for the cattle, I should locate a range and build a ranch, corral, etc., on one of the Laramie rivers, take up several hay claims, have the hay put up and everything ready as soon as the cattle arrived. I promised to do this or have it done but I would not consent to take any interest in the enterprise if the men with whom he had started to Texas were to be taken into the deal. The General felt rather put out at this decision on my part. He thought I was needlessly prejudiced against the three. He said they had been with Coe & Carter many years and he had always found them to be good, straight men. On bidding him good-bye he said I must reconsider my decision as he would like to have me take an interest in the deal. I told him I had made up my mind but that would not prevent me from locating the ranch and having everything ready for the herd when it arrived.

John Gilman made good his promise and sent away on other work several of his pets—Gladdon, Hugh Alley, Sharp, Rowland, and others, so that in the course of two months I had the camp of some six hundred men working smoothly and every man working for the best interest of the company. Mr. Gilman spent some time at the camp but more down at Laramie City, which had suddenly grown to many hundred people. Some of the buildings were of frame, some covered with canvas, some adobes, a few stores, the majority being saloons, dance halls and gambling places, all in full blast.

One day good Mrs. Iverson came to our camp from Laramie City, where her husband kept a general store, and asked whether I would distribute a boxful of Bibles if she sent them up. I told her I would be glad to accept and distribute them. The Bibles came and I handed one to every employee and to many others who came to our camp. No one can tell the good this act did. God bless her! I saw some of these men years afterwards and they told me they still had their Bibles and prized them very much.

I always tried to impress upon the minds of the men the evil effects of drinking, gambling and immorality. About this time I remember Mr. Gilman took a liking to an ex-lieutenant who had just received his discharge at Fort Sanders and engaged him to assist me in outside work in the purchase and receiving of ties and wood. One day I gave him, at Mr. Gilman's request, $1500.00 to pay down on several thousand ties that were offered for sale by a gang of tie choppers. In less than two hours afterwards one of our men reported to me that this gentleman was busy in a poker game in one of the gambling houses in Laramie City. In half an hour I was at his side and by persuasion and threats I secured a little over $1300.00,—all he had left. The result was that we parted with him very quickly.

Later, General Coe said he had a very good man, an intelligent old wagon master living at Nebraska City, whom he said was just the man we wanted. He came and within sixty days I discovered him steering our unsuspecting employees to a house of bad repute in Laramie City and dividing profits with the landlady. This smooth, pious-looking gentleman followed the lieutenant.

My duties were many and exacting. After a hard day's ride inspecting and receiving ties in the timber I would return to the store and post the blotter kept by one and sometimes two clerks. It was no uncommon thing to find me at two or three o'clock in the morning posting the ledger or going over the previous day's business by the light of a rag laid in a tin plate of grease. Candles at this time were a luxury and coal oil lamps had not reached us. This night work under such conditions began to affect my eyes and I had to discontinue it.

We had all classes of men among our several hundred employees, some that had fled from the States and were using fictitious names to hide their identity. It was no easy matter to get along with such men.

We paid thirty-five to sixty cents each for ties in the timber and received from the Credit Mobilier $1.00 to $1.30 each, delivered on railroad track near Fort Sanders, Sherman Station, Tie Siding, etc., and at these points we received from $12.00 to $16.00 per cord for wood, which cost us $6.00 to $8.00 per cord delivered. This looks like a good profit but not enough when we consider the great risk of fire, theft and an occasional raid on our live stock by marauding bands of Ute and Sioux Indians. At one time we had thirty thousand cords of wood ricked up at Sherman Station with a bad fire in it. Joseph Millard, the Omaha banker, had an interest in this until he heard of the fire and wisely sold his interest to other partners, sustaining but little loss. We would let many sub-contracts for cord wood, ties, poles, etc., delivered at Fort Sanders, Tie Siding, Sherman Station, and other points on the line of the Union Pacific Railroad.

I am reminded of one 500-cord contract let to an apparently good, straight fellow, to be put in on a contract of three thousand cords for the Government at Fort Sanders. The same was to be four feet long and piled in ricks eight feet high, the contractor agreeing to accept Government measure. One day I found the fellow "cribbing" and remonstrated, telling him he would get the worst of that trick, as such dishonesty would not only injure him, if discovered, but would reflect on our honesty. He said he would quit it. His contract finished, I called on the Quartermaster to measure it.

The Quartermaster was a young lieutenant, recently from West Point, and no doubt wanted to make a record of his thorough business ability. He had his tape line and note book carried by orderlies, while others held stakes at the corners. He walked along the sides of the eight-foot ricks, looked in every suspicious hole, measured many of the sticks and the length and height of the outside ricks, then with the aid of orderlies climbed on top of the ricks, on which he started to walk. It was not many moments before he fell down into the wood, evidently where it had been cribbed. I, and several orderlies, were quickly doing our best to extricate him. His dress parade clothes were torn, the chains attached from belt to sword broken and his shoes badly scuffed; no wonder he was making the air blue with yells and talk that would not be suitable to repeat in a Sunday school. We pulled him out and got him on terra firma. He spied the chopper who had piled up the wood and the tongue lashing he gave him made him very uncomfortable. The following day he called out a company of soldiers and had the ricks all torn down and repiled as closely as possible. This sub-contractor acknowledged that I had cautioned him several times not to crib. He learned a lesson that he remembered for a long time. The lieutenant learned that the sub-contractor was to accept and receive pay according to Quartermaster's measurement. After this sub-contractor received the lieutenant's measurement he quietly acknowledged to me that he wished he had not done it.

I shall never forget Christmas day in 1867. I attempted to cross the Laramie river with six four-mule teams loaded with logs to be used in building the ranch and corrals. I had decided to locate near a station on the Union Pacific Railroad, to be known as Wyoming. We, the teamsters and I, got stuck in the ice in the river. We froze our hands, feet, ears and noses very badly. This ranch was the second cattle ranch built in Wyoming, Creighton & Hutton, or Alsop, having built the first to care for Texas cattle.

Besides managing the tie and wood camp near Fort Sanders, I had superintended opening another tie and wood camp at Sherman Station. I had the ranch and corrals built and several hundred tons of hay in stack when the three thousand head of Texas cattle, mostly steers, arrived and General Coe, who came up with the herd in person, was pleased with what I had done, especially with the selection of the location. The General had discharged two of his pets, Knox and Brooks, at the crossing of the Red River. Mason, the man I disliked the most, came up with the cattle with the General. The cattle were a nice bunch in fair flesh, had been bought right and trailed up without great loss or heavy expense. I saw big profits in the deal and had it not been for Bob Mason's having an interest in the enterprise, under the General's continued persuasions, I might have taken the interest he desired. When I refused to do so he seemed to regret it very much.

A slaughter house was built and a meat market opened in Laramie City under the firm name of Mason & Company, and in a very short time Bob Mason was looked upon as a great man in Laramie City. Much dressed meat was shipped to the tie, wood and grading camps along the Union Pacific line. Casement Brothers had been grading, ironing and tieing two to four miles a day and the iron horse was pushing its way through the western part of Wyoming by leaps and bounds. The profits in supplying these camps were big. The firm of Mason & Company was making money fast out of their herd of cattle and had planned to drive up other herds the next year. Mason & Company's only competitor at this time was Iliff at Cheyenne. Bob could not stand the prosperity and temptations; fast women, drink and gambling took him off his feet in less than six months. L. N. Gallup and I were appointed receivers to close out the firm of Mason & Company. We sold the ranch and what was left of the cattle to Creighton & Hutton. At last General Coe realized that my opinion of Mason was correct.

One day in June, 1868, I received a message from Mr. Carter in Omaha, asking at what price per ton two thousand tons of good hay could be delivered in stack at Fort Sanders. Mr. Carter requested a quick answer.

I immediately saddled Mr. Gilman's private horse, a Kentucky thoroughbred, "Oak Rail," put a lunch in my saddle pocket and with my field glasses, compass, revolvers, Winchester carbine, bowie knife and a belt full of cartridges, was soon scouring the country between Sanders and the Laramie River and south of there. It must have been nearly five o'clock in the afternoon when a sudden thunderstorm sprang up. It was accompanied by considerable rain, wind and hail. The lightning was vivid and attracted by my brass Winchester gun, it once knocked my horse down on his knees. For a time I thought it had killed him but he gathered himself up and went on but not before I had taken off my overcoat and wrapped it around my gun, when I started again, see-sawing across the valley. Grass was plentiful but the old, long grass predominated. I had not proceeded far before a flash of lightning nearly blinded me and stunned poor "Oak Rail," who trembled all over. The lightning seemed to be playing up and down his ears and head. The poor horse was so frightened from the shock he received that I could scarcely get him out of a walk. As for myself, I felt dazed and the smell of sulphur was so strong that it made me sick. The storm had increased in violence. I finally dismounted, wrapped the Winchester in my overcoat and laid it down on the prairie, carefully marking the location and taking particular note of the surrounding country, after which I slowly continued my prospecting.

It was getting dark. I had gone probably two miles from the place where I left my gun and overcoat. I had satisfied myself that I could get that quantity of hay within fifteen miles of the fort and decided to return to camp via the route to the gun, which I found after much trouble. By this time "Oak Rail" was about all in. He breathed with difficulty. His hide was wet, not so much from the rain, which had abated, but with sweat. He staggered more or less every step he took. After finding my gun and overcoat I walked and led him and realized that I was elected to camp with him that night on the prairie. This I did, the greater part of the night surrounded by a pack of glistening-eyed, hungry wolves, that I had continually to scare way. Occasionally they would give a howl that made me feel lonesome. I did not want to shoot at them for this would locate me to any Ute or other Indians that might be camping on the river. I allowed "Oak Rail" to eat what grass he wanted as I coaxed him along at the end of the lariat. My clothes were wet and I was chilled with cold.

I arrived at camp about nine o'clock in the morning, having made up my mind for what the hay contract could be filled. As soon as I had put on some dry clothes I went to the Fort and wired Mr. Carter an answer. The reader can imagine our chagrin on opening the bids when Edward Creighton's bid was found to be three cents per ton less than Mr. Carter's. This Edward Creighton, of the firm Creighton & Hutton, was the builder of the telegraph line. So much for being president of the Overland Telegraph Company; all messages sent and received passed over his desk! Could I have used a cipher in this instance we might have secured that hay contract.

At this time it was a common thing to see men hung and hanging to telegraph poles or other convenient projections in Laramie City, Tie Siding, Dale Creek City, Sherman Station and Cheyenne. Some would weaken and confess, others die game.

After opening camps at Tie Siding and Sherman Station, I often had to go to Cheyenne to get funds to pay for wood, ties and logs. There were two banks at Cheyenne at this time, one belonging to Posy Wilson, the other to Harry Rogers. I would usually carry back on my person $5000.00 to $10,000.00 in greenbacks. It was not a comfortable feeling to have so much money with me since I would often meet ex-employees who knew that I always carried more or less money with me. I used the greatest caution in not exposing my money and in leaving these places I would steal quietly from the rear of the barn where I put up my saddle horse. Once or twice when I knew I was being shadowed, I waited

Surrounded by a Pack of Hungry Wolves

until dark and had one of Ben Gallagher's clerks ride my horse out to a certain point where I would mount and go across country to camp. With all this caution, one night, while leaving the city by a back street, a man sprang at my horse's head and grabbed for my bridle rein. Another time some one tried to lariat me and pull me off the horse.

To show how easy it was for some men to go wrong—one nice, clerical-looking gentleman, named Leighton, sent out by a missionary society to open a mission, took the $600.00 given him and opened a dance hall in Cheyenne. He said he could make more money that way.

One night I had business in Cheyenne. I was with Mr. Bulen, a preacher, and old Sam Watts, who at that time was clerking for Ben Gallagher. I thought I was in the best of company. It was proposed to go in McDaniel's dance house. I hesitated for a time but it seemed that in company with two such reputable citizens I had nothing to fear. Imagine my surprise when Reverend Bulen insisted on setting up the drinks for Watts and me. I was very nearly kicked out of the hall because I refused to drink with them and the proprietor of the place. Am sorry to say Bulen got so badly in his "cups" that we had to almost carry him to his room. He made amends for this by preaching a good sermon to the men at the camp the following Sunday, the subject being "The Evil Effects of Strong Drink."

I cannot close this chapter without mentioning a joke that John Gilman played on the people of Laramie City. While the men who were engaged in digging the well at the Union Pacific hotel were at dinner, Mr. Gilman scattered about $20.00 worth of gold dust in the well, which was probably eighteen to twenty feet deep. A party was at the well to see the first bucket come up. Noticing the free gold, a pan was promptly secured and some of the dirt washed. Surely the gold was there! The news spread fast and in almost less time than it takes to tell it, claims were staked off by the hundreds. The result was that one man was killed and several wounded. When the fact became known that Mr. Gilman had salted the well, it came very nearly going hard with him, especially on account of the man's death. It cost him many dollars for drinks and cigars and the price of a coffin.

While the Indians were neither so plentiful nor so desperate as around Fort Phil Kearny, yet an occasional band of Sioux and Utes would raid us, drive off some of our stock and run in our tie and wood choppers working in the fringe of the timber near old Fort Walbeck. Gold had been discovered in North and South Parks. Mr. Gilman had filed on several mining claims. I took one and hired the Shipmans, father and son, to work it for me. Unfortunately, the Ute Indians discovered this little mining camp of about twenty men, surrounded it, and the miners who did not escape in the night were hemmed in, starved out and later killed. The Shipmans and some others had sold their lives as dearly as possible. When we found them all were dead and badly mutilated. The Shipmans had even boiled their shoes, shoe strings and buckskin shirts and had lived on the soup as long as they could. As soon as we heard that the Indians had surrounded the miners, we sent out troops but they arrived too late. This massacre made us all very sad. We gathered up all the remains we could find and properly interred them in the Parks, with suitable head boards on the graves. Could I have found the home or any kindred of the Shipmans I would have sent the remains there, but I could not.

While hauling ties and wood at our Fort Sanders camp on the Laramie plains some of our work cattle died from eating loco weed, which is usually the first green forage to appear in the spring. It comes ahead of the grass. One day our bull wagon boss turned his work cattle into a thick patch of loco and about two hundred head became affected It took quick work with butcher knives that we stuck near their paunches to save them. This was done to relieve them of the gas that formed in them. Some very bad cases we drenched with hard oil and gunpowder and sometimes with a strong dose of warm epsom salts. As a rule, cattle will not eat loco unless hungry. Some animals, especially horses, act crazy after eating it, so if a horse or individual acts peculiarly it is a common saying that he is "locoed."

Game and fish were abundant, so our hunters, who were paid to supply the camp with fresh meats, had no trouble in bringing in deer, antelope, elk, buffalo and bear meat when needed. It was reported that General Coe (who won his military title by being appointed General of the First Regiment of Nebraska Volunteers at the time the Civil War broke out), in describing our tie and wood camp near Fort Sanders, said that in case a gun was discharged by accident, there would lay a dead antelope, and if any one went to the creek for a bucket of water, he would get a bucket of fish. Who can blame the Indian for not wanting to leave such ideal hunting grounds, even if the winters were intensely cold at times? It was such a dry cold that its intensity was not felt. The air was so light that we would often freeze before knowing it.

CHAPTER XXII

ABOUT the middle of June, 1868, our firm opened a new tie and wood camp about two and one-half miles north of Sherman Station and I was placed in charge. Here we got out and delivered on the line of the Union Pacific Railroad at this station and at Tie Siding several hundred thousand ties and probably one hundred thousand cords of wood. Later we established tie and wood choppers in the timber south of Tie Siding.

In riding over the country north of Tie Siding and Sherman Station I often wondered why the Union Pacific did not follow up the North Platte River valley and thus have a river grade instead of climbing the Sherman Hill, and I often said this would be done some day. It is being done at the time I am preparing this autobiography. The Union Pacific Railroad Company has started to build a river grade line from O'Fallons west. This may connect with the old line at Medicine Bow or Fort Steel.

About this time Gilman & Carter took a contract to get out ties to build the Denver Pacific from Cheyenne to Denver, agreeing to take pay for same in Arapahoe County, Colorado, bonds. We outfitted a large number of men and teams at our Sherman Hill camp and sent some with pack animals across country to the head waters of the Cache La Poudre where we had planned to get out the ties and float them down that river to a point where they could be taken out and hauled to the proposed line of road. It took some nerve to bid on this contract. While the price was a good one, the difficulties were many and great and the pay was not cash but bonds that our company, should it need money, might have to discount largely. In the space of two miles we had to build about thirty bridges in order to get our teams, men and supplies into the thick timber.

When our party of tie choppers with pack animals was ready to start, one particular Irishman, whom I had outfitted at Sherman camp, with his pack horse loaded high and heavily, grabbed a pair of buckskin gloves, saying he would take them to remember me by, and started out of the store on a run. I had to halt him with a revolver shot which grazed his boot-leg. He dropped the gloves, stopped and said he only took them for a joke. Starting the day after the Irishman left, to pilot another outfit, we overtook my friend, who had loaded up with some bottles of bad whiskey and had been joined by other tie choppers with pack animals. The third day out we got into the La Poudre cañons. The paths were narrow and the hills very steep. The Irishman was just a little ahead of us, urging his pack horse along over the narrow trail on a high ridge along the side of a deep cañon. I advised all to dismount; and all, except the Irishman, did. He continued riding and crowding his pack horse, whose top-heavy load caused him to lose his footing and bounce down the side of the steep cañon from rock to rock until the poor animal landed feet up, on the top of a tree. A shot put him out of his misery. Every moment we expected to see the Irishman follow the beast but he sat his horse, more drunk than sober, shouting: "Look at him! Look at him!!" as the poor horse rolled over and bounded from rock to rock. He damned his "sister's cat," saying, "There was the only property I owned in America and gone to h—l in a minute."

We had expended about $5000.00 on roads and bridges up the La Poudre when Mr. Gilman found out he had signed the contract on Friday. He said he had talked the matter over with his wife and brother and they had all agreed that the contract would prove a bad one and he wanted to get out of it. He requested me to take the matter up with Coe & Carter, which I did. Coe & Carter did not want to take any advantage of the Gilman Brothers and tried to persuade them to stay in the deal, but the Gilmans declined. If Coe & Carter would take the entire contract, the Gilmans agreed to lose their share of money expended to date. This was agreed to. Coe & Carter filled the contract and made $50,000.00 out of it. So much for superstition.

Settlers in that part of Colorado at this time were very scarce. There was, however, one great character, known as Buffalo Jones, living on the La Poudre where the river came out of the hills. He had several charming daughters who could lasso and ride the worst bronco or Texas steer that ever wore hair. The life history of these frontier people would make the most interesting book ever published. It is claimed that Buffalo Jones had a standing offer of $5000.00 to any good man who would marry one of his daughters.

I was kept busy in looking after the different camps until Mr. Emerson relieved me of much of the work on the Cache La Poudre.

I became well acquainted with Ben Gallagher, the merchant groceryman of Cheyenne, who also operated other stores along the Union Pacific Railroad under the name of Gallagher & Co., Gallagher & Nuckolls, Gallagher & Mc-Grath, and later under the firm name of Paxton & Gallagher of Omaha, where both partners later died.

S. F. Nuckolls was a Nebraska City product and a good, clean man. He was later sent to Congress as a delegate from Utah. I remember a story told by him. He said he and a former friend living at Cheyenne had a misunderstanding about a business matter and both decided to test the case in court at Cheyenne. Nuckolls hired A. J. Poppleton and his friend James M. Woolworth of Omaha. The case was called. Mr. Poppleton opened with a brief statement of the case and so lauded Mr. Nuckolls as an upright, honest man that Mr. Nuckolls was very much elated and had an idea that his case was won right there. Finally Mr. Woolworth rose and though small in stature, gave Mr. Nuckolls such abuse and painted him so black that Mr. Nuckolls could not stand it but got up and walked out of the court room. After a while he returned. The attorneys had been arguing some law points which the judge was passing on. During this lull in the proceedings one of the attorneys wrote a short note and passed it over to the other attorney, who, after reading it, crumpled it up and threw it under the table. Mr. Nuckolls had a curiosity to know the contents of that note and seated himself at the table, where, unknown to the attorneys, he pushed the paper near his chair with his foot and finally picked it up. Unnoticed he put it in his pocket, stole out of the court room and read it. It read: "What shall we charge these two damn fools?" He immediately called the man with whom he was having the suit, showed him the note and before they returned to the court room, they settled their difference, much to the disappointment of the two attorneys. Mr. Nuckolls told me this was his first and last lawsuit.

At Sherman Station I became well acquainted with Mrs. Larimer and her son, who kept a general store there, bought and sold ties and cord wood, while her husband had a star route mail contract from Point of Rocks north. She was a very bright, good, business woman. She also had a photograph gallery and one day upon my return from the timber she insisted upon taking my picture. Her ambition was to be the mayor of Sherman Station. There was also a Mrs. Kelly living near the station. These two women and Mrs. Larimer's son had been captured by the Sioux Indians near Fort Laramie. Mrs. Larimer and her son, after two weeks' captivity in the lodge of the chief, stole away one night and though the Indians hunted them day and night, they succeeded in eluding them and got back to the fort, after suffering unmentionable cruelties. Mrs. Kelly, not so fortunate, was taken by the Indians up on the Missouri River and kept with the band over six months. The squaws stripped her almost nude, appropriating her dress and skirts. She was finally captured from the band by a company of United States Cavalry after a severe fight. Mrs. Kelly never recovered from the shock and ill treatment she received while with the Indians. She made a fair living washing the clothes of our tie and wood choppers. All pitied and helped her in every

Brigham Young, Born 1801, Died 1877

Photograph of the Writer Taken by Mrs. Larimer

way possible. She was the widow of a soldier killed by Indians near Fort Laramie.

It was at the Sherman Hill tie camp that I nearly lost my life in the winter of 1868. Mr. Gilman had wired from Cheyenne that he would be up on the first train and requested me to meet him. I had made a hard drive with my team that day. One of my horses became lame and at the request of Harry Mullison, a sub-tie contractor, I had one of his horses hitched up in place of the lame one. I started for the station, only two and one-half miles south, in an open spring wagon a little before dark. It was snowing and blowing a gale and very cold. It was dark when I arrived at the station, having experienced much trouble and delay in finding my way through the many ricks of cord wood piled thickly four, six and eight feet high north of the station. Many of the ricks were partially buried in snow and the high drifts of snow between the ricks made it very difficult to follow the snow-covered road. After waiting about two hours the train pulled in with three large engines—one live and two dead ones—but Mr. Gilman did not come. I had given orders to our stable men to be on the lookout for us, knowing there was no place at the station to keep either of us or the team. It was ten o'clock when I started from the station for camp. The wind, which had increased in violence, was still coming from the north and I had to face it. It took me some time to get out of the woodpile into the open, where I had to take the middle of the three roads. I took careful bearings of the wind, got on the right road and had proceeded about one-half mile toward camp, when the storm coming to my right convinced me that I was off the trail. I headed my team to the wind but had not gone far before my face and eyes, as was also the case with my team, were plastered over with freezing snow and ice, making it impossible to see my hand before me.

Afraid of driving into some of the gulches from ten to two hundred feet deep that were filled with snow, I concluded it would be best to return to the station if I could and immediately turned my team's back to the wind. After considerable zigzagging, I got back on what I took to be the road. This I followed and was soon rewarded by my team's trying to wallow through the snow that had drifted on the north side of a six-foot woodpile and finally got back to the station. Harmon & Teats kept the store and post office at Sherman Station at this time. Mr. Teats who had not retired, was not much surprised at my return and insisted on my remaining, telling me to help myself to a bed on the counter and to make use of a pile of blankets and buffalo robes on one end of the same, but I could not bear the thought of that poor team's standing out all night in such a blizzard. After waiting about an hour, I started again. I got clear of the woodpile and must have traveled nearly a mile on the right road to camp when I again became lost. Had I driven my own team, it would have taken me safely to camp, but the Mullison horse being a stranger to that road and camp prevented my own horse from using his intelligence. I traveled around a long time, hoping that I would again cross the trail but did not. I became chilled and sleepy but well knew that sleep meant death. The storm was still raging. The falling snow was swept by a hurricane wind which was bitter cold. It was impossible to face it any longer. My hands and feet were becoming numb and my face was covered with a thick plaster of snow and ice. I finally found shelter for my team behind a large rock. I got out of the wagon and tied the team to the wheels, spreading over them what blankets I had. I then commenced and kept up a vigorous gait some twenty paces one way and then the other. I beat my hands and arms, pinched myself and rubbed my ears and nose and after a time succeeded in getting my blood to circulate. I had on heavy underwear, fur cap, overcoat, lined gloves and warm, heavy overshoes. If I could but keep awake I would come out all right. I appealed to Him who cares for the birds and imagined I heard a voice, louder than the raging storm around me, saying, "I will protect and see you through." It was none other than that Guardian Angel that my good mother turned me over to when I left home.

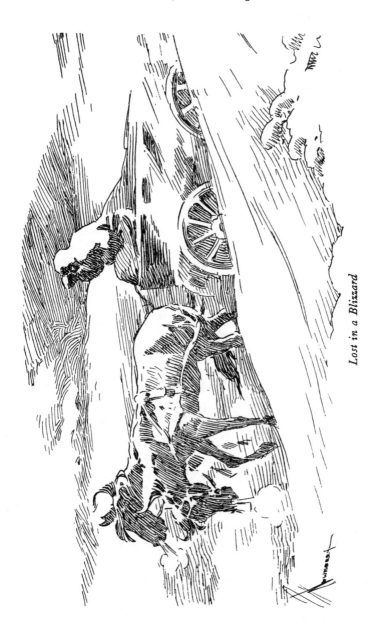

Lost in a Blizzard

I thought of many things during those long hours waiting for daybreak, which finally came but with it no cessation of the storm's fury. While well acquainted with the topography of the country, I could not tell where I was. It seemed that I was enveloped in a cloud of snow and storm. My poor team stood with heads down and backs to the storm. I pitied the poor, dumb brutes. Once I thought I would get on the back of my own driving horse, give him the rein and trust to him to take me to camp but I was too numb and stiff with cold to mount him. Not a speck of sunshine came out the next day, which was Saturday. I traveled and traveled with my back to the storm, walking beside the team and wagon, not knowing where I was or where I was going. Once in a while I would run up against a huge boulder, shy around it, then cross some deep gully filled with frozen snow. Several times I hallooed, only to be answered by the echo. The storm still kept coming but I could not tell from what direction. At last night came and found me sheltered with the team under a ledge of rock which protected us. As best I could I fastened the blankets over the horses, tied them to the wheels and put the spare laprobe around myself. I continued for a time to walk and stamp my feet, beat my hands, arms and limbs, and to rub my face and ears until my blood was again in circulation. I stood between the horses, hoping to keep warm and depending on them to awaken me should sleep overpower me. This must have happened in spite of my continued efforts to keep awake by moistening my eyes with my wet fingers. I felt myself falling against the Mullison horse, that had some broncho blood in him. He gave a sudden jump that awoke me. My thoughts rambled. What was I doing here? What day or night was it? Yes, the message said, "Meet me Friday evening." Why could I not have something to eat? And I began to beat my hands and arms, pinch them and my limbs, cheeks and body and then tried to run but could not. My feet and limbs were too stiff and numb.

This was the longest night I ever spent in my life. Daylight came at last but I seemed to be enveloped in misty clouds, which, after a long time, broke away and the sun began to shine. I had not the faintest idea where I was. The hills, rocks and trees were all covered with frozen snow.

After a long time, owing to my frozen fingers, I managed to hitch the team to the wagon and I started, sitting down in the bottom of the wagon. Every now and then I tried to shout but could not. Much of the time I was unable to guide the team and allowed them to take their own course. I crossed many gulches and canons filled with frozen snow.

I had crossed a wide and what must have been a deep cañon filled with snow when I suddenly saw some glittering object ahead but could not make out what it was until I came close to it. It must have been the railroad track. This I continued to follow until I knew no more.

It was getting dark when I came to my senses and found myself in my own room at camp surrounded by kind friends who had been working over me several hours, trying to thaw out my frozen face, hands and feet. Some of the sixty men who had been out hunting for me since Saturday morning, had discovered the team several miles east of Sherman Station. The team was walking west along the railroad track, the lines dragging and I was lying unconscious in the wagon. It was several days before I was able to attend to business. I had again many reasons to think that my Guardian Angel had still an interest in my welfare.

I could fill many pages of this autobiography with very interesting reading should I recite all the incidents that occurred while at this camp, but will mention only one more.

In order to help Mrs. Larimer, whose husband was away much of the time attending to his mail contracts from Point of Rocks north, I had agreed to receive and measure for her some cord wood and some ties that some Mexicans had been getting out on contract. A number of the ties were not up to specifications and I rejected them. I also found the cord wood cribbed and some of it very loosely piled, for which I docked them. This made them very angry. I told them that was the best I could do and if not satisfied, they could get some one else to measure and receive them. I gave them a statement to take to Mrs. Larimer. On leaving them I saw one of the Mexicans start off through the timber, carrying his rifle. I was on horseback and hurried along the trail, not wishing to let him get ahead of me. I had gone nearly half a mile when I suddenly turned my horse's head in a thick quaking asp grove and awaited results. In a few moments I espied through the branches "Mr. Mexican" coming up the trail on a run, carrying his rifle in both hands. When nearly opposite me I pulled my six-shooter, rode out to the trail, faced him and asked "Are you looking for me?" He did not know what to say but stammered out that he was chasing a deer. I marched him back to his camp at the point of my revolver, and turned him over to the boss contractor with instructions not to let him follow my trail or I would take him to Cheyenne. I am satisfied in my own mind that this Mexican intended to kill me if he could shoot me in the back. My facing him deprived him of his courage.

We had stripped the hills and cañons for many miles north of Sherman and Tie Siding Stations of the best of the timber, both for ties and wood, and had let many sub-contracts for ties, poles and wood to be gotten out of the South Side hills, twelve to twenty miles south of Tie Siding. There was a large number of tie contractors at work on both sides of the railroad, among whom could be mentioned Paxton & Turner and Sprague, Davis & Company.

I remember some tie choppers getting after Sprague, Davis & Company with a rope intending to hang all members of the firm because they could not get their pay. These contractors were not entirely to blame for this. Credit Mobilier Company was often short of funds. Some moneyed men of Wall street in those days looked upon the building of the Union Pacific Railroad as a wild undertaking. Its stocks and bonds could hardly be given away and it took nerve to get out ties, poles, logs and wood for a company so noted for slow pay as "Credit Mobilier." I, at one time, as cashier for Gilman & Carter, had over eleven hundred thousand dollars of this company's paper. Our firm did over three million dollars' worth of work for this company and to my knowledge never lost one dollar of it. All honor to the men who conceived and built the Union and Southern Pacific Railroads, thus uniting by the iron horse, the Atlantic and Pacific Oceans when the golden spike was driven at Ogden.

Driving the Golden Spike

Our company had established tie and wood camps at Rock Creek and Medicine Bow, but after Gilman Brothers had declined to continue co-partnership in furnishing ties, etc., to the Denver Pacific (the railroad planned from Cheyenne to Denver) a dissolution of the firm of Gilman & Carter was thought advisable. Mr. John Gilman wanted me to go with the Gilman Brothers, while Coe & Carter desired that I remain with them. I chose the latter. I had disbursed probably two million dollars but had a voucher to show for every dollar, except perhaps, postage stamps. All members of the firm had implicit confidence in my honesty. General Coe still insisted that I join them in the cattle business.

During the summer of 1869 Gilman & Carter took a 2800-ton hay contract to be delivered in stack at Fort McPherson, Nebraska, and I was sent there to fill the contract. It was arranged that after this was filled I take an active interest with Coe & Carter in the cattle business. General Coe had again gone to Texas to buy several thousand Texas cattle. The Gilman Brothers were very much disappointed when they learned I had decided to take an interest with Coe & Carter. All four were good men in their respective ways.

General Coe was exacting, overbearing at times. If his mind was made up, it was very hard to change him. He was sharp and shrewd, and knew all the tricks in the trade. At this particular time he was more wealthy than Mr. Carter.

Mr. Carter was plain, unassuming, easy-going, a deep thinker, the soul of honor, cool and deliberate and hard to change when he had made up his mind, but could be reasoned with at all times.

The Gilman Brothers' business was handled by John Gilman, who was a big-hearted fellow and had the gift of ingratiating himself into our confidence and we could not help but like him. He was remarkable for his genuine hospitality, frank business ways and sunny good-nature. He always had a good story to tell and tried to make people happy.

Reverting to Mr. Carter I will tell one transaction that sheds a flood of light on his true character. He and Mr. McDaniels had taken a mixed horse and mule train of flour to sell at Denver in 1860. On arrival at Denver they found the wheat flour market glutted but there was a big demand for buckwheat flour. They had been in Denver some time but could not get a bid for their flour. Mr. Carter had occasion to make a trip up Cherry Creek. He had been gone a couple of days and on his return Mr. McDaniels met him in camp and was elated to inform him that he had sold the flour.

Mr. Carter was agreeably surprised to learn this and anxious to know the name of the buyer. Mr. McDaniels told him that, since everybody wanted buckwheat flour, he had bought a lot of buckwheat flour sacks and about twenty sacks of buckwheat flour. He then put their flour into the empty buckwheat sacks with a little buckwheat flour on top in each sack and sold it all for buckwheat flour and had the money for it in his pocket. At this information Mr. Carter became very angry and told him that he would not have his name coupled with such a fraud and deception. They divided that night, Mr. Carter accepting as his share just what his share of the wheat flour was worth and Mr. McDaniels pocketed the balance. Mr. McDaniels remained in Denver and became very wealthy. Mr. Carter returned to the Missouri River where he later became associated with General Coe in freighting and contracting.

CHAPTER XXIII

Experiences at Fort McPherson and Wood River—A Government Hay Contract—Buffalo Bill and Other Friends—The Burke Family—The Fair Daughter—Embark in the Cattle Business—A Compromise with the Pawnees— Battle between the Pawnees and Sioux— Raw Corn Only on My Menu— Again My Guardian Angel Protects

IN the latter part of July, 1869, I arrived at Fort Mc-Pherson, Nebraska, with sufficient horse and mule teams and machinery to fill this hay contract. Charles McDonald, who kept the same store that we passed at this fort in 1866, was given a sub-contract by us of several hundred tons which he filled according to agreement.

I remember Mr. McDonald at the time we first passed through Fort McPherson. I did some trading in his store and saw him sell a stick of cord wood, four feet long and about four inches in diameter at the top end, to an emigrant for $1.00. The emigrant paid the price so cheerfully that Mr. McDonald stood and looked at him several moments after receiving his money. It was raining and buffalo chips would not burn. Mr. McDonald might have been debating in his own mind as to whether he had sold the wood too cheap. The emigrant might have paid more if asked, but Mr. McDonald wanted to be fair and reasonable.

While filling this contract here I first met W. F. Cody, later better known as Colonel Cody, or Buffalo Bill. He was employed at this fort as scout and guide. There were several companies of cavalry and some infantry stationed here, busy keeping the Indians in line. Indian raids on emigrants, freighters, ranchmen, stage coaches and settlers, including government stock, were frequent. The Sioux, under pretext of hunting buffalo, would often swoop down on the peaceful Pawnees, and many horrible, bloody battlefields between the Platte and Republican rivers resulted when these tribes met. The Pawnees usually got the worst of it. I remember seeing one of these battlefields near the Republican River and do not want to see another like it.

While we were filling this hay contract, many raids were made by thieving bands of Sioux on the government herds of horses and mules, also on nearby settlers. Among these settlers who lost their homes and all their stock may be mentioned John Burke, who had for the second time started a home about seven miles west of this fort, when thieving bands of Sioux swooped down on his ranch and drove off all his stock, including a large herd of valuable mules.

The Burkes were living at the Fitchie Ranch, which they later bought, together with the old Ben Holladay Stage Station about two miles west of the fort. This they later improved and made their home. It was here, seven years later that I wooed, won and married Miss Elizabeth Burke.

A few years before this, Mr. Burke had built a wagon bridge near the mouth of the South Platte River where it flowed into the North Platte, but high water had carried it away, much to the disappointment of the traveling public who wanted to go West by the way of what was then known as North Platte City. He then built his other bridges over the Platte River proper south of McPherson Station and northwest of the fort, to accommodate the hauling of freight, provisions, and feed for the troops stationed there and for which he received forty-five cents per hundred. Mr. Burke was an industrious, honest man, with a good wife, the mother of eight children—seven boys and one girl. He was a great worker, very enterprising, and did not know what fear was. He built the first irrigation ditch in Lincoln County, Nebraska, taking the water out of the south bank of the Platte River on Section 36, Township 13, Range 29, West of the Sixth Principal Meridian. He raised good crops of oats and vegetables which brought a big price. Later he built a railroad out of logs and ties in what was called Cut Cañon, crossing the

divide between the Platte River and Medicine Creek, south of
Fort McPherson, to facilitate the getting out of wood, logs,
ties and telegraph poles to fill his contract with the Government and Credit Mobilier or the Union Pacific Railroad
Company.

It was about this time that the Indians ran off all his
horse and mule stock. He followed the trail nearly two
months alone through Nebraska, Kansas, and Indian Territory but did not recover a hoof of the stock. Mr. Harvey,
who is now engaged in marking the Oregon Trail through
Nebraska, was engaged by the Union Pacific Railroad Company in classifying its lands north of Medicine Creek and saw
this band of Indians rush by him with Mr. Burke's stock,
only saving himself and men by remaining hidden in the thick
brush while the Indians passed.

Too much credit cannot be given to such pioneers as Mr.
John Burke, his wife Margratha and family, for the active
part they have played as early settlers of Lincoln County,
Nebraska.

I became acquainted with some of the officers at this
Post—all good, genial fellows—one of whom was Major
Walker, who, I believe, came with General Carr's Fifth
Cavalry. One Captain Hayes was Quartermaster—very ex-
acting but always reasonable. There were also several nice
families at the Post: the McDonalds, Snells, Ericssons,
Burkes and Codys, including the Colonel's two sisters, both
fearless riders. There was also the same old, genial Sam
Watts whom I first saw at Fort Sedgwick as acting Post-
master, and later at Cheyenne with Preacher Bulen, when he
took me into the first dance house I ever was in. Later came
Luke Healey, Maggie Cohen, John Murray, Louis Wooden,
George Dillard, Charles Hendy, and many other good people.

I had no time for sociabilities, hence did not go to any
of the Fort dances, which were said to be very pleasant affairs.

Among the noted frontier characters I met here was "Old
Turgeon," the Indian trader and inventor of the famous

"Turgeon Blanket." Turgeon accompanied Frank E. Coe, General Coe's son, and me on a buffalo hunt at the head of the Stinking Water, where he got mired and we had to pull him out with ropes.

Among other characters I met and grubstaked many times were Jimmy Cannon, who claimed to be the only surviving child of the Alamo Massacre; Edward Moran, after whom Moran cañon is named, and whom the Sioux Indians called "Iron Legs" because he could outwalk the swiftest-footed Sioux; Leon Palladay, a Sioux Indian interpreter, who later married one of Mr. Moran's daughters; Tod Randall, a squaw man and a recognized Sioux Indian authority; William Peniston of the firm of Peniston & Miller, proprietors of the Midway road ranch until the Sioux burned it, when they, like others, had to flee to save their lives and the lives of their families. Mr. Peniston was United States Commissioner and claimed to be a descendant of Lord Peniston of England. He was a good, genial fellow.

The noted Jack Morrow was still at his ranch some twelve miles west of McPherson but these thieving bands of Sioux never bothered him. He was usually the beneficiary of these Indian raids; so much so, that the commander at Fort McPherson gave Jack a hint to leave and he did. This broke up a bad nest of hard characters, both whites and Indians.

At the Fort lived E. E. Ericsson, Jacob Snell, and others. Poor Mr. Ericsson had incurred the displeasure of the commanding officer and that autocrat ordered the Ericssons to move, and because they did not do so promptly, had some soldiers tear the roof off their little home, thus exposing a sick wife and some small children to inclement weather until kind friends took them in and cared for them.

Sam Fitchie, about a mile west of the Fort, kept the Fitchie ranch, formerly the Ben Holladay Mail Coach Station.

Over at McPherson Station on the Union Pacific Railroad, about three and one-half miles north of Fort

McPherson, lived the Plumers, McCulloughs, Hanrahans, Wilsons, and our genial, sometimes dependable, friend Rooney who kept a small road ranch near the Station. Emigrants and others could stay at Rooney's, provided Rooney took a liking to them, but if he did not, woe be to them!

I was often called to the station to receive freight for our outfit and would sometimes go over with a team at night to receive it, the agent, Mr. Plumer, being very accommodating.

Sometimes I would stay all night at Rooney's, where I was always welcome. I remember staying there one night when the other guest, who was an emigrant, had incurred Rooney's dislike by kneeling in prayer and talking religion to him. After breakfast the emigrant asked what his bill was. Rooney told him $10.00, which was about $7.00 too much. The emigrant remonstrated against the high price, but to no effect. Rooney pulled a wicked-looking revolver from under the counter and told the emigrant to put the $10.00 on the counter and "skin." He obeyed and soon left, no doubt glad that he was living. Before I left, Rooney called Mrs. Rooney from the kitchen into the store and begged her to sing the song that won him, which she would have done had I not excused her at this time.

While filling the 2800-ton hay contract at Fort McPherson, I was suddenly summoned by an orderly to the Commanding Officer's quarters. Before reporting to that gentleman I thought best to see our wagon boss Robinson, who, on being questioned, said he had disobeyed my orders and had that morning taken in four loads of slough grass. I ordered him back on the trot with four teams and instructed him to pick up every particle of that slough grass and dump it on the manure pile. He did this before I had a chance to explain matters to the Post Commander, to whom I later reported. That officer read the riot-act to me and wanted to know what kind of hay I was bringing in. He said it was not fit for bedding and requested that I accompany him to see for myself. I did so, but on arrival at the hay corrals all the slough grass had been removed. The Commander was nonplussed and could not explain matters until I told him that, on learning that four loads of the poor quality of hay had been brought in, I immediately ordered the teams to gather it all up and dump it on the manure pile. The General stood and looked at me several moments and said he could not understand how we had removed it so quickly. I invited him to come and see for himself. He did so, and on seeing the hay, all bright but a trifle long, dumped among the stable refuse, he seemed satisfied and told me that he had confidence in me and was willing to allow me from that time on, in the absence of the Quartermaster, to pass on the quality of hay required.

Instead of stopping us when we had the 2800 tons in, the Commander allowed us to put in 3300 tons, and I was highly complimented by both the Commanding Officer and Captain Hayes, the Quartermaster, as to the manner in which I had filled the contract, which was at $8.45 per ton delivered in stack in the hay corrals at the Fort.

On the close of this contract, the last work I did for the firm of Gilman & Carter, I disposed of all the extra stock, wagons, harness, ox yokes, and machinery, retaining one span of mules, wagon, harness and mess kit, and two old employees, the Botkin Brothers, and started them with the outfit to "Dobytown" (old Fort Kearny), about the middle of October, 1869, to await the arrival of some 2500 Texas cattle that General Coe was bringing up. I had agreed to embark in the cattle business with General Coe and Levi Carter, under the firm name of John Bratt & Co., I purchasing Jack Wait's interest.

The outfit started. I took the train to Omaha with a view to settling up my accounts with the firm of Gilman & Carter, for whom I had disbursed nearly two million dollars. I am pleased to say that my accounts checked out within two cents, which proved to be a two-cent stamp for which I had not received credit. Both Mr. Gilman and Mr. Carter gave me considerable praise for my faithfulness in caring for their interests in the manner I had, and Mr. Gilman expressed his regret that I had concluded to cast my lot with Coe & Carter instead of with him and his brother Jed.

The settlement over, I hastened to Fort Kearny or "Doby-town," where shortly after I received the herd of Texas cattle brought there by General Coe and his Texas men.

This last herd had received hard usage from the start from San Antonio. Bad white men and hostile Indians had bothered General Coe en route. They had stampeded the cattle several times and a number had gone back (especially old brush steers) to the old range. Cattle inspectors had held the General up for blackmail and one mean, ugly, desperado inspector had been killed by the ranchman who sold General Coe the herd of cattle. The evidence at the trial justified the killing and the ranchman was acquitted. The result of all this delay was that the cattle arrived thin and many of them footsore.

It was decided that five hundred of the poorest ones be cut out and wintered near there on the Platte River if sufficient feed could be procured to care for them. With one Texas man and the two Botkin Brothers I took charge of this bunch of "skins" and "crips" and General Coe proceeded with the remainder of the herd to the ranch west of Fort McPherson. I fortunately ran on to some five hundred or more tons of hay that had been put up on the Denman island by James Jackson, who kept a general store at Wood River, about three miles north of the hay. This hay I purchased and found an ideal place—heavy timber, lots of brush and a nice flowing spring—on the north bank of the Platte River, where I could feed, shelter and water the cattle, safely protected from the storms. The location struck me so favorably that on finding it to be vacant government land I decided to preëmpt that 160 acres. After getting the cattle on it, making a road through the brush and a couple of channels to the hay stacks, and locating our camp, one morning I set out on horseback to Grand Island, about sixteen miles distant, intending to preëmpt this land, which I did.

At this time Grand Island was a small place of perhaps

four hundred people. Koenig & Webe had a store there, which I think was called "The O. K." There were several saloons.

I returned to camp next day. Imagine my surprise and chagrin at finding our cattle, horses and men surrounded by about seven hundred Pawnee Indians, who insisted on our moving at once, claiming that this particular location had been their winter camp for many years. I tried to tell them through their interpreter that I desired to hold these poor cattle here until the grass came in the spring, when I should be glad to move them to where our other cattle were near Fort McPherson. They objected, hence I was up against a serious proposition. Their chief told me I must leave before the next sunrise. I sent to the Jackson store for a wagon-load of flour, sugar, coffee, beans, syrup, crackers, soda, and other provisions, and that night killed two of the fattest cows in the bunch and gave the Indians a big feast, which pleased them, but they still insisted that I must leave. They said my heart was good but I could not stay. I spent a sleepless night on horseback watching the cattle with my three men.

The next morning I moved the cattle out of the brush and timber to the open prairie north of the Pawnee camp. I left one man in charge of the camp, the other two in charge of the cattle and horses, while I went to Wood River Station and wired the bank with which we did business in Omaha, to send by first express seven hundred ten-cent shin plasters. They arrived the next day—all new, crisp and attractive looking.

As soon as I arrived at camp I told the interpreter to have all the Indians—bucks, squaws and papooses—pass by the end of the wagon in which I stood and as they filed by I gave to each, even to the little babe tied on the mother's back, one little ten-cent greenback. This so pleased the Indians that after another feast, at which some dogs were killed and eaten and a big pow-wow held, I was given to understand I could remain there with the cattle until the grass came, on condition that I build a large log ranch or building, large enough to accommodate the squaws, papooses and old warriors in case of a Sioux or Cheyenne Indian attack. I readily agreed to this as timber was plentiful around us. I built a log building with port holes on all sides and assured them that in case of attack we would help fight their enemies, all of which pleased them greatly.

One Pawnee warrior, named "Skitty Butts," was so pleased with my action and our mild protests against his helping himself to our provisions whenever he wanted to, that he very generously expressed a willingness to give me his beautiful sixteen year old sister for a wife, but I courteously declined, telling him that I did not need a wife.

"Skitty Butts" was not the only one to crowd our little cook tent at meal times. Sometimes as many as fifty bucks, squaws and papooses would be hanging around for something to eat. The hatchet was buried. The pipe of peace was often passed around to us and in turn smoked. Twice during the winter a big feast was held by the Indians. Many dogs, skunks, beavers, and musk-rats, were served on these auspicious occasions, to which, as a rule, we were cordially invited. We dared not refuse to attend or to partake of the feast, which was presided over by their head medicine men, chanting war songs, praising the valiant deeds of their forefathers and invoking the aid and good will of the Great Spirit in their proposed buffalo hunts on the Republican River. I have often been compelled to eat at these feasts when the odor alone would make me deathly sick. I dared not refuse, since if any bad luck had occurred or anything gone wrong, all would have been laid to me and the penalty would have been death and the confiscation of our cattle and outfit.

On one of these buffalo hunts on the Republican River the Sioux attacked the Pawnees, killing nearly two hundred bucks and squaws, besides some papooses. I went over with a squad of cavalry from the "Dobytown" fort or garrison and saw the result of this fight, which was a complete victory for the Sioux. The Pawnees had sold their lives as dearly as possible, but the Sioux had the advantage of position and numbers and showed no mercy to the brave little band of Pawnees. Scalps

General Coe

Levi Carter

Sioux Squaw and Papoose

Pawnee and Sioux Indians

were taken and the bodies frightfully mutilated. Even a young squaw mother with a babe at her breast was not spared. A pack of hungry wolves and coyotes was feasting on the unburied bodies of the victims.

Be it said to the credit of the officers and soldiers of the squad who went over the battle ground, that the bodies were carefully gathered up, wrapped in blankets and buried not far from where we found them in that silent valley near the Republican River. Some posts were set up at the ends of the trenches in which the bodies were laid. I am told that nothing is left to tell the story of this bloody battle. The posts have disappeared long ago, the mounds have sunken and the battle ground is now a cornfield.

The Pawnees that remained at our camp and the few that got away and returned manifested their sorrow in different ways; some cried loudly like the Sioux on the death of a relative, others would sit for hours with faces covered with their blankets, weeping in silence and vowing vengeance on their deadly enemies for the brutal butchery of nearly two hundred of the flower of their tribe.

"Skitty Butts" sister, who could shoot an arrow as straight as her brother and who, it was said, had killed several buffalo and other game, went with this hunting party, was captured and carried off by a young Sioux chief.

Time passed quickly. We were kept busy feeding and caring for the cattle, and while much snow fell and the winter was a cold one, the cattle went through without much loss. We caught some thieving white men driving some of them off to an island in the Platte River, where they butchered them, took the meat to Grand Island and sold it.

As stated, we had turned the large log house over to the Indians and the men and I lived in the two tents. It was an agreeable change when spring came and the grass was high enough so the cattle began to leave their hay and graze on the open prairie.

About May 10, 1870, we broke up camp and moved the cattle across Wood River to Prairie Creek, bidding adieu to our Pawnee Indian friends, who bade us an affectionate good-bye. I met some of these later while supplying their agency at Genoa with beef, and others a few years later acting as scouts for the Government under Major North. Later, in 1876, the tribe was removed from Nebraska to a reservation of 283,000 acres in Oklahoma, since which time their number has greatly decreased.

We had not been many days in camp on Prairie Creek when my three men struck for higher wages. I was paying them $45.00 per month and board. They wanted $55.00 per month and board. The Sioux had just been making some raids on the settlers, mostly cattlemen, on the Loup rivers, and my men thought we would be the next to be attacked on another raid that the Sioux had planned on the Pawnees. Our temporary camp on Prairie Creek would be on the route should they carry out this threat. I sent word to the Pawnees at our old camp to be on the lookout for this proposed attack, which they headed off by all moving back to Genoa on the double-quick. This information being sent to the war party of Sioux probably saved us from attack. I tried to reason with my men. I told them I could not afford to pay them the wages demanded and that I did not think the Sioux would bother us, but this did not satisfy them. They demanded their time and I paid them.

Just about this time, 3:00 P. M., it commenced to rain and the cattle started to scatter. Before leaving camp to round up the cattle I luckily tied up an extra horse to the wagon. It was just getting dark when I returned to camp. The rain continued falling. I changed horses, put the one I had been riding on a stake rope, then went to the cook tent and grub box, thinking I would find a few cold biscuits, but the men had taken all the cooked food. I picked up a couple of ears of corn and put them in my saddle pockets. It is not necessary to state that I had a hard night's ride. The cattle kept drifting until I got them in a bend of the creek where the banks were steep. Here I succeeded in holding them in spite of the rain. About 10:00 A. M. it began to let up. I headed the cattle toward camp and after changing horses again, about 2:00 P. M. I rode to Wood River station and Jackson's store, where I succeeded in hiring John Smont and other men, whom I brought out to camp on extra horses.

Since the men left I had had no time to cook anything. My menu had been the raw corn off of several cobs. The men I had just hired cooked a hasty supper consisting of biscuit, coffee and bacon, which I enjoyed. With one of the men, I then rounded up the cattle and herded them half the night, when we were relieved by the other two men.

It was while holding the cattle on Prairie Creek one windy night, that a heavy field desk lid, which I had set up against the torn corner of the tent to break the wind, fell on my forehead while I was asleep. This must have stunned me, for I awakened in a pool of blood. The iron-capped lid had struck me on the forehead, which scar I will carry as long as I live.

While on Prairie Creek another little accident, which nearly cost me my life, befell me. I had gone to Jackson's store with a mule team to get provisions. Wood River was high and going over one part of the bridge. I got my supplies and started back to find the water apparently about one foot deep flowing over the bridge. I thought I could get across and touched up the mules with my whip. Before I realized my danger my mules, the wagon and I plunged into about twelve feet of flood water. I cannot tell how I got out. The mules were drowned and the wagon recovered several days afterward, but the supplies had sunk into the mud or been carried away by the current. Again I was reminded of that "Guardian Angel."

At this time there were no settlers on Prairie Creek and many of those on Wood River had left on account of Indian raids. Some had gone to Grand Island, others to old Fort Kearny, or "Dobytown." Among the settlers on Wood River I remember, besides Jackson, the Olivers, Lambertsons, Dugdales, Charles Walker (whose wife many called Ironsides), Pat Walsh, that Prince of Democrats who used to take pride in carrying the ballot box with its vote to Kearney. Some one stuffed the ballot on him once with an obnoxious ballot, which made Mr. Walsh very angry.

I could mention many other good Wood River people with whom I became acquainted, among them Otto Legg and Sol Rickmond. The last I saw of Legg was when he borrowed some funds from me to take him to Kearney. I have not seen nor heard from him since.

George Williamson and the McGees had claims near mine. The former was a hot-headed fellow, who later killed his man and had much trouble in keeping his neck out of a rope loop for his crime.

Here I must close my experience with the cattle wintered in 1869 and spring of 1870 at Wood River.

CHAPTER XXIV

ABOUT June 10, 1870, grass became good enough so
the cattle could live and hold their own on the trail
if handled on easy drives, hence I started my little
herd of invalid cows and heifers, many of which had calves
by their sides, necessitating easy drives.

In passing Stevenson Siding, John Long, the section foreman, bantered me for a trade of twenty head of the light end
of the herd, mostly yearling heifers. I told him I was afraid
he was not fixed to handle and care for them and that the
cattle were Texas cattle and somewhat wild when people
went around them afoot, but he said he knew his business
and had quite a number of section men whom he could use
in handling and herding them. I hesitated about selling him
the cattle and told him that as fast as the yearlings were cut
out of the bunch they would be considered his property, to
which he agreed. The price was $22.00 each, cash as soon
as cut out. John had six section men employed to hold the
heifers as fast as cut from the bunch. They simply scared
the cattle and about the time the twentieth had been cut out,
the other nineteen had disappeared over the hills. John
began to realize that he did not want them and asked me to
take them back. I could find only nineteen of them. Finally
I sold him an apparently good milk cow with a young calf for
$50.00. I left Smont at the section house that night to hunt
up the missing yearling, but he failed to find her. Strange but
true, we found her three years after in a herd of cattle on
the South Loup. She had a calf by her side.

Smont, on his overtaking us, told about John Long's experience with the milk cow. We had tied the calf for him, but the poor mother was so wild and scared at those section men chasing her afoot that she was much inclined to abandon her calf. Long got up at peep of day, thinking he would be able to rope the cow while she was near the calf, but on seeing him and the men she made for the hills. Mrs. Long and the little Longs had anticipated having some milk for breakfast and asked John in a very pleasant way if he had "pailed" the cow. John answered rather savagely, "Pail h—l and damnation. You might as well try to pail a buffalo." Smont finally roped the cow and tied her up near the calf and after throwing her down a few times she reluctantly consented to be milked. We often did this to break Texas cows for milking.

Several calves drowned in crossing the Platte River, which was swimming in several places. Outside of this we got the cattle through in good shape.

Shortly after my arrival at what we had named Fort McPherson Herd Camp, according to prior arrangements with Isaac Coe and Levi Carter, I bought out John Wait's interest in the cattle, numbering several thousand head, and a co-partnership was formed under the name of John Bratt & Co. Wait had established a small camp in one of the deep pockets of the short cañons leading on to what was called the Burke Flats, a little east of what was known as "Point Lookout" just west of Moran cañon, and about midway between Fort McPherson and North Platte City.

I could write a chapter about this particular Point. Many a stage coach, freight and emigrant train, soldier and cowboy have been chased and shot at, and some captured and killed by war parties of the Sioux hiding behind "Point Lookout," from which they would swoop down on the unsuspecting travelers without a moment's warning. I and some of our cowboys had a narrow escape from capture by a small band of Sioux, who came charging down on us from "Point Lookout." They did their best to cut us off. While on our way down the bottom the band split, part going in front and part behind us. We saved ourselves by dashing into the brush and fording the river. One of our line riders, William Rix, in disobeying orders "never to ride the same line twice in succession," received two bullets in his body, one going through him, the other lodging near his backbone. He was shot by Indians hiding behind "Point Lookout." Rix recovered and finally went to Utah.

Our cattle ranged between the Platte River, Medicine and Red Willow creeks, west of Fort McPherson and east of O'Fallons' Bluffs. Our ranch brand was an oblong circle on

Our Ranch Brand

the left hip and loin and ear mark, thus: ⊂⊃⊖ Our cattle were known among cattle men as the "Circle Herd."

During the Fall of 1870 we commenced building what was later known as The Home Ranch on Section 13, Township 14 North, Range 30, just north of the old Jack Morrow Road Ranch, south of Fremont slough, being about four miles southeast of North Platte City and about fourteen miles west of Fort McPherson. We built our ranch house and stables out of sod. The walls of the ranch house were four to six feet thick and fitted with port holes to enable us to stand off an attack by Indians. We built strong corrals, and branding chutes, out of cedar logs and rails and fenced in Section 13, on the east, south and west, with strong cedar mortised posts and red cedar rails, four rails to an 8-foot pommel. Many of the posts are standing there to-day, the 10th day of July, 1912, forty-two years, as sound as the day they were put in the ground. At this time the cañons had plenty of cedar trees in them of which we made free use.

I remember we moved into our ranch house, with its sod and dirt roof laid on cedar rails, on Christmas Day, 1870.

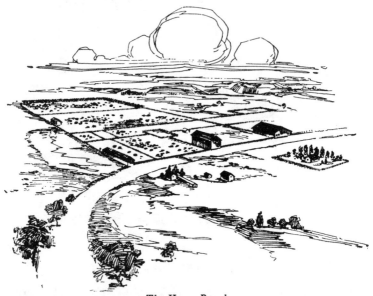

The Home Ranch

We also completed our stable with its sod walls and hay roof. It was quite a relief to myself and men when we had a rail pasture to turn our horses into, a stable in which we could tie a couple of dozen at night and a good house in which to protect ourselves from Indian attacks. This was a great improvement on sleeping out around our horse herd in the open with a lariat fastened around a saddle horse's neck and tied to our arms.

Our employees, some twenty or thirty, were mostly

Texans or Mexicans. All could swing a lariat, use a revolver or ride a broncho, but understood little and cared less about buildings or making fence.

The many little thieving bands of Sioux and Cheyenne Indians kept us busy before we finished our ranch, corrals and pasture. They would take a sneak on us and drive off a few horses every chance they got. About forty Sioux Indians stole up on us one dark night and took seventy-five head of horses out of a herd of one hundred twenty-five in spite of the fact that some twelve herders were sleeping around them with saddle horses tied to their arms, legs or bodies. In the stampede some of the men were dragged a great distance over the prairie. One man's arm was broken. As soon as we could get our forces together I had the men take up the trail while I went to Fort McPherson to get a squad of cavalry to help us follow the Indians. Lieutenant Thomas, a brave little officer, was detailed with a company of cavalry to help me follow the Indians with the stolen stock. Buffalo Bill went along as guide. We caught up with our men about dark near the head of Medicine Creek. They had the trail, which was quite fresh. It seemed to lead to the head of Red Willow Creek, which we reached a little before daylight. At break of day we saw the Indian camp and some of the stolen horses. The order was given to surround the camp, if possible unknown to the Indians, but this could not be done. Many of the Indians had laid down beside their ponies, the loose horses apparently grazing in the center of the tired and sleeping Indian guard. Before we had surrounded them, the guards were aware of us and were on their ponies, trying to stampede the loose horses. The rough lay of the country aided the Indians more than us, but it was not long before we had many of them hemmed in a "pocket," from which a few escaped.

I remember one incident that occurred in this fight. One of our men, Gokey by name, a half-breed Frenchman with some Indian blood in him, was galloping his horse alongside of mine, when we spied an Indian trying to hide behind a tree.

We stopped. Gokey dismounted, saying, "I shoot you, I shoot you." Old Gokey very deliberately took aim at the Indian, resting his gun on the side of a tree. The Indian commenced dodging. Old Gokey, getting "a bead" on the Indian, pulled the trigger, but his gun failed to go off. He mounted his horse in disgust, saying, "I believe I won't either." The Indian, no doubt, was pleased but not for long, since a ball coming from another direction, soon sent him to join his thieving comrades.

Enough to say, the fight lasted about two hours. We took no prisoners and not many Indians escaped. We brought in all of the horses and ponies that were not killed or crippled, except some that a few of the Indians got. One of our men was killed and four wounded. The papers that loved the Indian better than the honest settler and brave soldier, who were always ready to do or die, styled this Indian fight a needless butchery and brave, gallant Lieutenant Thomas was courtmartialed. Scout and Guide W. F. Cody, not as well known as he was later, did good work in this fight. We recovered most of the horses. The Indians let us alone for a few days after this "drubbing," when they came and took a few more of our horses, shot our lineman twice through the body and stampeded the Government herd of horses and mules at Fort McPherson.

While these roving, thieving little bands of Sioux Indians were bad and committed many depredations, yet the Sioux Indians, as a nation, were not at war with the whites. Spotted Tail, the great Sioux Chief, was keeping his word. He promised his daughter before she died of a broken heart at Fort Laramie that he would never go to war against the whites again. He exacted this promise from many of his subchiefs and later from Red Cloud. Some of these Sioux Chiefs, especially Spotted Tail and his followers, would often come to our Home Ranch and stay a couple of days on their way to and from their buffalo hunts on the Republican River and its tributaries. On these occasions we would make them a feast, killing a couple or more "beeves," give them flour, sugar, coffee, syrup and beans, and if winter, hay for their ponies. They were familiar with our brands and ear marks, both on cattle and horses. I had a list of brands and many times animals would be recovered and returned to proper owners by this friendly coöperation.

Spotted Tail showed his honesty and good will toward us many times by telling us where certain bunches of our cattle were. He and other Sioux Indians, in the spring of 1872, told us where we would find the remains of several hundred cattle that had been needlessly butchered by several little war parties of Sioux Indians, all because they did not happen to run across any buffalo. Some of our men and I went over in the country indicated by Spotted Tail's band and found the carcases of nearly four hundred cattle that had been killed, not for the meat but for pure, unadulterated meanness. We found scores with their tongues cut out, many others killed for the sinew, some for their hearts, others for their brains and many had just a little meat taken from the loins. These animals had been in good condition. We were out several weeks, getting at the facts, numbers, sex, ages and value and found our claim footed up to nearly $13,000.00, for which we put in a claim to the Government. This was scaled down some and then paid, when unprincipled squaw men went to the chiefs of these thieving bands and told them that the Government, the "Great Father," was going to deduct these claims from their annuities and that they could get out of paying for the cattle by saying they did not kill them. These lies were put in form by unscrupulous agents and others to cover their negligence in allowing the thieving bands of Indians to leave their reservations. The Indians being promised that the money paid us for these cattle would be given to them, persuaded many of these Indians to tell the basest falsehoods, on the strength of which, though we had several hundred Indians testify to seeing these cattle after they were killed by the marauding bands, we were compelled to pay back a part of this already scaled-down, just claim to the Government—all this after our kindness to these untruthful Indians and to many who took pleasure in raiding us and destroying our property. We were thus defrauded of several thousand dollars justly and honestly due us and made to appear in the light of cheating the poor Indians. Spotted Tail and other noted chiefs, acquainted with the facts, always said that we were cheated out of our rights.

The life of the cattle man in the days from 1867 to 1889 was anything but a Sunday-school picnic. We drove up many herds from Texas to our range in Nebraska, the first herd going to Wyoming, where I built the ranch in 1867, near what was later called Wyoming Station. The Texas cattle breeder had no use for the money of the Northern people, the greenback. They insisted that we pay for the cattle in gold, and to get the gold there safely was a difficult problem. We would carry all we could in belts around our bodies under our heavy shirts. We made double bottoms to our wagon beds and carried much of it there. We usually took a few picked men with us—men that we could rely on in any emergency. Some of these did not know where we carried our money. After a few drives we became better known to the Texas cattle growers and once gaining their confidence, the task of dealing with them was easier. Later herds would be counted out to us—so many yearling heifers, so many yearling steers, two-year old heifers, two-year old steers, so many dry cows, so many cows with calves by their sides, so many three-year old and so many four-year old and upward steers, so many males at so much per head for each class, or the total number at a stated sum for the average, nothing under yearlings counted. These herds would average in cost, during the years 1867 to 1895, all the way from $5.00 per head to $20.00 on the Texas ranches. It would cost from $1.00 to $2.50 per head to trail the cattle from Texas to "Dobytown" (old Fort Kearny), Fort McPherson or Ogallala, Nebraska. The cost would depend on what luck we had in getting the herds off their breeding grounds, what number of bad white men, Mexicans, half-

A Stampede

breeds and Indians were encountered on the trail, whether feed and water were plentiful, the number of stampedes, the luck in crossing swollen streams, and last but not least, the number of good, reliable, trusty employees we happened to have.   No matter how careful in this we would frequently hire a man, who, unknown to us, had killed his man, and with chips on both shoulders was always ready to drop another on the least provocation.   In the early days it was hard to get one who did not drink, gamble and swear.   It took courage and some good judgment to handle and get along with them.

We would drive herds of fifteen hundred to twenty-five hundred head in a bunch, usually requiring ten to fifteen men, who would have from five to seven horses each.   The cook would drive the mess wagon, usually pulled by two to five yoke of cattle.   In a big outfit there would be two or more horse wranglers for night and day service.

With an exclusive steer herd the greatest caution would have to be taken to avoid stampedes.   The approach of a pack of wolves, coyotes, elk, deer, buffalo or other game, all of which were plentiful in those days, would jump a sleeping herd to its feet in an instant and if the night herders did not know their duty and act promptly to sooth and pacify the frightened animals, a stampede would be certain.   A small band of Indians or desperate white men could and did sometimes turn in an instant a docile, sleeping herd into enraged, maddened, crazy animals, that, once started on a run or stampede, would sound like the noise of a cyclone or tornado. The bellowing of the cattle, the knocking of horns, the pounding hoofs that seem to make the earth tremble, caution the experienced cowman to get quickly out of the way and on the outside of the stampeding cattle, which he begins to circle around and around, thus changing the straight course into a milling whirlpool; and after a ride for life, all the while singing some soothing song, he and his fellow herders, if not thrown by their horses stepping into some prairie dog, wolf or badger hole, finally get the herd stopped, if not quieted.

As a rule, after such scares and stampedes, the cattle continue to be excited and restless the balance of the night and sometimes for many days and nights thereafter. After a stampede the cattle were usually counted the following morning and if any were missing, several herders were detailed to scout the country and adjacent herds (if any) and to bring back the missing cattle, which were picked up on either the ranch brand described in the bill of sale or the road brand. We found it good judgment to put a road brand on all herds we bought—some plain letter or figure—even if only a dim or hair brand, as it was usually called. I know of cases where coast or brush steers have traveled forty miles or more in one night in a stampede and were it not for the road or trail brand we could never have recovered them, for they would have gone back to the same range where they were bought.

Another grief to sometimes try the herders' nerves and rob the venture of considerable profit would be the crossing of swollen creeks and rivers. To do this without loss required nerve and good judgment. The most experienced men would be placed on both sides of the cattle, well up toward the lead and, once in the river, these men would do the pointing, while others behind would keep the swing cattle moving, following the lead of the herd. Other herders would gently keep the tail of the herd moving along so there would be no gaps or chance to break back. All should be done without hurrying the cattle or exciting them, or the horses in the least. A herd of cattle, excited or frightened in crossing a swollen stream, will usually go to milling with the result that some are drowned. Experienced cowboys well know how to stop this milling by riding into and breaking the whirl and getting the cattle strung out again.

In crossing some rivers quicksand is encountered and always dreaded. Many a cow and horse have lost their lives in this. I have seen horses with their riders almost disappear and have to be pulled out with ropes.

The most treacherous river I ever crossed on horseback was the Snake River near Shoshone Falls in Idaho. We rode into it, seeing the bottom of the river, when in an instant we disappeared in water fifty to nearly two hundred feet deep, to be almost sucked under in a blind whirlpool.

One time in crossing the Red River on the Texas Trail with a herd of cattle, General Coe discharged two of his old foremen, Mate Brooks and John Knox, because they refused to swim it prior to crossing the cattle. The General wanted to see what kind of a "getting out" place it was.

It was on this drive and on the banks of this river that a couple of herders came into camp for dinner and complained about there being no clean plates, cups, knives, forks and spoons. Just then the General stepped into camp, and after learning the trouble, picked up every plate, cup, knife, fork and spoon and dumped them into the river, telling the men they could get along without those luxuries, and they did until the next store was reached, when each herder bought, used and kept his own.

Another arbitrary and very important, fearless fellow that we had to contend with was the brand inspector of some of the different counties the Texas Trail went through. Some of them were satisfied to be fed and would pass the herd easy and allow it to proceed without delay. Others, more mean and exacting, would hold up the cattle for all they could get, delay the moving for several days under the pretense that some of the brands were not plain and distinct. Some met their death in this game of bluff. As a rule there was always a match for this kind of a fellow.

Life on the Chislom Trail, beset with dangers on all sides, was a hard one. The herds would usually make two drives a day of seven to eight miles each, depending on the condition of the cattle and whether there was sufficient grass and water. In later years, on account of many herds being driven up from Texas to the Northern States, feed became very short late in the season, resulting in many thin herds arriving and consequent losses during the hard Nebraska, Colorado and Wyoming winters. Methods changed as the years went by.

Instead of taking our gold with us in our belts or false

wagon boxes, as we had done, we would take part in gold and exchange on St. Louis, Kansas City or New York for the balance of the purchase price of the cattle. Later the owner of the cattle, or some relative, would come up the trail with us and take the pay for the cattle in Eastern exchange back with them. Getting better acquainted with the Northern cattlemen, the Texas cattle raiser began to drive his own herd to Aberdeen and other points in Kansas and later to Ogallala and other points along the Union Pacific Railroad in Nebraska, Colorado and Wyoming.

On the Texas Trail

Among these Texas drivers, whole-souled and big-hearted, could be mentioned Millet and Mayberry, Faut, Prior Brothers and Uncle Billy Stevens. They were the soul of honor and their statements never questioned.

Among the pioneer ranchmen in Nebraska, besides us, were Keith & Barton, Bent & Evans, Edward Creighton, who had cattle interests in Wyoming, Ed. Welch, Ben Gallagher, Russell Watts, John Burke, Sr., Major Walker, W. A. Paxton, Bosler Bros., Sheidley Bros., Iliff, Fussler Bros., Bay State Cattle Co., Ira Nichols, and many others who embarked in the business. The first cattle queen near North Platte was Mrs. Randall, later Mrs. Ritner. Then came a host of small cattle ranches. All prospered and did fairly well in the business until hard winters and lack of feed hit some herds hard.

Our range at this time, 1870 to 1873, was from the Platte River to the Republican and from Fort McPherson on the east to Fort Sedgwick on the west. The main ranch was what we called the "Home Ranch," about four miles southeast of North Platte. We had a number of ranches and camps on the outside, one at Fox Creek, one at the mouth of Curtis Creek, one at the head of the Medicine and Red Willow creeks, another near Bishop's old ranch and one near O'Fallons' Bluffs. Some of these were temporary camps and used only at certain seasons of the year or in cases of emergency. We ranged from ten thousand to fifteen thousand cattle at times and about one thousand horses and mares, branding three thousand to five thousand calves and two hundred to three hundred colts a year.

My life was a very busy one, full of hardships, sleeping wherever night overtook me—sometimes in a ranch but often in the open with my saddle for a pillow and slicker and saddle blanket for my bed.

We filled the beef contracts at Fort McPherson for over twelve years, the North Platte garrison for several years, besides several temporary contracts, to two-company camps at the mouth of the Red Willow Creek, also other places where troops were stationed to keep the Indians in check. We also filled several Indian contracts for beef and breeding cattle at the Rosebud and the Pine Ridge Indian Agencies and operated a meat market at North Platte.

These side lines—keeping track of our cattle and horses, as well as bunches of thieving Indians and whites, fighting prairie fires, following trail herds through our ranges, going on round-ups, branding calves, shipping "beeves" and dry cows, putting up ten thousand to twelve thousand tons of hay annually, building ranches and corrals, kept me and our employees rather busy.

I had to deal with all classes of men from the "goody-

goody" fellow (not many of these), to the horse thief, desperado and general, all-round bad man. It was hard to keep them in the straight and narrow path. I tried to set them a good example and encouraged them to quit their bad habits of gambling, drinking, and swearing. I was kind to them but firm, and insisted that all orders be carried out. I encouraged them to save their money and to be honest with each other. We supplied the different ranches with good, wholesome reading matter and each ranch had its Bible. If an employee could not be braced up and taught the better way after a fair trial, I would finally let him go, rather than quarrel with him. When hired I would always tell him what his duties would be and that any time when he found he could not discharge them faithfully, not to be afraid to tell me, and if we could not come to a mutual understanding we would part friendly if possible. In event of injury or sickness of any employee we would see that he received the best medical care and proper nursing until well. Up to 1880 each employee carried his gun or revolver with plenty of ammunition if going on long trips, also bowie knife and field glasses, as a protection against roving bands of thieving Indians and wolves, and to supply the camps with game. Such was the custom, and to discontinue it the writer had to use much will power, especially when going on round-ups, but we finally discarded our weapons.

The ranch or stock business grew rapidly and many people engaged in it, even women. I refer to Mrs. Randall, widow of Ex-Governor and Postmaster General Randall. later Mrs. Ritner, a very intelligent lady.

The cattle business was not, as many expected, all profit. Hard winters and prairie fires would scatter the cattle and entail much loss where the hay was scarce. Some cattlemen did not put up any hay, and of course these lost heavily. Again herds passing through the range would often take some of our cattle along, mixing during the night, notwithstanding the fact that we had cowboys go through and camp with these outfits. Yet in spite of this care and diligence we would occasionally hear of some of our cattle or horses being discovered in Wyoming, Colorado or Dakota.

Later came stock associations. I was elected President of the first stock association formed in Lincoln County. Other counties and Western states soon followed in organizing, and in a few years we had a good working mutual system. Brand books were published, giving a list of recorded brands and marks on cattle and horses in each state. Better stock laws were put on our statute books. Round-up districts were formed. Date and place of starting and rules governing same were published in the different stock papers. Annual meetings were held at different places in the different states. At these meetings all topics governing or pertaining to the stock industry were freely discussed. Many stock growers attended these gatherings and took great interest in them. Brand inspectors were appointed to watch the different shipping points and run down cattle and horse thieves, commonly called "rustlers." We had an executive committee that would think nothing of following a bunch of cattle or horse thieves through every state of the Union and into old Mexico or farther. This vigorous policy broke up many of the gangs, but constant vigilance was necessary. What was done created a better feeling among stockmen generally. The ranchman who had adopted the brand B 4 was no longer afraid of his neighbor's adding the letter U to his animal. At the same time we had to be always on the watch.

Just before beginning a round-up on the east end of our range on the Birdwood, I caught one of my neighbors driving off our range to his own a bunch of about five hundred mixed cattle, for the purpose of securing the unbranded calves, or mavericks, in the bunch. I was surprised and angry at his doing this and told him so. I gave him a severe quirting for about a mile and then took the cattle back to our own range west of the Birdwood. The man did not return the next day, but his brother did with a Winchester rifle, threatening to kill me. I told him these things did not scare me, and that I would serve him the same if I ever caught him doing the same dishonorable trick.

For the information of the reader I will here explain the word "maverick."

In the early history of western Texas, in the forties, there lived a shrewd, far-seeing, business man named Samuel Maverick, whose ambition was to be able to travel from San Antonio to El Paso and from El Paso to the mouth of the Rio Grande on his own land, and at one time it seemed his dream would be realized for he secured title to two million acres of this land. A part of this passed out of his hands before he died. The remainder was willed to his wife and by her to their grandchildren, some of whom are now living near El Paso, Texas.

Once upon a time Samuel Maverick had a debt against a stockman which he could not collect, so he accepted four hundred cattle at $3.00 per head in full for all demands. He placed a trusted negro in charge of the stock and paid no further attention to the cattle. At the end of four years he sold the original cattle at $6.00 per head but did not take into consideration the natural increase. He had branded none of the calves and the consequence was that there were on the range a large number of unbranded cattle. Therefore, when stockmen came across unbranded animals, they would say they belonged to Maverick or they are Maverick's. This is how the work "maverick" originated and began to be applied by cowboys and stockmen to all unbranded stock.

During the early round-ups it was no uncommon thing to have a killing, either of a stock owner or cowboy. Shooting at each other on the least provocation was common and more than once have I seen a good fist fight. I remember Mr. Iliff (one of the old pioneer cattlemen whose range was in western Nebraska and eastern Colorado and Wyoming) had a fistic encounter with a cowboy who gave him the worst of it and in order to prevent his eyes from getting black from the punishment received from the cowboy, a young steer was killed and some thin slices of beef plastered over both eyes, which, however, did not prevent the flesh above and below the eyes from becoming badly discolored.

I happened to see this fight. Both men were game, fought hard and asked no favors. At the end of the fight Mr. Iliff shook hands with the cowboy, told him it was all right and that he had no hard feelings against him.

Mr. Iliff accumulated a great deal of wealth in the cattle-growing business. In addition to his large cattle interests he operated a large meat market in Cheyenne. He shipped a great deal of fresh meat by the carcass to section houses and grading, tie and wood camps east and west on the Union Pacific Railroad.

Mr. Iliff died many years ago, leaving Mrs. Iliff rich. Some years afterward, being a great worker in the Methodist church, she married Bishop Warren of Colorado.

CHAPTER XXV

*The Round-Up—Initiating the Tenderfoot—Dangers of the Cowboy
—Organization and Management—Tribute to the Cowboy*

A ROUND-UP as conducted in these days was quite interesting. The time and place of starting the round-up
for the different sections of range country having been
agreed upon at the annual meetings of the different stock associations held in Nebraska, Wyoming, Colorado, Montana,
and in other stock-growing states and territories, the owners
would send their outfits, or representatives, to meet at a certain time and place. The route was mapped out and
thoroughly worked so all owners would get what stock belonged to them, the brands and marks on the animals being
prima-facie evidence of ownership. If an animal was not
branded or ear marked, it was known as a "maverick" and
properly claimed by the owner of the cattle belonging to the
range being rounded up. The owner of the cattle on said
range, if competent, would be expected to act as superintendent of the round-up and boss the work.

The spring round-up would usually commence between the
15th and 30th of May, and the fall round-up about the
10th to 15th of September, at or near the east line of our
range, commencing on the Dismal River, thence west through
the Lake country south of Hyannis, thence south, taking in
the West and East Birdwood creeks, to the north bank of the
North Platte River. At the mouth of the Birdwood Creek
we would be joined by small representatives who had worked
the cattle country on the South Loup and down the Platte
River as far east as Brady. Other outfits would commence
work at the forks of the Platte River, working west between
the rivers, while still others would commence rounding up
the cattle as far east as Plum Creek, working the cattle country
west on the south side of the South Platte River. Small
parties would take in the range country as far south as the

Medicine and Red Willow creeks and other outfits would cover the range country tributary to the Republican River. So that nearly every mile of the range country would be ridden and all cattle grazing on these different ranges would be rounded up and all cattle or horses bearing other owners' brands would be gathered up and if not too many in number, would be thrown in a joint herd and moved on with the round-up, until they reached the range where they belonged, when they would be separated from the other animals and left.

Initiating the Tenderfoot

As a rule, I would be chosen superintendent to boss our range and usually was asked to boss the round-up through adjoining ranges.

It was no easy job to handle two hundred or more cowboys with nearly a dozen different outfits and one thousand to twelve hundred horses, keep the work moving intelligently, find camping places for each outfit and see that all, even the lone representative, had an equal show and a square deal, but I had the reputation of doing it. It was difficult to secure sufficient experienced cowboys for these round-ups and we often had to fill in with what were termed "tenderfeet."

For these the older experienced cowmen would usually have something in cold storage that would, as a rule, take the conceit out of them. Should he make the remark that he could ride anything, he would be given the chance to ride the worst bucking outlaw horse in the bunch. If he stayed in his saddle his fellow cowboys would show him more respect but should he "pull leather" or get thrown, the cowmen and cowboys would joke and ridicule him unmercifully. When these practical jokes would be carried too far I would interfere and protect him. With sympathy and encouragement I have seen some of these timid tenderfeet turn out to be some of the best riders, ropers and expert cattlemen in the outfit.

The life of the cowboy, especially on these round-ups, was a hard one and full of perils. The percentage of deaths and disability on the range at this time was said to be greater than in a military campaign. He had to conquer the "outlaw" and vicious broncho; the pitfalls of the plains—prairie dog, wolf and badger holes—were often in his track; he swam swollen rivers, crossed wash-outs and quicksand, stopped the mad rush of stampeding herds, faced pelting rains accompanied by terrible thunderstorms, the bolts of lightning often killing cattle in the bunches he was herding. No wonder he suffered the pangs of rheumatism brought on by excessive rough-riding and too much sleeping on round-ups (generally about four hours out of the twenty-four), under the stars in all kinds of weather with sometimes nothing but his slicker and saddle blanket to cover him.

Still there was always enough splash of adventure in the life to lend it a charm. He was paid $35.00 to $45.00 per month and furnished with board and outfit. He would be supplied with five to eight horses, depending on the class and condition of the animals and the lay and character of the country to be worked.

The round-up crew consisted of a foreman, a cook, a horse wrangler for day and another for night herd, and as many cowboys as the occasion demanded. The foreman's authority was absolute. The cowman or cowboy must obey his orders in all matters or quit. The horse wranglers had charge of the band of cow ponies that accompanied each outfit on a round-up.

After the night herder had brought the horses at peep of day into the rope corral (formed by ropes tied to the hind and front wheels of the mess wagons) he was supposed to hold them there until all the cowmen present had selected their mounts and a change of horses for all the other cowmen who might be out with the cattle. These herders were relieved by others who had had breakfast, when the day wrangler took charge of the horse herd, letting it graze on the best feed near camp until the mess wagons were ready to move, when the horse herd was moved behind them.

The horse wranglers were supposed to assist the round-up cook in making and breaking up camp, setting up and taking down the cook and sleeping tents, seeing that the cook had wood and water, loading und unloading the rolls of bedding, stake ropes, etc., always keeping an eye on his loose bunch of horses so that they could round them up and bring them into camp on a few moments' notice.

The cook had charge of the cook wagon with its load of provisions and camp equipage. Like the cowboys, he got but very little sleep, often up at three o'clock in the morning and until very late at night. He drove the wagon from point to point from six to eight miles at a time, according to instructions given him by the foreman of the outfit, who received his instructions from the superintendent of the round-up. The distance of the drives depended upon the number of cattle to be rounded up, the lay and character of the country to be worked and the supply of water for the men and stock. The cook was supposed to be able to rustle a meal in a very short time.

In the early round-up days we would depend much on wild game, ham, shoulders and bacon, beans, syrup, sugar, coffee, soda bread or biscuits, and sometimes honey. The game con-

Caught in a Prairie Dog Hole

sisted principally of antelope, buffalo, deer and elk. Later we fared better, using canned corn, tomatoes, condensed milk, potatoes, onions, beans, baking powder biscuits, sugar, syrup, and when game was scarce all the fresh beef we needed, to say nothing of vegetables and often canned fruit, dried apples, prunes, and other dried fruits.

When the meal was ready the cook hallooed, "Grub pile," and each cowboy, without ceremony, grabbed a tin plate, cup, knife, fork and spoon and helped himself, then retired, either outside or in one corner of the tent.

A Hasty Meal

Before the meal was finished the horses were driven into the rope corral, ready to be roped by their respective riders, or in case of their absence, by the foreman or wrangler, and tied to await the arrival of the absent cowmen.

If cattle were plentiful on the range and not too many cows and calves, and brands showed up plainly, we would round up, work and separate three thousand to five thousand head per day, putting each brand of cattle in its proper herd, working two to four bunches of three hundred to five hundred head in a bunch at a time. The cows and calves would be cut out first.

After all stray cows and calves were cut out the bunch

was turned over to the outfit having the largest number of cattle. The duty of the foreman or experienced cowman in charge was to see that the bunch was handled quietly—not "ginned" around—and that no cattle were cut out except those which the parties working the bunch had a right to take, especially mavericks, unless following the mother.

Sometimes disputes would arise over certain brands and if the contending parties were hotheads, the contention might result in a quarrel and end in a killing, in the early round-up days when "might made right." But a killing was an exception to the rule. Later nearly all disputes were settled by arbitration or an appeal to two disinterested, experienced cattle owners on the ground. In this way we got along better.

In a subsequent chapter I may refer to one case where neighboring cattle owners tried to take advantage of the writer.

These round-ups would take from three to six weeks in the spring and about thirty or more days in the fall.

All the cattle back on their own range again, then would come the branding of calves and mavericks. These we would gather together one day and brand the next. The cows and calves would be taken to some corral on the range, held in the pens during the night, and early the next morning the calves would be separated from their mothers, when the task of roping, throwing, branding and marking would be easy. Eight or ten men and I would brand and mark five hundred or more calves in one afternoon. I would invariably handle the branding irons myself, allowing one of the men to do the ear marking and keep tally. Occasionally if we found a bunch of cows and calves a long distance from one of the corrals, we would rope and brand the calves on the prairie.

In branding large herds of grown cattle we usually used the corrals and branding chutes when near. If not we would rope, throw and brand them on the prairie.

Our flesh brands and ear marks were as follows: Common herd, ⭕ on left hip and ⭕ on left loin. Ear mark ⧓ (crop off the right and slit in the left ear) and in addition to the above, for several years we used a horn brand. Our native herd was branded ⭕⭕ on left hip and ⭕ on left loin, with same ear mark as above. Our thoroughbred herd was tagged in left ear and numbered. We also branded about three thousand yearlings one year thus: ⟱ with the regular ear mark, i. e., crop off the right and slit in left ear. These we shipped to Mountain Home, Idaho.

A Branding Scene

The three classes of cattle were kept separate, the common herd, north of the North Platte River; the native herd of five hundred head or more, at Fox Creek; and the thoroughbreds at the Home Ranch. To relieve the congestion on our ranges we placed some out on shares with small stockmen, in Deuel, Keith, Grant, Cherry, Custer, and other counties, giving the parties one-half the increase, they to make good the original number except those that died from natural causes.

Of course, it was impossible for me to keep track of every detail. I was extremely fortunate in having good, trusty employees and I at all times appreciated them. I would always share their lot, the same bed, the same food and the same strenuous hard work, and I would never ask an employee to do something that I would not do myself. I held their respect and good will. I would say "come," not "go," especially if something difficult was to be accomplished.

In 1885 our company, known as John Bratt & Co., bought from the Union Pacific Railroad Company 123,673 acres of land, lying west of Birdwood Creek, east of White Tail Creek and north of the North Platte River, which we fenced, thus enclosing with the government sections nearly 250,000 acres, but we never built a stick of fence on government land.

This dispensed with expensive round-ups and gave us a better chance to provide feed for our stock in winter. The river bottoms were fenced off from the range and divided into many hay meadows, in which we put up thousands of tons of hay in shock at a cost of not to exceed fifty cents per ton. Fire guards around the hay bottoms and around the range were plowed and a wide strip burned out and every precaution was taken to protect the range from prairie fire. Still the fires would come dashing in on us from hunters or other careless people despite our precautions.

Even though beef went to a low price, we made some money. We paid our men good wages, gave them good food and cared the best we could for their moral and physical welfare. We kept them winter and summer, unlike some of our Western stock growers, who discharged the most of their men in the fall, thus doing more to make horse and cattle thieves out of them than anything they could do. The summer's wages of a cowboy would often be spent in a night. What was he to do through the winter? He had to live, and to live he was forced to steal.

I was a member of the Executive Committee of the Wyoming Stock Association for several years. Much thieving and rustling was going on. We were following some of these rustlers into Texas, and even into old Mexico, and I frankly told the members of this committee that they did everything they could, indirectly, to make horse and cattle thieves out of their employees. Some agreed with me, and later allowed many of these employees to remain at their ranches through the winter, boarding them without charge, while others paid their men half wages and boarded them for the little work they did around the ranches. Later, with improved breeds of cattle, ranch improvements, with a mild attempt at farming by irrigation, some of these cowboys, who at first insisted on doing all the farming on horseback, caught on to modern methods, and now do not look with contempt on the plow, disc, drill, mower and binder.

Times are changing, and the old cowman has changed also. Not so long ago, when wishing to retire at night, he would seek his roll of bedding, sometimes doubling up with another cowboy, untie or unbuckle his tarpaulin and spread out the bedding on some level place near camp, free from cactus and sagebrush. The tarpaulin was laid next to the ground and was about twice the length of his bed. The bed consisted of one or more pairs of blankets and sometimes a pillow. If not, he used his saddle, warsack or boots. The bed made, the other half of the "paulin" was pulled over the bed, making a shelter from the cold and rain, should any fall during the night; then he turned in, when the following verses would philosophically describe his feelings:

When the storm is blowing,
Do not curse your lot.
If it wasn't snowing,
Might be blazing hot.

When the sun is pelting,
Fire brand, don't scold;
If it wasn't melting,
Might be freezing cold.

Take life as you find it.
See, the rainbow's curled.
Trouble? Never mind it.
Good Lord runs the world.

THE COWBOY'S HYMN

Last night as I lay on the prairie
And gazed at the stars in the sky,
I wondered if ever a cowboy
Would ride to that sweet Bye and Bye.

The road that leads to that region
Is narrow and dim, so they say;
But the trail that leads down to perdition
Is staked and blazed all the way.

Some day there will be a great Round-up,
When cowboys, like mavericks, shall stand
To be cut out by those Heavenly riders,
Who are posted and know every brand.

I wonder if ever a cowboy
Was prepared for the great Judgment Day,
And could say to the boss of the riders,
"I am ready to be driven away!"

They say He will never forsake you;
That he notes every action and look.
So for safety you had better get branded
And have your name in His great tally book.

A CHRISTIAN COWBOY'S CREED

I am no profess'n' Christian of the sort the cities hold.
Haint been gathered with the chosen in the chosen's sacred fold.
An' I've never grown in spirit while a-thinkin' o' the way,
That the reckless unbelievers sin around me every day.
All the creed I try to practice is the ol' time Golden Rule.
Never hear no sacred music but the breezes fresh and cool;
An' the only church o' worship onto which my fancy clings
Is the outdoor church o' nature whar the Lord's a-runnin' things.

I can get more soothing comfort from the music o' the brooks
Than the preachers o' creation ever rassled out o' books;
An' the sighin' o' the breezes an' the singin' o' the birds
Brings a sort o' Christian feelin' you can never get from words.
There is sermons in the sunshine, there's discourses in the flowers.
There is heavenly baptism in the gentle springtime showers.
There is life an' inspiration in the brooks an' in the springs,
Out in nature's sanctuary whar the Lord's a-runnin' things.

While I'm ridin' on the night herd, every star that gleams above
Seems a sparkling' gem that's speaking o' the Master's kindly love.
An' the flashin' o' the lightnin' an' thunder's angry roar
Tells me o' the power majestic, o' the Being I adore.

When the storm in awful fury is a-bawlin' in its wrath,
Like as if it'd sweep the cattle jes' like feathers from its path,
I'm contented as the sage chicks underneath their mother's wings;
Out in nature's big cathedral whar the Lord's a-runnin' things.

When I hear the final summons, sent to tell me I mus' go
To the Round-up in the Heavens from the ranges here below,
Not a song nor not a sermon nor a ceremonious play
Do I want in the perceedin's, when my body's laid away.
I would rather far be buried on the ranges all alone,
With the spot whar I'm sleepin' never marked by board or stone;
So's when Gabriel sounds his trumpet I kin rise and spread my wings
From the grassy slopes of nature, whar the Lord's a-runnin' things.

JAMES BURTON ADAMS IN D. P.

Whole-souled, generous, big-hearted, fearless and ever-faithful cowboy! May your every wish be fulfilled, your ashes rest in peace and your soul dwell in happiness and peace forever with the faithful who have preceded and will follow you to that great and glorious Kingdom, when you will be forever safe in the Great Range Master's care.

CHAPTER XXVI

Our Cowboys—Characteristics—Adventures

L EW PARKER was a Texan, who rather than let go of the lariat, held on to an outlaw broncho until he pulled the thumb off his hand.

There was Will Rix (mentioned in a previous chapter) who rather than go a quarter of a mile out of his way around Point Lookout, took his same old trail, contrary to orders, and as a result was shot twice through the body by Indians lying in wait for him. Rix tore the handkerchief from around his neck and as soon as the Indians quit chasing him, plugged the bullet holes in his body with bits of his handkerchief to stop the bleeding. He had to be lifted off his horse on arrival at the Home Ranch. His clothes, saddle and horse were almost covered with blood from his wounds. He got well in about two months and later went to Salt Lake.

Little Jim, the Texas horse wrangler, rode a horse from Ogallala to our Home Ranch, a distance of sixty miles, in five hours, rode up to me and asked for a change of horses. I told him to go into the corral and help himself. He did, then went to the kitchen, grabbed some biscuits and meat and without any explanation, started south as fast as his horse could go. Half an hour later the sheriff of Keith County came rushing up on a horse covered with foam. The sheriff was in hot pursuit of Little Jim, who had shot and killed the foreman of Fant's herd because he had blacksnaked him. I learned later that the sheriff never caught him.

Nibsey Meiggs, the son of a rich South American contractor, was cast adrift by a proud stepfather. He was placed aboard a Peru naval vessel by his father. He had no taste for that kind of life, and one dark night, while the vessel was lying at anchor in San Francisco harbor, jumped overboard, swam ashore and worked his way to North Platte and finally to our Curtis Ranch, where I hired him. Nibsey was honest, truthful and afraid of nothing. He worked for us several years. In the winter of 1872, on the information of Spotted Tail and his band, he rode alone nearly two hundred fifty miles to the head waters of the Republican River and brought back sixty-six head of our stray cattle. On a dare he jumped upon the back of a wild six-year-old Texas steer that was being branded in the chute at the Home Ranch and rode the steer nearly two miles before he slid off. While corralling a bunch of beef cattle one night at the Burke Ranch, in chas-

Nibsey on a Wild Steer

ing one that broke away he fell, with his horse, into an old abandoned well. We had to dig them out, the well being about six feet wide and twelve to fifteen feet deep. The horse's neck was broken but Nibsey was unhurt. At Fox Creek Ranch he rode a horse so wild that we had to throw him to saddle him. With Nibsey in the saddle, the broncho dashed through the thick timber and brush, stripped himself of the saddle and landed Nibsey, head down, in a five-foot snowdrift at the head of a small pocket, where we found him with just his feet sticking out of the drift and very nearly gasping his last breath. This is the same Nibsey, who, while cooking for six of us when we were building the Curtis Ranch near Medicine Creek, made us a batter pudding and finding nothing to boil it in, tore the back out of old Gokey's dirty shirt and boiled the batter pudding in this.

"Billy—the Bear" got lost from a round-up in the Lake country near Spring Valley, southwest of Hyannis. We finally found him after three days' search. He had become temporarily insane and was on top of a hill pawing dirt and bellowing like a mad steer and came charging at us when we surrounded him. We had to rope and tie him down in the wagon until we got him to the ranch, where, after a month's nursing, he regained his senses.

This is the country where one cloudy morning on a round-up I turned loose sixty cowboys to work the country and drift the cattle to Three Mile lake. All the men got lost but George Bosler, Jerry Drummer, John Burke, Jr., and myself. We happened to have pocket compasses, otherwise we would have been lost also.

Another faithful cowman (a crack shot) whom we kept at the outside ranches on range lines, was John Hancock. One night while on a round-up he tried to sleep in the Burke Grove near Fort McPherson but could not do so on account of the numerous mosquitoes. He stood them off for a time by smoking but they became so persistent that they did not mind tobacco smoke, when John suddenly took off all his clothing, ran out into the open, commenced to beat his hands and arms and hollered for nearly half an hour: "Come at me now! Come at me now! Come and eat me up, you sons of guns!" They took him at his word and it was misery for Hancock to wear his clothing for some days afterwards.

He and that prince of cowboys, "Dick Bean," were great chums. When the Cheyenne Indians under chief Dull Knife came up from the Indian Territory through Kansas and Nebraska, Hancock was holding our west line on the North Platte River near White Tail Creek, and Dick was foreman at the "Keystone," the Ogallala cattle ranch about a couple of miles west of our ranch. Bean and Hancock saw the Indians coming across the river and kept under cover ahead of them until the Indians went into camp on the White Tail Creek, when they returned to the Keystone ranch and there learned that Major Thornburg and his command, in pursuit of Dull Knife's band, had just formed camp without lights on the south bank of the North Platte River. Hancock and Bean, although it was a rather dark night, went across the river and told Major Thornburg that they could take him to Dull Knife's camp in about one to two hours' ride. The Major declined the offer, saying that he was not going to tackle Dull Knife's band in an unknown country on a dark night like that. The Major waited with his command until daybreak and lost the opportunity of his life. He and his men rode hard on the trail of Dull Knife and his band for several days, only to capture now and then a played-out Indian pony or an old buck, squaw or papoose. They never overtook Dull Knife, who with Old Crow, Wild Hog and about sixty other warriors, was finally located near the sinks of Snake Creek by U. S. Cavalry under Captains Johnson and Thompson, aided by some twenty-two Sioux scouts under American Horse.

I may refer again to Dull Knife, whom I first met while our ox-train was about to cross a dry fork of the Cheyenne River in 1866 and again in 1872 between Medicine Creek and Platte River. The story of the capture and death of himself and brave band is one of the most pathetic in Indian history and sheds no glory on the humane side of our "Great Father's" management of the Cheyenne Indians under Dull Knife at Fort Robinson.

Pardon for digressing, there was Jim Noble, who, while herding our thoroughbred cattle near the Home Ranch, resented some imaginary wrong done him by a nearby homesteader, pulled his revolver and tried to shoot him but sent the ball through his pony's neck instead.

Jim's brother, "Faithful Zack," was foreman at our

Birdwood Ranch and Cowboys

Some of the "Circle" Cowboys in 1888

Trego   Rupp   Coker   Schick
Cowboys of the "Circle" Outfit

Home Ranch for several years. He was one of the best we ever had and did not believe in plowing corn on horseback. He and his good wife boarded the men, who could not say too many kind things about each of them.

Then we had good, honest Dick Davis and his amiable wife. When consulting him about the work at the ranch he would sometimes say, "I will talk it over with Ed," meaning Ed Gentry. Both heads were usually level. Dick later was appointed by me as Chief of Police of North Platte during my two terms as Mayor, and a more faithful, efficient officer never lived. He made it warm for the gamblers and law-breakers, ridding the city of both nearly at the cost of his life.

Here I am reminded of faithful Silas Sillasen and his brothers Jens and Andrew. The latter died at Birdwood ranch from drinking part of the contents of a bottle of carbolic acid which in the dark he mistook for a bottle of medicine. Everything was done to save his life by good Mrs. John Coker and others but without effect. He was given a cowboy funeral from the Lutheran Church in North Platte. His favorite cow pony, carrying his empty saddle, was led behind the hearse.

The cowboys tell a story about Silas's waking Tom Stowe to go on relief herd one night. Silas went quietly up to Tom's bed, which was in the open covered by the starry canopy, pulled the bed "paulin" back from over his head and shook him gently, saying, "Tom! Tom!! Your time has come." Tom jumped up, grabbed his gun and answered, "The h—l it has!"

I cannot conclude this chapter without referring to Jake Rupp, whom some of the cowboys persuaded to wash his head and face in coal oil to make his hair, whiskers and mustache grow. It did the opposite. Poor Jake, it is claimed, later became mentally incapacitated to look after his interests, worth several thousands of dollars, accumulated mostly while in our employ. Honest Nate Trego, another faithful employee, and others, are looking after Jake's affairs and no doubt doing what they deem best for him and his interests. Yet I think Jake is perfectly harmless and with a little kind supervision could be allowed to manage his own affairs. I saw the superintendent of the Sanitarium at College View, Nebraska, where Jake is being treated, and he assured me Jake was all right and could go home to his ranch. I shall try to see that his suggestions are carried out. The actions of some mercenary relatives have helped bring about his condition.

Another great cowboy character was Buck Taylor, who ate twenty-four biscuits at one meal and told the boys he would eat twenty-four more if they did not stop teasing him. He later became a prominent rough rider in Buffalo Bill's show.

Bill Jackson was a colored cook who came up with one of our herds from Texas. I had to sit up with him all night in order to prevail upon him to give us an early breakfast.

Al Raynor, another cook whom I scolded for being so slow in getting up, contended that he was quick at that. I told him I thought it took him nearly half an hour that morning to pull his boots on. This he denied by saying that he always slept with his boots on.

James Jasper, nicknamed "Arkansas," came up with another of our herds from Texas. He could not tell a copper cent from a five dollar gold piece or a one dollar bill from a twenty. When I paid him off, after buying his railroad ticket to San Antonio and giving him $5.00 for expense money, I gave him $428.00, balance due him, in one dollar bills, which I made him sew inside the lining of his coat and then safely put him on the train with a letter of introduction to the conductors of the railroads I routed him over.

John Miller was another cook. When I came in at the Birdwood Ranch unexpectedly one day, Miller was talking to himself, saying "Bald-headed and nearsighted! The last of a played-out race, and it shall stop right here." Then he went to Frontier County, married a widow and became the father of a large family.

Ed. Coates was another good fellow, who would either pour a cup of coal oil on the fire or drop in the stove a 44 metallic cartridge when he wanted a little more room around his cook stove.

Another cook, Jim Carson, became angry and snapped a six-shooter at me six times because I asked him to get up at ten o'clock one night to cook supper for a bunch of hungry cowboys who had ridden hard all day without anything to eat. He frankly told me that he would not get up and cook supper and I told him if he did not he must leave the ranch that night. He said he would do neither. Carson got up and dressed. I made out his account and gave him his check and told him he must leave. He pulled his revolver and snapped the six chambers at me. I have never been able to figure out why they did not go off. Jim's intentions were to kill me. He reached for a Winchester standing in a corner of the ranch house, but by this time I had my own revolver covering him. He tied up his blankets, slung them over his shoulder and I escorted him out of the ranch, across the slough bridge and bade him good night, to which he replied he would get even with me yet. The hungry cowboys got a good supper. They approved of what I had done, except that they thought I would have been justified in killing Carson.

I would be an ingrate did I not briefly describe some of the characteristics of several of our foremen and other faithful employees before closing this chapter. They show that, while cowboys in those days led a hard, rough life with only limited chances to better their moral and mental condition, yet there was always a high sense of honor among them, showing that there were many good hearts beating under those woolen shirts—hearts full of sympathy in case of injury or death. I saw a large group of cowboys weep when poor Tom Lonogan met his death on a round-up on Willow Creek bottom, in trying to stop a cow from going into another bunch. The horse and cow came together with such force that all went down. Tom's neck was broken.

Volney Frazier was the "Adonis and Apollo" of the cow camp. When I introduced him to his future wife, he wanted to know how soon I thought he could win her for his wife. It took nearly six months.

E. W. Murphy, who could do more work on less sleep and food than any man I ever knew, when asked to take a very nice girl for a horseback ride, hesitated and said he had no time to take girls out riding. But he took her and finally won her for a wife. They are the proud parents of a very nice, happy family. He hated profanity unless suitable to the occasion. He would not be imposed upon. Colburn, who shut up one of Mr. Murphy's cows, discovered this when he broke a fence rail across Colburn's back and turned the cow out of the corral.

William Burke, a six-foot, good-looking Missourian, when he heard that the city marshal of North Platte had mistreated one of the cowboys working under him, came down from the Birdwood ranch and broke a chair over the marshal's head. Burke had no bad habits and was always in for fair play.

Jim Reed was a good-natured fellow but John Challener would not allow him to lie down or sit on his bed. Why?

John Lockwood was always faithful and watched over our interests. Grandpa and Grandma Lockwood and daughters were good people whom it was a pleasure to meet and to know.

Robert McKnight at the Home Ranch would write on the barn and granary doors: "Mr. Bratt says, 'Be sure and close the granary door for if you don't the hogs will eat the corn.' 'Be sure and water the horses, if not they will get thirsty.' "

Donald McAndrew, or "Scotty," was a good, all-round foreman. He knew how to farm to get good results.

Hans Gertler, good old Hans! and Mrs. Gertler, were typical Germans. They kept the Home Ranch for several years and boarded the men who worked at the ranch. The employees thought Hans and his wife were just perfect. They liked to call her Minnie until she resented it by asking one of the men: "Whose Minnie am I? Yours or Hans's?" I remember roping a two-year-old steer in the corral one day. I caught him by the foot and "snubbed" him to the fence, requesting Hans to get me another rope. This he did and I commenced swinging the rope, at the same time walking up to the steer, who started for me, having slipped the rope off his foot. He came at me so swiftly that I had not time to get out of his way. I ducked. The steer went over me and struck poor Hans squarely in the stomach, knocking him to the ground. If the steer had not had flaring horns he would have killed Hans, whom I did not know was behind me. For a long time it was a debatable question in Hans's mind how I, in front of him, escaped, and he, behind, got hurt. Sam Van Doran, then a little boy, was with his father looking on through the fence and will vouch for this story.

Leonard Cornet, who had charge of our share cattle in several counties in the northwestern part of Nebraska, could be depended upon in every emergency, always honest, untiring and faithful. He was always ready at a moment's notice, and the night was never too dark, the journey too long, or the river too wide and deep. As manager of the Union Stock Yards here he is still found by his employers to be the same trustworthy man as in past years.

Joe Atkinson, droll, funny, old Joe! could change a discouraged camp of cowboys into one of laughter and good nature in an instant by his jokes and witticisms, always happy, good-natured and full of sunshine.

John Challener was a typical Englishman, who came to America to learn the cattle business. John was red-headed, wiry, full of grit and energy and a real good fellow, who prided himself in wearing a neat, well-fitting suit of corduroy

knee breeches, which some of the cowboys spoiled by dropping a lighted match in an almost empty nail keg upon which
John was sitting. It had two pounds of loose gunpowder
in it and John and the keg went up in the air. The former
was not presentable on the return trip. To try John's nerve
and swimming qualities, they had one of their number feign
sickness and hurried John across the North Platte River,
which was swimming over half way across, to Paxton for a
doctor. John came back with the doctor, who balked on crossing on his horse when he came to the river. He told John what

The Fate of the Knee Breeches

to do for the sick cowboy, who was better on John's return.
This is the same Challener, who, when a thieving band of
Sioux Indians took our horses from his camp at Bald Hill in
the Lake country, came out of the camp and, though alone,
and many miles from other ranches and men, commenced
shooting at the Indians. They came back to John's camp, bent
on killing him. John shut and barred the door of the ranch and
shot at them through the window. The Indians finally got
on top of the roof of the ranch and sent many bullets through
it, hoping to kill John, but they did not hurt him, although
several shots came very close to him. They took his four

head of horses. John was game. He sent several bullets after them as they rushed the horses up the valley towards the head of the Dismal. John finally went into the cattle business on the South Loup River. He later sold out and went back to England, where I hope he is prospering and happy.

Next we have Marion Feagin who was never known to tell an untruth, chew tobacco, or drink anything stronger than coffee or water (?). He married a nice Iowa girl and brought her to the Birdwood Ranch, which she kept for a long time. The first night at the ranch must have been strange to her. I happened to be there with some twenty cowboys to gather a bunch of cattle. Beds were spread all over the dining room floor. I noticed Mrs. Feagin locked the ranch door before retiring to her room, a very unusual thing to do at a ranch where cowboys are coming in at all hours of the night. I got up and unlocked the door to let a cowboy in, when Mrs. Feagin came out of her room and locked it again. I think about half a dozen more cowboys came in before daybreak. I know they kept her busy nearly all night locking and unlocking that door. Marion told her not to mind it. She told us the next morning that she had not been used to sleeping in her Iowa home with the doors unlocked. She soon got over that at the Birdwood Ranch. Later Feagin went with Isaac Dillon near the Powder River in Wyoming where he established a horse and cattle ranch. He died there some years ago, leaving his widow and two sons considerable property. "Good-bye, Marion. Your name will be in the right book on the final round-up, where you will meet many good souls like your own."

Then comes Ed. Richards, one of the best, all-round cowboys that ever sat a horse or roped a steer. He could sit the worst bucking horse, throw and tie the wildest steer or lick the biggest bully in camp. He would think it fun to ride twenty to thirty miles to take some nice girl to a dance, take her home just before breakfast after dancing all night and be ready for a hard day's ride that day. Ed. finally married a nice girl near Chadron Creek. He started a ranch and did well until the Great Herd Master called him.

Next comes trusty George Potter, who was never happy unless in the sight of "Old Baldy." He had charge of our herd of some six hundred males where we usually wintered them at what we called Mile camp some eight miles west of the head of the Dismal River. George could swear once in a while, shoot straight and speak his thoughts when necessary to big or little. I often used to visit George, making the drive of seventy-five miles from the Home Ranch to Mile camp alone in one day. Sometimes I would never meet a soul during the entire trip, going and coming. It gave me a chance to commune with nature. Sometimes I would meet or see at a distance a pack of wolves or hungry coyotes and many deer, elk and occasionally a buffalo. George later married a widow in the Lake country, who prevailed upon him to sell out a valuable homestead that I had persuaded him to take and prove up on. He moved to California, where he died some years ago.

Now a word as to Hank Chestnut, one of the best-hearted cowmen that ever lived and one of the kindest to his horses. He could go into a corral of bronchos and within an hour have the meanest one in the bunch eating out of his hand and following him around like a dog. He had just one failing that he tried to overcome but could not. I furnished him funds twice to take treatment. Under encouragement and fatherly advice he quit it for over one year. He married a good woman, who was wife and mother to him. He meant well and was loved by all who knew him, but his failing finally beat him at the game. I could write a chapter on good old Hank. I tried hard to make a man of him. I humored, petted, pleaded, coaxed and begged him to quit his drinking habit. He would promise. The spirit was willing but the flesh was weak. Poor Hank! I think a kind, just God, when the books are opened on the judgment day, will say to Hank

them come out of the channel, cross the island and watched them carefully as they went over the bank into the South Platte.

All were in the river when Kerr rode up. He and his outfit had seen from the hills the commotion we were making and he wanted to know what was the matter. I told him nothing except that some of the men present were trying to steal our cattle. Kerr yelled, "Show me one," and plunged into the river. I told him I thought the bunch was clean and to come out and follow me.

The three men who took the black steer had been doing their best to push him into the river, but the steer would not be pushed. On the contrary, he was now on the fight. We rode up to them and told them we had nothing to say to them, as they had done their duty for the men for whom they were working, but we would take the steer and we did.

The next morning I went to North Platte and was surprised to find Barton in our attorney's office. He had cooled down and we frankly talked matters over. The attorney told him I was right in demanding that the disputed cattle should be run through our chute.

Heretofore the words and deeds of this strong cattle company had always been taken for law. Might made right. Had I conceded one inch to these men our brand of cattle would have shown up prominently in their herds, and instead of being prima-facie evidence of ownership, would have been the opposite—a farce.

I had no further trouble with these gentlemen, who, from that time, respected our rights.

Brave and faithful John Jones did his duty. He helped me win this uneven battle for the right. Neither of our horses were worth a dollar after that day's work.

Kerr's outfit had again been absent several months, picking up and bringing back cattle, many of which were found south of the Republican River. I had received no word from them except through bands of Sioux Indians, who occasionally stopped at our Home Ranch on their way to the Rosebud and Pine Ridge Agencies from their buffalo hunts. I had become alarmed for the safety of our men and one Sunday I saddled up one of the best horses, buckled on my revolvers and bowie knife, and with my Winchester rifle and field glasses, I told Jones I was going to take a ride toward the Medicine Creek to see if I could see anything of Kerr's outfit.

I rode within a few miles of the breaks of the Medicine. I saw some coyotes and wolves and one lone animal standing on a side hill by itself. I could not make out with my field glasses whether it was a cow or a buffalo and concluded to ride closer. I found it to be a cow and in a little hollow below several wolves were devouring her calf. I left the poor mother, who seemed to appeal to me to save her offspring. I would like to have done so but knew it was useless to drive her away. She would come back if I did.

I rode up on a high hill and looked the country carefully over with my field glasses, when to my joy I saw a mounted party of about eight some two miles northeast of me. I decided it was part of Kerr's outfit and put my horse on a lope towards them and waved my hat at them. They had evidently seen me and were waiting for me to come to them. When not quite a mile from them I discovered they were Indians and not cowboys. This caused me to stop and take a quick survey of the surrounding country with a view to securing the best position I could in case of an attack. I knew it would not do to run away from them or show that I was afraid. They being between me and the Home Ranch, it would have been an easy matter to cut me off. I finally rode up to the top of the highest hill and waited for them to come to me. My horse acted foolishly as soon as he scented the Indians and would not stand as they tried to approach and shake hands. There were six bucks and two squaws. In the leader, who could talk a little "Pigeon English," I discovered my old friend, Dull Knife.

He told me he had just come up from his people in the

south and was going to visit Red Cloud, Spotted Tail and other Sioux with a view to gaining their friendship and permission to make his home with the Oglala Sioux. He said his people did not like it in the south, that quite a few had died and if they had to live there, all would die.

I brought them to the Home Ranch, where Jones and I gave them a good supper, fed their ponies and allowed the Indians to sleep on piles of hay that we brought in the ranch.

After breakfast the next morning I thought best to take Dull Knife and his party to Major Brown, then in command of the North Platte Garrison. That officer put them in the Guard House and virtually made them prisoners until he could get orders from the Department commander at Omaha. I told Major Brown that Dull Knife and his party were good Indians, going on a friendly visit to the Oglalas and I asked that they be given some rations and allowed to proceed on their journey, which was done after going through much red tape.

After being detained a week by Major Brown, they were escorted to the south bank of the North Platte River, where I bade old Dull Knife good-bye. He said that he remembered my giving him my dinner at the crossing of the Dry Fork of the Cheyenne River six years before when on our way to Fort Phil Kearny. He remembered all the incidents and told about one of our bullwhackers stealing a buckskin from one of his tribe. Poor old Dull Knife! He had a good heart and died a martyr to save his tribe from death and starvation. Read Edgar Beecher Bronson's story, "A Finish Fight for a Birthright," if you wish to have the facts.

CHAPTER XXVIII

*Hardships of the Cattle Business—The Disastrous Prairie Fire of
1874—"Buffalo White" Takes an Icewater Bath—Cattle
Companies Become Numerous—"Buck" Taylor's
Threat—How "Sleepy" Was Made an
Early Riser*

IN the fall of 1874, before we had gathered and shipped
our beef cattle, the worst prairie fire I ever saw swept
over our range and adjacent country from Plum Creek
on the east to Julesburg on the west and from the Republican
on the south to the Platte on the north. It was said that the
Indians set the fire to drive the buffaloes north of the Platte
River. I think it was the work of careless hunters—white men
hunting buffalo.

I was out with fifty men with camp outfit for over two
weeks, trying to stop it. None of us had our clothes off
during the entire time. We slept by spells. Sometimes the
men would drop down in their tracks and fall asleep before
they knew it. We fought the fire from the Medicine Creek
to Red Willow Creek and back to the Platte River. At one
time it looked as though we could save a big half of the range,
but changing winds and back fires springing up behind disappointed us. At night, with no wind, we could extinguish
many miles of it.

I killed two horses, cut their heads off, split them down
the back and with lariats attached to a hind and a front foot
of the carcass, two cowboys, one on either side, dragged them
over the line of fire, with ropes fastened to the horns of the
saddles. They could put out many miles of fire, when followed up by a couple of men with wet sacks to extinguish any
little fire that was missed.

This fire fighting at night in a broken, hilly country
like Well, Moran and Fox Creek cañons was rather dangerous
work. I remember a German and myself were busily putting

ranch. If the winter became severe, we would ride through the cattle, pick up any thin ones, then put the calves and other cattle picked up earlier into fresh hay pastures and turn the last gathered cattle into the hay pasture that the calves were taken out of. Toward spring we would rake several hay shocks into one, on which we would throw a little salt; then the cattle would eat all the hay so the hay meadows were kept clean all the time, much to the surprise of Mr. Carter (a native of New Hampshire) who argued that the hay bottoms would all be ruined on account of the butts of hay left on the meadows, but they were not. By this method our total losses would not average three per cent. We could, with free range at this time, raise a three-year-old steer for twelve dollars. Of course we had to contend with severe winter storms and sometimes blizzards and prairie fires.

I remember one blizzard that drifted sixteen hundred mixed cattle through several wire fences and over snow banks into the North Platte River. Four hundred head, mostly yearlings, being unable to climb the high river bank, drowned.

Again, although we would take every precaution to keep fire out of our range by plowing some two hundred fifty miles of fire guards of four to six furrows each, about two hundred feet apart, and burning off the grass between these fire guards, yet sometimes careless white men, trappers and hunters would allow fires to get away. Scarcely a night passed when the grass on the range was burning, whether at my home or at some of our ranches, that I did not get up once or twice during the night, if I did not sleep where I could look over the horizon fringing our ranges. If there was a light in the sky I could tell the locality of the fire, and many times I have started out in the middle of the night with a wagon-load of men, sacks, water barrels, plows and all the cowboys I could mount, putting the team on a lope to head off or put out some ditch fire.

Had we had the telephone over the ranges and connecting the ranches in those days, what a large amount of work and anxiety it would have saved us!

The foremen and men at every one of our ranches had positive orders to be always on the lookout for fires and, when discovered, to hasten to put them out.

In the big prairie fire that burned off our range in 1874, which started between Willow and Medicine creeks, and was driven by a high south wind, I happened to be at our Curtis Creek ranch when I saw the fire spring up. After telling one man what to do to save the ranches and our stock grazing in that section of country, I saddled up the best horse we had there and started for our Home Ranch, foolishly without matches. The fire jumped the Medicine Creek and crowded on the heels of my poor panting horse. Several times the fire came so close to me that the intense heat and great clouds of smoke almost enveloped me. Sometimes I wished that I had climbed a tree and turned my horse loose, but the thought of losing our Home Ranch gave me courage and impelled me to go on. I got to the ranch a few minutes ahead of the tongue of the fire and with the force of men we had at the ranch managed to save the buildings but lost some of our fences and corrals. I had scarcely broken a lope, except in going over deep holes and steep cañons, from the Medicine to the Platte via the head of Fox Creek and Moran Cañon.

To add to our troubles, the western cattlemen in eastern Wyoming and Colorado and western Nebraska, whose strong (principally steer) cattle had drifted on us in the winter storms, would usually insist on commencing the round-up shortly after the first of May, when our cattle, consisting of what would be called a "she herd," would be at their weakest. To prevent this imposition and damage to our cattle in that vicinity, mild remonstrance having failed, I swore out over sixty warrants, and had many of our own and neighboring cowboys working at adjoining ranches sworn in and deputized to serve the warrants under the direction of Sheriff Groner of Lincoln County. This action bluffed these representatives, with the result that the round-up was postponed twenty days. After this, we cattle owners at the east end had something to say as to what date the round-up should

The Fire Crowded on the Heels of My Horse

commence on the east end of the range country without
damage to our cattle.

It is said that Buck Taylor and another cowboy rode
up to a bunch of western representatives, all heavily armed,
riding near the head of the Dismal River, where the round-
up was scheduled to commence work, and asked them what
their business was. They replied that they had come to
attend the round-up and told what cattle companies they
represented. Buck told them in very plain language that
the first man that started to round up a "critter" would be
killed. The representatives rode away, whispering to themselves: "That's Bratt, that's Bratt." I did not know I had
such a reputation until I was asked by some of the cattle
owners who sent these representatives why I had threatened
to kill them if they started the round-up at that time. I told
these owners that I was a law-abiding citizen and was only
seeking to protect our interests and did not remember of
threatening to kill any one. Later they found out that Buck
Taylor and not I had told their men that.

During round-ups we had to cross the North and the
South Platte rivers occasionally, even when high, the few
bridges at this time being many miles apart. Desiring to
attend a round-up between the rivers at a point a few miles
east of Paxton station, we decided to cross the river, which
was very high, about one mile east of Cedar Creek, but owing
to the high, steep banks we could not get our horses into the
river. We, twelve cowboys and I, were about ready to give
up the idea of crossing at that particular point when I asked
the cowboys if they would follow me. They all answered
they would except one young man, who remarked that he
was ready and willing to follow but wanted some of us to
stay by him in event he went under, as he said: "I can't
swim." We told him we would see that he got through all
right. I slackened my latigo straps, rode back about one
hundred fifty yards from the bank and put my horse on a
fast run and before he knew it, we were both out of sight in
swimming water. The others followed as fast as they could

Leonard Cornet

"Buck" Taylor (Later a Rough Rider in
Buffalo Bill's Wild West Show)

come, even the young cowboy who said he could not swim. I had put two expert "water dogs" in charge of him and he came through without being washed out of the saddle and was proud of his achievement. A camera focused on us about the time we all struck the water would have made an interesting picture. We had to swim about half the width of the river, which at the point where we jumped the bank was nearly three-quarters of a mile wide.

We gathered a number of cattle and put them in a bunch that was going to be crossed at the mouth of Blue Creek. We

How Sleepy Was Made An Early Riser

recrossed the river west of Paxton. The tenderfoot covered himself with glory.

I here relate how we cured a cowboy who would not get up when called.

We were in camp on the West Birdwood Creek, near the big spring. All the men were up, had had breakfast and were ready for instructions for the day's work except one man, nicknamed "Sleepy." He had been called but did not get up. I called a couple of mounted cowboys and told them to quickly fasten the ends of their lariats, one to each corner of the opening of the "paulin," near the sleeper's head, and when fastened, proceed on a quick run, with the lariats around the horns of the saddles, down the steep bank of the creek, then slowly through the creek in order to give "Sleepy" the benefit of a good bath—the water in the West Birdwood Creek at this point was two to four feet deep—then pull him gently up the creek bank and leave him with his saddle horse. All of which was quickly carried out to the disgust of "Sleepy," who never had to be called twice to get up after this while working for the Circle outfit.

CHAPTER XXIX

Citizen Duties in Addition to the Cattle Business—Swim the River to Elect a Teacher—A Snake in a Tobacco Pocket—Two Hotheads—Ogallala in the Early Days—Honorable Cattlemen

DURING this strenuous time I was not unmindful of my obligations and duties as an American citizen. My friends insisted on putting my name on the Democratic ticket as a candidate for the legislature. I am afraid I made a poor candidate since I did not want the office, neither could I discharge its duties, if elected, without neglecting my own and those entrusted to me by others. I took no part in the canvass of the district, while my competitor went over every foot of it. I was pleased when the votes were counted showing my opponent a twenty-two majority.

I took interest in our schools and churches, contributing liberally towards their establishment and support. I was elected a member of the Board of Education of North Platte two terms, serving one term with Frank Reardon, James Belton, Morgan Davis, James Reynolds and Nels Nicholls. The question came up about hiring Miss Graves again as a teacher. Miss Graves afterwards became Mrs. Eells. Some members of the Board objected to her because she danced. To me this objection seemed narrow—very narrow. The vote stood three and three. Those who opposed waited until James Reynolds was in Texas and the writer one hundred twenty-five miles west on the North River round-up, when one day M. C. Keith sent me word that there was going to be a school-board meeting that night and if I wanted to save Miss Graves I must be present. I received the message at 8:00 A. M. The man bringing the word had ridden hard all night, changing horses at the Keystone Ranch. I picked the best horse in our bunch, turned the work over to our foreman and it was not long before I had left McCulligan's Butte, south of the North Platte River, behind me. I do not think I broke a lope for ten miles. The river was bank full, covered with froth and foam in the many swift, deep channels and much driftwood coming down. I rode down opposite the Seven Crook Ranch, but the boat was on the south side. I came on to the Keystone Ranch to meet with the same ill luck—the boat was on the south side, hence there was nothing to do but to take to the river. My good, faithful horse was about all in and no saddle horses in sight at the Keystone Ranch. I loosened my cinches and started across the water. It was deep in places on the north half of the river but became deeper as I neared the south bank. Old "Babe" went under twice; the current was too swift for him and threw him on his side and me out of the saddle for a moment. We both floated down some distance under the bank, finally to float in a sand draw, where I was not sorry to get on terra firma once more. I urged my horse forward all I dared. I was greatly pleased as I clipped off the last two miles on the down hill toward Ogallala to see a freight train standing on the track ready to pull out. I waved my hat to the engineer, who saw me coming. He guessed my purpose and after whistling and opening the throttle a little, started the train slowly. I rode along the side of it, jumped off my horse, turned him loose and swung on the side of a freight car. I called to a friend to take my horse to the livery barn, climbed upon the freight car and walked back to the caboose. I knew the conductor and explained to him my haste to reach North Platte and before we were six miles out of Ogallala I realized that the little, old freight train of nineteen cars, pulled by one of those little Giant engines of the 600 class, was in a mad race of about thirty miles an hour. Without waiting for anything to eat or a change of dry clothes, I rushed down to the board meeting, entering as they were having the roll called as to whether Miss Nellie Graves should be hired as a teacher. I voted yes. The tally stood two and two—a tie—with two members absent. They had expected one of these to be present but he failed to show up. They did not look for me. I dropped in like à clap of thunder from a clear sky. The friends of Miss Graves called a mass meeting, at which, while no ink wells or law books were thrown at each other as happened sometimes, some very plain language was expressed. Good Alex Stewart was chairman of the meeting, which ended by the passage of a resolution instructing the school board to engage Miss Graves as teacher for the ensuing year, and that dancing was no detriment to her as a teacher. This settled, I took the first train for Ogallala and leading "Babe," crossed the river in a boat, at the Seven Crook Ranch, where a few miles above I met the round-up boys returning with our stray cattle.

Colonel E. D. Webster, former editor of the Omaha Republican and during the Civil War private secretary to William H. Seward, accompanied us on one of these round-ups in the interest of himself and Mrs. Randall, who jointly owned the "H" brand.

The different outfits were camped along the North Platte River, opposite the mouth of Lost Creek, now better known as Oshkosh.

We were holding about six thousand head of range cattle that had been gathered that afternoon out of the Blue Creek country, besides many bunches belonging to different owners east and west of the Bosler Brothers' range. Thomas Lawrence, who was in charge of the Bosler Brothers' outfit, was in charge of the round-up work and had arranged for night herders for the six thousand head bunch that had not been worked, by calling on the different outfits for their quota of men to hold this large bunch, consisting principally of large steers. This, with their own outfits, put nearly every man in the saddle that night.

About midnight a terrible thunderstorm sprang up, followed by a heavy rain that fell for several hours, coming down for a time in sheets and swept by a heavy wind. The sky became so dark that we could scarcely see our hands if held up before us.

The result was a big mix-up. I, like many other owners, was out with our men all night. By hard, constant riding, we held our bunch but could not prevent several hundred other cattle from drifting in on us. The lower bottom where our camp was, was covered with storm water to a depth of one to two feet. Daybreak found us all—every camp—very much demoralized. The water was a foot deep or more in our camp.

Colonel Webster came into our camp. He was all in and resembled a drowned mouse. He threw himself down on a pile of sacked corn that we had in the tent and fell asleep. The Colonel had a great dislike for snakes. Tom Ritchie had killed a big rattlesnake at the foothills and put it in the pocket of his slicker. Noticing the Colonel sleeping, he slipped the rattler into his tobacco pocket. In a few minutes a cowboy entered the tent and inquired if any one had any tobacco. Some one said the Colonel had, when the inquirer went up to him, awoke him and asked if he had any tobacco. The Colonel growled at being disturbed and began feeling in his pockets, finally putting his hand on the snake. He jerked it out of his pocket, gave a high leap, nearly breaking his head on the ridge-pole of the tent, his face changing from red to purple, then to white, as he leaped off the corn sacks into nearly a foot of fast running storm water, swearing a blue streak that he would whip the man (calling out a very ugly name) who had put that snake into his tobacco pocket. Ritchie was bent on licking the Colonel on account of the name he had called him but we managed to keep the two apart.

Much bad feeling existed between the Ritchie Brothers and Webster & Randall on account of crowding of ranges, and the snake episode was the real cause of an open rupture between the two men. I never saw the Colonel smoke or chew any more tobacco on that round-up.

This reminds me of a similar rupture between W. C. Irvin, one of the foreman of the Bosler Brothers Cattle Co., who claimed the range from some miles east of Blue Creek to west of Brown's Creek, up to Dennis Sheedy's range.

The Boyd Brothers had come in just east of Blue Creek with several thousand cattle, expecting to claim the Blue Creek country as a range. The Bosler Brothers, who had a ranch at the mouth and west side of Blue Creek, strenuously objected to the Boyd Brothers' action and quarrels were constant between Sam Boyd, who had charge of the Boyd Brothers' cattle, and the Bosler Brothers and their foremen, W. C. Irvin and Tom Lawrence.

In riding up Lost Creek valley on one round-up with Sam Boyd and W. C. Irvin, both fighters and hotheads, I dismounted three times in riding one mile to prevent the two men from eating each other up alive. Each continued to hand back to the other all sorts of accusations, when both men would dismount with a challenge to whip the other. I would get between them and order both to get into their saddles and quit such boys' play. Both had grit enough to fight a buzz saw.

In these days Ogallala was a wide-awake, wild, and sometimes wicked town. For many years it was the distributing point of the Texas cattle, but later owners began to bring up their own herds to sell to the Northern cattle growers. I have many times seen as many as fifty thousand cattle ranging, being held in different herds along the bottom and foothills on the south side of the South Platte River, strung along from ten to fifteen miles east, west and south of Ogallala. Ogallala had its numerous saloons, dance houses and gambling dens, all running in full blast both night and day. The town marshal was a brave fellow, but there were times when he went to cover, being unable to control the bad ones, not a few of whom had to be killed.

I remember one night, while sitting talking in an upstairs room at the Leach House, northeast of the depot, with one of the Bosler Brothers, Wm. Paxton, Judge Faut, Uncle Billy Stevens, Colonel Mayberry and one of the Sheidley

Brothers, that about fifteen shots were fired through the window of our room which faced the street. Our little hand lamp, lighted and standing on a wash stand, was shot to pieces, as was nearly every pane in the window. I do not see how we all escaped being wounded or killed or why the hotel did not burn down, but none of us got a scratch. It is unnecessary to say that there was quick dodging and scrambling to get out of that room. We learned later that the cowboys got into a fight in Tucker's saloon and after breaking every mirror, bottle and glass in the saloon, came out on the street,

A Crack Shot

and the light in our window being the only glim in sight, the boys made up their minds that it must go out, and it did.

I have seen cowboys ride into this saloon and jump their horses on to the pool and billiard tables, and some crack shot would shoot the glass out of a man's hand while it was up to his mouth. Another would see how much he could shoot off a cigar in a man's mouth without grazing his nose with the bullet. The village authorities tried to maintain order but were often powerless.

Louis Auftengarten kept the principal outfitting store and

and I started to Emil Ericksson's. Mr. Ericksson was justice of the peace and lived about three miles east of the Fort.

After Kirby took the oath of office, we started back to the Fort. Kirby was a heavy man, unaccustomed to the saddle, and the little ride to Judge Ericksson's had cooled his enthusiasm. He wanted to know why we could not delay the trip until morning. I told him we had only until six o'clock the next night to organize the county and had fifty miles to go to get to the county seat and in case of accident we might not make it and could not afford to take the chances. Finally he promised to go if we took two canteens of liquor along, to which I agreed.

We started up Cottonwood Cañon about 1:30 in the morning on two nervy, but not sharp-shod, horses. I was careful to give Kirby the gentler horse, which, before we had gone two miles up the cañon, lost his feet and went down with Kirby on an icy stretch of the road. Kirby was angry and refused to remount until coaxed with two large drinks out of the canteen, when he changed and took my horse, believing him to be the better. The fact was that I had had hard work to keep my horse on his feet. It was Kirby's way to ride with a slack rein and holding to the horn of the saddle.

After going less than a mile his horse went down but he kept his seat in the saddle by "choking" the saddle horn. He did much swearing and declared he would go no farther. I again made the appeal that all the would-be county officials would be waiting for us and would not forgive us if we neglected to perform this duty. After more canteen, we started again, he allowing me to lead his horse until we got out of Cottonwood Cañon and up on Rattlesnake Ridge (the narrow divide between the two cañons leading to Fox Creek), when he insisted upon possession of one of the canteens. I gave him the one with the lesser contents. He also insisted on guiding his own horse, which I reluctantly allowed.

We had gone about three miles down the six-mile ridge, which was bare of snow, when we met a small herd of buffalo.

Kirby's horse took fright and started to shy and run. I started my horse on a fast lope and caught it by the bridle rein as it was madly dashing towards the precipice of a cañon pocket, where both Kirby and horse would have been killed had the horse not been stopped. Kirby had let go of the bridle rein and was holding to the horn of the saddle. He was too much in his "cups" to realize his danger. However, he consented to allow me to continue leading his horse, minus the canteen, which he had dropped in his efforts to hold to the saddle horn.

We finally arrived at Fox Creek ranch between five and six o'clock in the morning, where the cook and cowboys, who were to accompany us to Stockville (Hank Clifford's tepee), had a good breakfast of buffalo meat, biscuits and coffee awaiting us. Breakfast over, I left Kirby dozing in the ranch.

One horse of the team sent out with the books, commission blanks, etc., the day before, had become lame and we were compelled to put in his place a wild Texas horse that had never been harnessed before. We had to throw him to harness him.

We loaded into the spring wagon the two boxes of books and other materials, awoke Kirby out of his sound sleep and got him aboard and settled in the seat beside me, when shortly before sunrise I gave orders to the man at the horses' heads to turn them loose. The Texas broncho became quite active in standing on his hind feet and lunging forward, apparently trying to get out of his collar. The new road cut through the heavy brush and timber, leading from the ranch to the main road around the head of Fox Creek, was not any too wide but it assisted materially in keeping "Texas" in the trail. The team kept up their lope down the creek and up the pocket north of where the Fred Schick ranch was later built. We had hard work to keep our seats in going up this pocket on account of washouts and buffalo trails. Kirby was jolted around considerably and finally grabbed the back of the seat to prevent his falling out of the spring wagon. We finally reached the head of the pocket and the little neck

We reached the forks of the Birdwood, the Hinman ranch, about daylight. Here we ate a little lunch and held our horses by the lariat, allowing them to eat the long, straggling grass that projected above the snow.

We had been here about an hour when Lieutenant Wheeler's company joined us. It was arranged that we should proceed up to the east fork of the Birdwood, locate the Indians and make the attack together, the Lieutenant remarking that he had positive orders not to fire on the Indians, but he said: "If you commence it and it is necessary, I may have to take a hand in it to defend ourselves." He said that after resting his horses a couple of hours he and his company would follow our trail. Judging from the reports received from our range riders, he concluded we would find the Indians near the mouth of Squaw Creek.

We held a short council of war and it was arranged that three men, familiar with the country, should be started up on the east side of the creek and seven others, also familiar with the country, should be put out as scouts on the west side. The bottom of the creek was narrow, very soft in places and difficult to cross. Neither of the three parties was to fire a shot, and in case either party located the Indians, such party would be expected to send a man back to notify me and I would do my best to get in touch with Wheeler and his company. If the Indians were located, we expected to make the attack together. I did not want to have it said that this was a cattlemen's or cowboys' Indian fight. Possibly many of these Indians were my friends and I did not want to take any advantage of them until I knew for a fact that they were stealing our or neighbors' stock.

With this understanding the seven guards in charge of Volney Frazier, our Home Ranch foreman, left us with the further understanding that in case of an attack, they would be expected to drive the Indians from under cover of the creek bank so we could get at them. The first shot fired by us or the Indians was to be the signal to close in, capture all the Indians' horses and take the Indians prisoners, either dead or alive, provided they had stolen stock in their possession. We did our best to keep in sight of our scouts, at the same time keeping one man well in the rear to signal Wheeler as to our course up the creek.

We had followed many Indian tracks leading from the creek into the bluffs on the east side, but finally quit this since they would invariably return to the creek by a different pocket.

The snow lay on the ground two to ten inches deep but drifted. The sun was out bright but the weather was freezing cold. It was getting past four o'clock. The sun was sinking fast under a cloud, yet no Indians and no Wheeler. We came within a mile and a half of the mouth of Squaw Creek, when, on going to the top of a small hill, we found our three scouts on the east side of the creek in a small side pocket, awaiting us. They had located the Indians, their horses and camp, about a quarter of a mile ahead of us.

We dismounted and several of us crawled as close as we could to the Indian camp. There, grazing on a flat just above the bed of the creek, were about forty head of horses, most of them loose but guarded by a mounted Indian, who was riding around the bunch. We could not locate our seven men on the west side of the creek. This left us eleven men, counting myself.

After locating the Indians and their camp by the little curl of smoke coming out of the creek bottom, which was down between the hills and could not be seen from our position, we retraced our steps to where we had left the horses in charge of the other guards. Then we all mounted and rode back from the creek under cover of the bluffs, with the object of finding a position for attack. We found just what we wanted—a great sand blow-out, in which we could hide our horses. We quickly turned them over to five of the guards while we other six, with our long Springfield rifles and a brace of revolvers each, climbed to the top of the sand hole, where we made a footing; and six guns were soon pointing at the Indians' horses, with a good marksman stooping over each and looking carefully down through the sight at the end of the barrel. The eleven of us were within a quarter of a mile of the Indians' horses and, by the aid of our field glasses, had no trouble in locating certain horses in the bunch that had been stolen from Mrs. Randall, our neighbors and us. The mounted Indian, suspicious that all was not right, had disappeared under the creek bank, probably to give the alarm to the Indians in camp. A few moments later a big portly Indian, wearing a red blanket, came strutting in front of the Indian ponies, carrying a Winchester rifle. He had caught sight of some of our heads peeping above the rim of the sand hole, since he shouted to us in tolerably plain English: "Hunter wa sichee," meaning "Go away, cattlemen." Without orders Bill Thompson sent a shot at the Indian. The ball went between his legs, causing him to jump several feet into the air and run down back of the horses under the creek bank. This was the critical moment when the seven guards west of the creek could have done good work by driving the Indians from under the bank, thus enabling us to get a fair show at them, but they failed to show up. They later stated that they had to make a large circle around the head of a cañon in order to get within range of the Indians.

Several shots were fired by our party at what were thought to be Indian heads peeping above the creek banks. The scattering bunch of Indian ponies handicapped us by obstructing the view of the creek bank, and Major Walker courageously offered to go and surround the ponies, which had scented our horses and had come closer. I objected to the Major's proposition. It was a brave one, but the Major would have been killed the moment he got on the other side of the ponies. Nothing could have saved him, as it was proven later that there were twenty-two Indians, each having a repeating Winchester rifle with magazines full. It would have been the same if the Indians had attempted to take the ponies. We could have killed a part of them. The Indians saw this and that our position covered them as they continued to come closer of their own accord.

It was getting dark. None of the seven guards on the west side of the creek had indicated their location, neither had Lieutenant Wheeler and his company, for whose safety I was becoming alarmed. The Indians might at that moment, in event they had seen his command, be leading them into a trap. None of us had any idea how many bands of Indians there were on East Birdwood Creek. The tracks we had seen indicated more than we had already discovered on the creek. We had our hands full watching the surrounded Indian ponies and guarding against any flank movement that might be attempted by the Indians. Notwithstanding these odds against us, I determined to send one of our guards as soon as I could to head off Lieutenant Wheeler and his company.

At this moment a bunch of cattle came running out of the head of a cañon that led from the creek bottom where the Indians were camped, indicating that the Indians were following them up. Here one of our guards, Frank True, without warning, started his horse on a fast run toward the head of this cañon, where for his protection, I thought best to follow him. Catching up with True I remonstrated with him for taking such desperate chances—that he was liable to get killed. He said he did not care. He was going to kill an Indian anyway.

We had reached the edge of the cañon, the banks of which were somewhat steep. In the bottom of the cañon I saw several Indians coming on a run, each carrying a Winchester in hand. True, on seeing them, jumped off his horse, turned him loose, threw his Springfield rifle to his shoulder and fired at the approaching Indians. I also sent the ball in my gun among the group of Indians. These two shots checked their advance and caused them to stop and surround one Indian, who, I am satisfied, had been wounded. As quickly as I could I grabbed the reins of True's horse, urging him to mount quickly, which he did, when both of us started across the little, flat valley as fast as our horses could carry us. Bullets dropped around us thick and fast and one struck True's horse in the left cushion, knocking him off his feet, at which the Indians gave a wild yell, thinking they had killed both horse and rider. Another ball struck the brim of my hat.

At this time the guards, left with the Indian horses, commenced to fire at the Indians, causing them to dodge and keep hidden under edge of the cañon. This timely action perhaps saved both of us from certain death. I think it taught True a good lesson. A braver boy did not live, but he lacked judgment, and the first principle of a good soldier or guard is to obey orders. I had cautioned our guards many times not to take any chances and for all to adopt the Indian method of fighting under cover.

We soon joined our rescuers. They had surrounded the Indian horses and were closely herding them, expecting the Indians to make a dash on them every moment and try to stampede them.

As soon as I joined the guards I sent a good man to head off Lieutenant Wheeler and his company. The Indians were completely routed and lost everything they had except the blankets they wore over their shoulders or around their bodies. While part of the guards held the horses, others went by the Indian camp with a few pack horses, on which we loaded everything of value at the camp—blankets, tepees, buffalo robes, buckskins, wolf, coyote, beaver and skunk pelts, paints and extra moccasins, and just as it was getting dark we started our prizes for the Hinman ranch at the forks of the Birdwood creeks.

We arrived at the Hinman ranch at nearly midnight, about which time, we later learned, the Indians passed the Cody and North ranches at the head of the South Dismal on a brisk walk. Between that point and the North Dismal the wounded Indian gave out, dying some time during the night. His body was discovered several days later and buried.

The next morning twenty-one Indians were seen passing near Rankin's ranch on the North Loup—all more or less frozen. They arrived several days later at Rosebud Agency, frozen, hungry and the most dejected looking Indians that were ever seen.

That night we hobbled many of the horses, and divided our force of guards, including the seven that had come in from the west of the creek, into three reliefs. Those not on herd kept their saddled horses on a stake rope ready for emergency. The guards off duty curled themselves up like kittens anywhere on the dirt floor of the Hinman ranch and dropped asleep. There was but little chance to sleep. Lieutenant Wheeler and command fared as well as we did, since they had tents, hot coffee and hard tack, while we had frozen biscuits and Birdwood water.

Lieutenant Wheeler seemed sorry that he was not able to catch up with us. He claimed to have gotten lost while following Indian trails in the hills east of the Birdwood Creek. We will be charitable and give him the benefit of the doubt. I know one thing—had he joined us about the time we had the Indians in that cañon and had helped us just a little, not many Indians would have arrived at the Rosebud Agency. He took up the Indian trail the next morning. Perhaps he wanted to show his willingness to accomplish something personally. I thought it a useless trip and hard on both men and horses. Much snow was on the ground and the thermometer ten to fifteen degrees below zero. I believe the seven guards did their best to reach us.

At peep of day we packed our captured articles on the backs of several Indian ponies, took the hobbles off our horses and started for North Platte, sending some of our men by way of the Birdwood Ranch with the stolen horses which we had recaptured. Others went with the pack horses and some by way of Mrs. Randall's and Major Walker's ranches in order to leave the stolen horses belonging to them.

When turning Mrs. Randall's horses over to her man at the ranch he became rather cross because we had not brought the halters along. I think the Indians had cut these up for belts.

On the way to North Platte it was suggested that we paint our faces Indian fashion with the paints found in the Indians' camp. We arrived at North Platte between three and four o'clock that afternoon and assembled in the Court House yard, where the local photographer insisted on taking our pictures.

It was a hard trip on the guards and their horses. We had been gone two nights and two days. We had been thirty-three hours in the saddle, had ridden over one hundred fifty miles and had each averaged about three hours' sleep. Our fare had been scanty—frozen biscuits and ice water. Our horses had been without a feed of grain. Many of the guards had frozen their hands, ears, noses and feet, the first night riding thirty miles facing a furious snowstorm, rushed by a strong, bitter cold, northwest wind. This was all the glory the North Platte Guards got out of this trip, and we were thankful that we were not sent to the Happy Hunting Ground by this bunch of thieving Indians, all armed with modern guns against our old, Long Tom Springfield rifles graciously loaned to us by our state authorities.

Such is the true story of the last Sioux Indian raid on the ranchmen and settlers of the Platte Valley west of North Platte and in the neighborhood of the Birdwood Creek. Our guards may have lacked discipline, for they had no time to drill. They were nearly all cowboys and ranchmen. What they lacked in dress parade tactics they made up in courage and in deeds. This is not a reflection on that good army officer, Major Walker, who accompanied us and shared our hardships. He was always ready to do and dare. "All honor to you, Major!" and to all the guards who stayed with us and helped to make it one of the most successful, though nearly bloodless, victories ever won by a few whites against a bunch of thieving Sioux Indians.

CHAPTER XXXII

Interesting Developments—A Trip to Pine Ridge and Rosebud Agencies—Spotted Tail—A True Friend—The Town of Whitman—A Prayer Meeting in a Dance Hall

THE following spring I determined to go and see the Indian agents at Pine Ridge and Rosebud, also to have a talk with Red Cloud, Spotted Tail and other prominent chiefs of the Sioux nation at those agencies. Accordingly I left Sidney in the early part of April, 1879, traveling by stage coach, which was loaded with passengers—men and women—en route to the Black Hills mining camps. I was glad to leave the coach at Fort Robinson, from which point I traveled by buckboard to Pine Ridge, better known in these days as Red Cloud Agency.

These famous Pine Ridge hills extend for fifty miles through Sioux and Dawes counties and all who have viewed this region consider it one of the most picturesque places in Nebraska.

At Pine Ridge I met the agent, also Red Cloud and other prominent chiefs, and my young friend, Billy Garner, who was interpreter. He was the same Billy Garner, stepson of John Hunter, to whom I loaned a couple of revolvers and boxes of cartridges in 1867 at Fort Mitchell. I also met my old friend, Leon Palladay. Both assisted me greatly in explaining my mission to the agent, Red Cloud and the other chiefs. I gave them a list of the horse and cattle brands owned by the cattlemen in the Platte Valley and in return I received a list of their brands. I also told them of the Big Turkey raid, what we did to them, and referred them to the letters I had written. All of this met their hearty approval. My visit created a good feeling between the Pine Ridge or Red Cloud agency Indians and the stockmen of the "Shallow Water," the Platte Valley.

My friend Palladay loaned me a horse and saddle to take me to the Rosebud Agency, one hundred twenty-five miles distant. The second night my horse played out while going down the White River bottom. I tied him to a tree and laid down on my saddle blanket, using my saddle for a pillow. The next morning I was awakened early by some peculiar sensation. I found my horse jerking on his rope and on opening my eyes, discovered I was surrounded by eight Indians. They asked me many questions in Sioux: Who I was? What I was doing there? Where I was from? Where I was going? I told them I was "Yellow Hair," a "tagaliska wasichi" (a cattleman) from the Shallow Water valley (the Platte), and that I was on my way to see Spotted Tail and the "Great Father's" man, their agent at Rosebud, but my horse played out where they found me sleeping; that the horse had been loaned to me by my friend Palladay, the interpreter at Pine Ridge Agency, and that as soon as my horse had rested I was going on to Spotted Tail's camp.

One of the Indians could speak a little English. He told me they were Indian police and were going to Rosebud Agency, which they said was about twelve miles distant and I could accompany them.

I had eaten the small sack of "pappa," consisting of wild meat and berries, given me by Palladay for lunch the day before, and gladly accepted a small chunk of dried antelope from one of the Indians, cutting it into thin slices and eating it as we rode along.

By degrees I learned that these Indians were out looking for horse thieves and am satisfied they took me for one when they first saw me. The Indian who spoke a little English told me a great deal about the white man who had the gold tooth. This was the gentleman for whose capture $1300.00 had been paid. They claimed that many of their horses had been stolen. When I showed them a list of their brands and told them what we had done, they treated me more kindly. I told them what we had done to Big Turkey the previous fall on the Birdwood. They knew about this, also that one Indian was killed and the others sent back without any clothes on and that later we had sent their captured horses back to Rosebud Agency. They also knew that my trip to their agency was to have a talk with Spotted Tail and other chiefs, and the agent at Rosebud, the same as I had just had with Red Cloud, his chiefs and agent, who approved of what we were doing and promised to coöperate with us—the stockmen of the Shallow Water valley—to break up these gangs of horse thieves.

Before starting they had relieved me of my gun, revolvers and knife, also of my field glasses, so I felt that I was not only their captive but at their mercy, until I had thoroughly explained my mission when they regarded me as a friend and treated me as such, but took special care of me until they turned me over to the Indian agent with all my belongings.

The agent treated me very considerately and sent for Spotted Tail and other chiefs, many of whom had visited our Home Ranch, where I had many times fed them and their ponies.

After shaking hands with the Indians, who appeared glad to see me, at the suggestion of the Indian agent we went to the Council Chamber where, by the aid of the interpreter, Tod Randall, I explained why I had come to talk with them. The agent had my letters to him and Spotted Tail read these and they were explained to the Indians by Spotted Tail and the interpreter. All approved of what we had done and were doing to break up the stealing of live stock and all agreed to help me and the stockmen of the Platte Valley to put an end to it. I told them what we had done with Big Turkey and his band who came down to steal our horses and I asked that the Indians do the same with all white men who came to steal their horses.

The meeting proved a very satisfactory one. I had printed lists of all known horse and cattle brands in Nebraska from Plum Creek west to the Wyoming and Colorado

Miss Elizabeth Burke

Spotted Tail

lines. In return I received from the agents at Pine Ridge and Rosebud a list of horse and cattle brands claimed by the Sioux Indians. Before adjourning the council the pipe of peace was lighted, smoked and passed around from one to the other. The best of feeling was manifested by all.

I was invited by the agent to dine with him, but I did not like to turn down Spotted Tail's invitation, which was also extended to Tod Randall, the interpreter; hence both of us accompanied Spotted Tail to his lodge. Here I met several other sub-chiefs, No Flesh, Big Crow and some whose names I cannot recall. A big feast was prepared for us, consisting of a large, fat dog, fried venison, coffee and biscuits. I took the venison, coffee and biscuits.

I was asked to tell the particulars of Big Turkey's raid, which I did, and all present said we had done right in treating Big Turkey and his followers the way we had, and it would have served them right had we retained their horses instead of returning them and some others that were said to have been run off by "Gold Tooth" and his rustlers.

That night I slept with Randall in Spotted Tail's tepee and before retiring Spotted Tail called us both aside and cautioned me to be on the lookout for Big Turkey and the relatives of the Indian who died from the effects of the wound received that night on the Birdwood. Spotted Tail put a guard around the tepee. Nothing disturbed us except the barking of many dogs.

After breakfast the next morning Spotted Tail, Randall and I went to the agency and visited the store, the agent's office and other buildings.

I had closed up my business matters with the agent and was returning to Spotted Tail's tepee when we were met by several squaws, young bucks and papooses, who were crying without shedding a tear. I had heard this cry before at other places and knew what it meant. Big Turkey and other warriors joined them before we reached the lodge. Spotted Tail told Big Turkey and those who were in that Birdwood raid that I was one of the cattlemen who sent them back without their horses and without any clothes on. He told this little band of Indians to stop their noise and return to their lodges. Some obeyed, others did not but went on a distant hill and cried louder than before until Spotted Tail sent some of the Indian police to warn them, when they ceased and disappeared. I presume they returned to their lodges.

I had arranged to return on horseback by way of Valentine and across country by Whitman to the Birdwood ranch. I borrowed a good horse from Randall and sent the Palladay horse back to Pine Ridge by the mail carrier. I left Rosebud about midnight with an escort of six agency police, who accompanied me several miles on the road, when they returned and I proceeded on to Valentine, where I arrived shortly before noon. Five days later I arrived at our ranch at the mouth of the Birdwood, feeling that although the trip was a hard one it had not been made without some good results to both the Indians and the cattlemen.

I cannot mention the town of Whitman, a station on the B. & M. Railroad, east of Hyannis, without referring to an experience I had there shortly after it was located.

We were on a spring round-up, ready to commence work on the Dismal rivers. We had several representatives of Western cattle owners who had come to gather the brands of cattle in which they were interested and some of these had ridden over to Whitman to participate in the opening of a dance house. I sent a trusty man over to tell these men that we were ready to commence work and could not wait for them much longer. They sent word back that they would return in a day or two. I hated to commence the round-up without them and thought best to ride over to Whitman myself on Friday night. I arrived there late, staked my horse near the station and there being no spare beds, I slept in the station that night, not caring to mix with the cowboys, graders, and others in the dance house, which was going full blast. The next morning I rounded up all the cowboys. Some, I regret to say, were nearer drunk than sober. They asked me to remain until that night when the expected dance was to come off. I reluctantly consented. There were some forty or fifty men and probably twenty women. These women at one time had been good girls, but now, God pity them!

I took a look into the dance hall, which was dimly lighted with several coal-oil lamps standing on brackets fastened to the sides of the hall. A screeching violin was furnishing the music and a half-drunken gambler was calling off the dances, which lasted on an average of five to ten minutes, when the dancers were expected to go up to the bar and drink. The smell of liquor and tobacco smoke, the yelling and cursing, the obscenity of language and manner of both men and women were sickening and disgusting, and I was sorry I had consented to remain.

The dancers had forced a good old preacher on the floor and were making him dance with a lewd, drunken woman. Some of the men occasionally took a shot at his feet, bidding him to step high. Another knocked the crown of his plug hat in and down over his ears. The old man had come up to this terminal of the B. & M. Railroad to do missionary work among the graders and floating scum of humanity that usually follow in the wake of a frontier town. All seemed to be bent on giving the good old man the time of his life. He stood it all good-naturedly until completely exhausted. He got into one corner of the hall and sat down on the floor. After resting a while and during a lull in the dancing, the old man got upon a gambling table and commenced to talk to the crowd. He said he had attended their dances every night and done everything they wanted him to do, including many things that were not right. "Now," he said, "with your permission and God's help, I will hold service in this hall to-morrow, Sunday night," and asked them all to come. They told him they would be present. I could not help but admire the old man and told him I would remain with the cowboys from our round-up camp and would personally help him all I could.

The next morning I skirmished around and found that the station agent had an organ and his good wife consented to play for the service. We carried the organ over to the dance hall, swept out the hall and secured a promise from the proprietor of the hall not to sell any liquor during the service. The old missionary made out a program for the service and that afternoon, with the help of a few good people, we practiced the singing of the hymns to be used. They were "Rock of Ages," "Jesus, Lover of My Soul," "My Country, 'Tis of Thee," and others.

At the appointed time the hall was nearly filled. On a card table stood a coal-oil lamp, the Bible and hymn book beside it. The old missionary opened the service with a good, kind, fatherly talk, then we sang "Rock of Ages." Tears came into the eyes of some of the women and all seemed deeply interested, until some one shot the lamp to pieces on the table. This mean act incurred the displeasure of nearly all present. Another lamp was secured and "Doc" Middleton walked up to the side of the old preacher and said, "Whoever did that was damn mean and if he does it again, I'll kill him." The man who shot the lamp left the hall and the service proceeded without further interruption. When the preacher finished, I proposed to pass around the hat to take up a collection for him. I counted some one hundred thirty dollars and presented it to the good old man, who thanked his audience very earnestly. The next morning he took the first train for the East, probably glad that he was living and no doubt thinking there was some good in the worst of us.

The writer was relating this experience and others a few years ago to a life insurance agent, Mr. C. K. Huntington of Lincoln, Nebraska, who came into his office. Imagine the surprise of both to find that Mr. Huntington was the station agent at Whitman at that time and it was his good wife who played the organ. Mr. Huntington said that he could vouch for the truth of every statement in regard to this incident as told by the writer.

The cowboys and I came on to the round-up camp on the Dismal River where we had left it. On the way some of the boys talked freely and regretted what they had done and promised to do better. Some of the readers will agree with the writer in his estimate of "Doc" Middleton, who may have committed some crimes, but nevertheless had a good heart in him and his later life seems to prove it. He spent many years in Crawford, Nebraska.

"Shen-tag-a-lisk," my friend, better known as Spotted Tail, whose tombstone stands in Rosebud cemetery, should have chiseled on it: "Brave in war and faithful to his promises in peace."

CHAPTER XXXIII

Active Men and Strenuous Activities—Colonel W. F. Cody—
Major North—A Speedy Run—Crooked Tie Inspector—
Credit Mobilier—A Dangerous Undertaking

I FIRST met Colonel W. F. Cody, better known as Buffalo Bill, at Fort McPherson in 1869, when I was filling a twenty-eight hundred ton hay contract for the United States Government.

At this time W. F. Cody was scout and guide and was kept busy in leading troops to head off Indian raids on emigrant and freighting outfits, stage coaches and settlers going over the overland trail and those trying to establish a home in western Nebraska. He led a strenuous life and was an all-around good fellow, whom everyone liked, not a few taking advantage of his generous nature and well-known hospitality. His good wife, two sisters and small daughter, Arta, shared his little cottage near the McDonald store. His life, prior to this, while here, and subsequent doings, have been published and are a matter of history and linked with the early settlement of western Nebraska, Kansas and other states and territories. I could tell of many Indian raids where he displayed both courage and good generalship, sometimes superior to those higher in command.

Before taking up the Wild West show business he embarked in the cattle business on the head of the South Dismal River in company with Major North and other Columbus gentlemen. Some years later we bought their stock interest and ranches, for $75,000.00, after which the Colonel gave his undivided attention to his show business, of which he made a grand success.

As a rule he would spend several days with us on the annual round-ups, when there would be something doing besides actual round-up work. To make things safer and more Sunday-school like, all revolvers and guns would be gathered

"Doc" Middleton

Col. W. F. Cody (Buffalo Bill)

up and kept under lock, since some of the cowboys would take advantage of the Colonel's hospitality by going to his wagon and helping themselves to his cigars and sampling his liquors that had been brought along as an antidote against snake bites and other accidents. There would be broncho riding, roping, racing, riding wild steers, swimming contests, and sometimes a friendly poker game to see who would stand on night herd the longest. The cowboys were always glad to see the Colonel and the cattle owners and foremen would vie with each other in showing him a good time, and would prepare special feasts and meals for him when he came to or near their ranches. Nothing was too good for Colonel Cody.

I remember attending one elaborate ranch dinner given for the Colonel by the Laing Brothers at their ranch east of the Birdwood. The first course was soup, then came a large kettle of boiled beans. All passed off nicely until some of the hungry ones, among them George Bosler, James Ware, Thomas Lawrence, Dick Bean and Jerry Dummer, passed their plates back to Seine Laing, who was doing the serving at the head of the table. Seine got pretty well down to the bottom of the kettle, which stood before him on the table, when he struck something that would not "cup up." Seine called the cook whom he called "Squire," to bring him a fork. This was done and Seine brought to view out of the bottom of the kettle the blackest, dirtiest, greasiest old dish cloth or stove rag I ever saw. This ended that choice Delmonico dinner rather quickly.

Nothing pleased the Colonel more than to be allowed to go into a bunch of cattle and cut out strays. He was too strenuous a worker in a bunch of cows and calves. He did better in a bunch of steers, dry cows and heifers. As soon as he spotted one in "milling and ginning" these around, it would have to get out or soon be carrying a lariat around its neck. When I was bossing the round-up and the bunch became excited, I would call Cody out. All of which he took good naturedly, knowing well that rough handling of stock meant loss in flesh and shrinkage in value.

When he started his Wild West show we sold him a large bunch of outlaw cow horses and some of our expert riders and ropers joined his show, which was a success and one of the best educators of early life on the frontier that the public ever saw.

Another well-known good citizen, a former partner of Colonel Cody and a neighbor of the Colonel's in the cattle business, was Major Frank North, Commander of the Pawnee Scouts, who did great service in heading off and chasing down renegade bands of Sioux and Cheyenne Indians who would often steal away from their reservations and make a business of stealing stock and other property that they found unprotected. Major North was also captain of our company of North Platte Guards. It was fortunate for Big Turkey and his band of twenty-two Sioux that we chastised on the east Birdwood, that Captain North and his scouts were not along. There would have been no Big Turkey or band to march back to Rosebud. The Major was a thorough Western man, big-hearted, broad-minded, always on the side of right. The hardships he had endured in leading his scouts to victory in many campaigns had undermined his strong constitution and health but had not dampened his spirit and energy. While we would be enjoying his and Colonel Cody's hospitality in comfortable beds on the ranch floors at the ranch at the head of the Dismal River, poor Frank, apparently satisfied with his lot, would be sitting propped up in a chair, unable to lie down on account of asthma. In Eugene F. Ware's work, entitled "The Indian War of 1864," all reference to Major Frank North and the work of his scouts will be read with interest. For a short period he was associated with Colonel Cody in his show business. He died as he had lived—unassuming and faithful to every trust—and lies in a grave at Columbus, Nebraska, honored and loved by all.

In addition to buying the Cody and North brand of cattle, we shipped in several trainloads of cattle from Kings River, Nevada. I had divided our cattle into three separate bunches, using the same circle brand but in different places on the animal. We kept the thoroughbred cattle at the Home Ranch in winter and summered them east of the Birdwood Creek. The native cattle were kept at Fox Creek and the other, or common cattle, were kept north of the North Platte River, west and north of the Birdwood Creek, in order to better systematize our business.

In shipping the cattle from Kings River I met the first train at Winnemuck and came on with it to its destination, Ogallala, Nebraska. Everything went smoothly until we started to reload at Medicine Bow, where we stopped to graze them. The station agent at the Bow had interested himself in our shipment and secured me right of way and clear track to Laramie, provided we would be ready to leave at a certain time. I put what I thought to be two good, competent men to count and tally out the number to each car. I took the balance of the boys to the loading chutes. Everything worked like clockwork until one of the counters came to me and said he had about forty head in excess of what he should have for the last two cars. I told him I was sorry but it could not be remedied now and to push them into the last two cars. They went in and were resting their front feet on each other's backs and horns. The doors were closed and by that time one of the boys returned with six bottles of beer from Trobin's store. Three bottles were given to the engineer and fireman and three to the conductor and brakeman, with request that they get me into Laramie as fast as they could turn the wheels. I began to think they were doing it for before we had crossed Rock River the twenty-eight cars of cattle were moving like a cyclone. The engineer commenced to whistle for brakes. The conductor was tempted to set some but hesitated when I told him to let go and that we would come out all right. We went through the snowsheds like a flash. On a curve the wheels hardly touched the track. We flew down the grade from Cooper Lake like an avalanche. I had not touched a drop of that beer. I had every man in the train scared and almost believe that the conductor would have fallen off the caboose had I let go of his coat. I was sure I would get to Laramie with that train of cattle. Everyone was out of his office, including Ed. Dickinson, the chief dispatcher, who shook his fist at us as we rushed through the Laramie yards and passed them nearly two miles before the engineer could stop his train. As soon as stopped and we had backed up, I told Mr. Dickinson what I had done and if there were any damage I would pay for it and assured him the crew obeyed my orders. I asked him to have the switch engine take off eight cars at the west end of the train so I could unload them and level the cattle up, which was done. Some of the cattle in the two rear cars were down and badly trampled but all got up and walked out of the cars. The engineer and conductor were laid off for a few days but I paid them for their lost time. Mr. Dickinson impressed upon my mind very forcibly that in the future I could not run any trains over his division but I told him I had no inclination to repeat that run. If that train of cattle had gone in the ditch I would have been responsible for all damages.

After leveling up our overloaded cars, Mr. Dickinson gave us two fresh engines, with right of way over east bound freight to Ogallala. To this point we had another good run. The cattle were all unloaded, not much the worse for the bad treatment received in the two rear cars from Medicine Bow to Laramie.

Had this incident occurred in these modern days of railroading, all concerned would have been not only discharged but perhaps railroaded to the penitentiary for life. These times were hard and very trying to railroad presidents and managers of the Union Pacific Railroad company. What about the dark days when the pay car would not visit us once in three months? Yet, no one ever accused a single Union Pacific official, big or little, of doing wrong.

I will take that back. I do remember a tie inspector's going crooked once, not for money but for two bottles of whiskey.

I had refused to receive a bunch of about six thousand ties gotten out for us on contract by a bunch of Canadian

Frenchmen because they did not come up to specifications.
The Canadians contended I was too exacting. I told them I
could not help it and that I would pay them for every tie that
measured up to specifications. They finally asked if I would
pay for all ties received by the railroad company inspector.
I told them I was obliged to do so. They finally got the inspector to their tie camp one bitter cold day and with the aid
of the whiskey got him to spot every tie. Many were short
and did not have a six inch, let alone an eight inch face.
When I found out what the inspector had done I remonstrated with him for his actions in thus defrauding the
company. He gave as an excuse the answer that the men
were poor, that they had been very kind to him in giving him
whiskey and he thought he would do them a good turn, and
besides, the Casement Brothers needed the ties badly. He
asked if I would not put teams enough to haul them so they
could be loaded the next day. Before the week was out these
ties had been ironed. The Casement Brothers were building
two and a half to three and a half miles of railroad at this
time in a single day and maybe the tie inspector's conscience
overlooked his idea of right and wrong by blinding it with
the shadow, "Had to have them."

We paid the contractor as agreed. He afterwards quit
the tie-making business and embarked in the cattle and sheep
business, at which he made over half a million dollars.

I met this same gentleman some years ago in Salt Lake
and rode with him to his home station in Wyoming. The
poor fellow was all in physically. He justified his action in
giving the whiskey to the tie inspector by saying if he had not
done so, the inspector might have frozen and would have
failed to inspect the ties and in that event, his men would not
have received the money for the ties, which the Union Pacific
needed badly, hence it was a blessing all around. This was
another side to it as told by good-hearted Tom Sims.

These were dark financial days for Credit Mobilier. It
took nerve to continue putting money into that hopper to
build the Union Pacific Railroad. When I was manager for

that great tie and wood firm, Gilman & Carter, composed of Isaac Coe, Levi Carter, and John and Jed Gilman, we were paying out daily five thousand to ten thousand dollars of good greenbacks for Credit Mobilier paper of questionable value and of which we had already an accumulation of over eleven hundred thousand dollars. Heretofore, we had sent these accumulations to our bankers in Omaha, but these gentlemen told us they had about all they could use for the present.

General Coe came into camp about this time and asked what amount of money it would take to run the camps for thirty days. I told him as nearly as I could and he told me to keep right along and draw on him. Before leaving, I loaded him up with all the Credit Mobilier paper we had and he took the first train for New York with a determination to interview Thomas C. Durant. A few days afterwards he wired that money was tight but he had succeeded in getting a part of our claim.

Many other tie makers were getting cold feet. The men of the Sprague & Davis Co. (who had quarters near us) so scared that firm with a rope with a noose in it, that they pulled out between suns. What would be our fate? We had faith but it took more than faith to pay for ties, logs and poles. We followed the line of road along established camps on the Laramie, Medicine Bow, Fort Steel, and other points.

Credit Mobilier had carried out its promises as far as able. It had taken no advantage of us and with the present management in control we had little to fear. We were getting good prices for our material. Union Pacific stocks and bonds were being tossed around in Wall street from front door to rear. There was no market value for any of them. Jay Gould and his trimmers were in control. The pessimists were thick and noisy. They gave it out that the road could not be built and if built, it would never pay. Not satisfied with this dirty work, the would-be "rule or ruin" fellows started a government investigation of Credit Mobilier accounts. All this was done for spite and to harass the Credit Mobilier Co., that had many good defenders both in the House and Senate, also able defenders like George Francis Train and Dr. George L. Miller.

While the Union Pacific had had some good men at its head, it also had its Adams. It now had the noblest Roman of them all—S. H. H. Clark. He was broken down in health, but his name was a talisman in the household of every employee on the system. If the pay checks did not show up in time, a word from Mr. Clark would set everything right. He was loved by all and no other railroad president ever lived who carried such loyalty of employees. The humblest section hand was always welcome to talk with him and shake his hand.

Credit Mobilier had carried out its obligations with its sub-contractors. We had not lost a dollar by it, though our Company had backed it with its capital and all of its credit. It had accomplished its object—the Union Pacific Railroad had been built and the Golden Spike uniting the Atlantic and the Pacific oceans had been driven.

I happened to be in Omaha when rumor had it that the city was overrun with United States Secret Service men hunting for Credit Mobilier information and its books. I was approached by some of these gentlemen and questioned somewhat closely as to the extent of our Company's business relations with Credit Mobilier. I told them frankly that its relations with us had been strictly honorable, that at one time we had carried over eleven hundred thousand dollars of its paper, that we had backed it with every dollar of our Company's cash and credit, and would not be afraid to do it again. I could have told these gentlemen where its books were had I been asked, and perhaps have received a valuable remuneration for so doing had I desired. Enough to say, that about 8:30 that evening a certain trusty man was called to accompany two baggage cars, a private car and special engine with right of way. Engines were changed at Grand Island, North Platte, Cheyenne and other terminals. It is said the little train became lost near Point of Rocks. The weather became so intensely cold that the contents of the boxes had to be burned to prevent the man in charge from freezing. He returned to Omaha later but has now passed away. I once talked with him about this matter and he told me that the books were straight and the only thing they might have possibly revealed was the limited holdings of some of the Credit Mobilier stock by a few senators and congressmen. It was "much ado about nothing."

In closing this article there are no apologies to make for any Union Pacific official. If any crime was committed, it was done by others and not by them.

During the fall of 1884 we sold to Patrick Brothers of Omaha some four hundred beef steers to be delivered the following February at one of the breweries at Peoria, Illinois. When ready to ship there was six to eight inches of drifted, frozen snow on the ground, making it impossible to drive the steers to North Platte without making their feet and legs sore. A few days before the time of shipment arrived, another snow of about three inches fell, making it more difficult to drive the steers to North Platte for shipment. The Birdwood Creek for nearly two miles distant from its mouth and the North Platte River in that vicinity, were frozen solid. I had crossed the river just above the mouth of the Birdwood many times with teams and to test the ice further, had loaded two wagons heavily with dirt and crossed them several times, which satisfied me of its strength to hold the steers if we could keep them strung out, so I ordered the cars sent from North Platte to O'Fallons' station, determined to ship from there. The day previous to shipping we made several trips with teams, loose horses and work cattle, scattering hay on the snow, making a very plain trail across about forty to sixty feet wide. During the night there blew up a very strong wind that swept every particle of snow and hay off the track we had made, leaving the ice bare and slippery. At three o'clock that morning I had several teams and many men sanding the river, making a track as wide as before. By noon we had the crossing complete after having driven over it many times with teams, loose horses and work cattle. The ice still seemed solid. I knew the risk I was about to take—that I might lose a lot of steers—but I had confidence that I would come through all right.

We had an early dinner and when ready to start, I put Mike Foster in the lead with a good team hitched to a spring wagon. Following this I had a four-horse team hitched to a hay rack full of loose hay. Next followed about twenty head of gentle work cattle, then the beef steers with a total of about sixteen good cowboys for the flanks and rear of the steers. All had proper instructions as to places and what to do in emergencies in event the steers commenced to crowd or bunch up. I took the east or left flank a little ahead of the center of the bunch so that I could move quickly to the lead, center or drop to the rear, wherever needed. All went smoothly for the first quarter of a mile until we reached the ice over deeper channels, when the ice began to crack, frightening the steers, and they began to bunch. I motioned to the driver of the hay team to keep going and to the men to close up on the cattle in order to keep them moving. The cattle did so, but only when forced vigorously by the cowboys. The continued cracking and later the heaving and sagging of the ice frightened and excited the steers, which kept on bunching, the ice gradually sinking. The hay team was ahead and out of danger. Not so with Mike Foster's team, which I saw was gradually going down on a large cake of ice. It took every man and all his nerve to stay by and hold those steers from breaking back. The ice went down and with it the steers and every man into four to six feet of water. For a time it looked as though many of the steers and riders would be sucked under the ice by the swift current. Where I and some of the cowboys were on the lower side it looked like certain death, as large floating cakes of ice ten to fourteen inches thick kept breaking loose by the milling of the steers and floating down on to us on the lower side. I realized that our only show was to crowd the steers forward. Sometimes they were two and three deep, some down on the ice in the water, others climbing over and on their backs. In this way they commenced to break and loosen the ice ahead as they continued wallowing over it until they got into shallower water where the ice was strong enough to hold them up. We thus kept them going until we reached the south bank of the river with the entire bunch, including the work cattle and loose horses, which took their baths more philosophically than the steers. Our cowboys were all accounted for and Mike Foster, with the little black team but minus the seat on the wagon, came as far as he could at the tail end of the cattle. We had to pull the wagon out of the broken ice with saddle ropes in order to give the team a footing on the icy trail again. We experienced some trouble in getting our saddle horses out of the water upon the ice. Many of us had to dismount in doing so. Every man was wet all over and his clothes were frozen stiff on him a few moments after getting out of the water. As soon as all were out a couple of men and I went ahead to get the loading pens and chutes in readiness.

We got the steers into the pens all right and in less than two hours had them loaded and started on a train for North Platte en route to Peoria in charge of faithful Mike Foster and another good man. I sent the little team and the four-horse hay team to the Home Ranch that night and I returned to the Birdwood Ranch with the rest of the cowboys. In re-crossing the river with the work cattle and loose horses, we all had another cold bath.

"Negro" Johnson, our broncho buster, and another cowboy, tried to cross the river about four hundred yards above us. They got safely across the deep channels by crawling over on their stomachs, but their saddle horses went in.

That night I drove back to the Home Ranch and after a change of clothes, took the train east to Council Bluffs, where I awaited the arrival of the steers, that we finally unloaded at Peoria. They had had a hard trip and were rather gaunt but there were no "crips."

I cannot close this tale of that remarkable crossing of those "beeves" over the frozen North Platte River, without a word of praise for our faithful cowboys, among them

"Negro" Johnson, who did his part nobly during that thrilling adventure.

Johnson later worked for a well-known cattle and horse man residing in North Platte. This gentleman was in the habit of swearing at Johnson, which he at last resented, telling him that if he had to take these cursings, he would want more pay. He was asked how much more he wanted and said it was worth $5.00 per month more. The deal was closed and the cursing continued more vigorously.

*Many Irons in the Fire—The Birdwood and Blue Creek Canals—
I am Introduced as "Mr. Kelly"—The Equitable Farm and
Stock Improvement Company—Dissolution of Partnership*

IN addition to managing our large cattle interests, we built, with the aid of proposed water users, the Birdwood Canal, some twenty miles long. The water for this canal was taken out of the Birdwood Creek and diverted into the canal about one mile above its confluence with the North Platte River. The Birdwood Creek is fed by springs of soft water that evidently come from what is termed the Lake Country, ranging from seventy-five to one hundred fifty miles north and northwest of the heads of the East and West Birdwood Creeks. These numerous springs remain about the same the year round and make a perpetual stream in what may be termed the Birdwood proper of about two hundred fifty cubic feet per second, one-half of which can be turned into the Birdwood Canal and is capable of irrigating some 75,000 acres of hay and tillable land lying below it. The cost of water and of maintaining the canal for years after its construction was a very trifling sum annually. After we disposed of our interests in the canal, unfortunately it got into the hands of schemers and promoters, who persuaded the owners of land under or adjacent to it to form an irrigation district and bond it for about $25,000.00. The promoters pocketed several thousand dollars of this.

In order to work this scheme through, a certain per cent of the proceeds from the sale of the bonds was paid to those having original water rights in the canal. These now realized the fact that they had to pay principal and interest on these bonds, besides a heavy annual maintenance tax to keep up the ditch and pay officers' salaries. The original owners of the ditch may have received $3.00 per acre for their equity and before they got through the deal might cost them $8.00 per acre. This is high finance. The promoters of this scheme must have pocketed $10,000.00 pure velvet.

There is no better or purer water than that Birdwood Creek water. It possesses great medicinal properties and has been known to cure several bad cases of Bright's disease and kidney troubles. It should be piped to the city of North Platte for domestic use and could be made to supply the Union Pacific at Hershey, Birdwood Siding and North Platte, where it would have a fall of one hundred forty feet, giving the best fire protection. The expense of pumping could be saved, and North Platte would have one of the best water systems in the state.

We also built the Blue Creek Canal, from seven to nine miles long. The water was taken out of the Blue Creek on its east side a little north of the town of Lewellen. This stream, like the Birdwood, gets its source of supply from the Lake Country. The water is pure and soft and no doubt possesses similar medicinal properties. This canal is known as the Bratt ditch and is one of the best little canals in the state. It waters several thousand acres of land that never fails to raise good crops.

We also made part of the survey to build a canal about seventy miles long, taking the water out of the north side of the North Platte River a couple of miles west of Oshkosh. We spent over $10,000.00 in preliminary surveys for this canal, the tail water of which we proposed to turn into the West Birdwood Creek. The object of building this canal was for the purpose of irrigating what we could of the Ogallala Cattle Company's land east of Blue Creek and some of our 123,000 acres that we owned east of White Tail Creek, northeast of Ogallala. We would probably have constructed this canal had we not disposed of our land.

I must here tell a little story.

When I went to file on the location for the water right for this proposed canal I took with me our surveyor, Charles Walker, and Ed. Richards, our foreman at the Birdwood ranch, both well known in that country. I was only known by a few old timers and it was suggested that Walker and Richards introduce me as Mr. Kelly, a sheep man, looking for a location to place a band of sheep.

On our route from the Birdwood ranch with team hitched to a light wagon, we were lucky to make Mr. and Mrs———'s ranch for dinner. The gentleman of the ranch was not there, but the lady, knowing ·Richards and Walker well, served us a nice dinner. Of course, I as "Mr. Kelly," talked about nothing but sheep. When we got through and were ready to depart, Richards asked the lady what the bill was. Knowing that he worked for us, she innocently inquired whether they or Mr. Bratt had to pay it, remarking that if Bratt paid it, it would be more than if we three paid it. Richards told her that Bratt did not pay for the dinner, so I presume the cost was less, which Richards paid with a smile. That night we stayed at Bob Graff's, where I was well known, and I think the next morning the lady found out that I was Mr. Bratt and not "Mr. Kelly."

I have seen this good lady since. Maybe she remembers Richards' deception, as well as my own as "Mr. Kelly," the sheep man, and maybe she knows the reason why I should pay more for the dinner than the other fellows—I don't.

Enough to say we located the water right under the name of the Midland Irrigation and Land Co., of which Frank Murphy, President of the Merchants National Bank of Omaha, was president, and Mr. Markell of Omaha was another officer.

In order to handle our business in better shape we incorporated the firm of John Bratt & Co. under the name of the Equitable Farm and Stock Improvement Co.

After disposing of our north side lands we closed out our cattle interests. We did not come out with as much money as we should have owing to some very unfortunate deals made by one of our partners, who seemed bent on a "rule or ruin" policy, no doubt due to advanced age and broken-down health.

Of Mr. Carter I can say none but kindly words except that had he felt like protecting our interests, he could have

Waste-gate No. 1 on Birdwood Canal

JOHN BRATT
Taken in the year 1892

done so, since the two of us held three-fifths of the stock in the Equitable Company. Several bad deals could have thus been prevented; but family ties, and a dislike to antagonize the General, no doubt caused him to acquiesce in the General's unfortunate exchange of the Equitable Company's Nebraska interests for encumbered Ohio and Kentucky property, in which we got the worst of the deal by nearly one hundred thousand dollars. I remonstrated many times against these deals but to no purpose. After the exchange was made I was sent down to look over the property, examine titles, and care for other details. The price of every piece of property we received was padded 25% to 50% and some of them were not worth the mortgages against them. All of which General Coe, as President of the Equitable Farm and Stock Improvement Co., assumed and agreed to pay.

But no matter. Both partners are now dead. Let them rest in peace. As I sit writing these truthful facts of inside history of our copartnership, I am happy in the thought that I never took advantage of either of these partners, although I could have defrauded them out of thousands of dollars without their knowing it. For a period of five years neither of them saw our stock and ranches. Both had implicit confidence in my management and honesty. No matter how hard the task, often at the risk of my life, I always tried to do my duty. Whether I did it or not, the reader can judge.

CHAPTER XXXV

Conclusion—Two Terms as Mayor—Real Estate and Insurance Business—A Threatening Letter—Brief Review of My Career

I HAD closed up company matters with Coe & Carter and disposed of my stock in the Equitable Farm and Stock Improvement Co., when in the spring of 1898 I was urged by many good citizens of both parties to become a candidate for mayor of North Platte.

The city had been mismanaged and exploited for years. Both money and credit were gone, not by theft but by reckless mismanagement of its financial affairs. It owed some $7000.00, drawn on the general fund without any authority of law and no provision made to pay it. All could have been repudiated, but it had been the custom to contract debts in this manner, hence the holders of this illegal paper were entitled to their pay. This was the way I looked at it. In addition to this the former city attorney had stipulated all the city's rights away and virtually confessed judgment to the North Platte Water Company for $11,057.90 for back hydrant rental, which Judge Norris, the trial judge, said the city must pay, notwithstanding the water company had received every dollar that a seven mill levy raised.

The city was run "loose." Gambling was a recognized vocation and drunks on the streets were a common sight.

Immoral houses were numerous and it seemed that the good people of North Platte were helpless. Saloons were run without restraint.

With this picture before me I must have been seeking trouble when I consented to become a candidate and told the delegation of non-partisan business men who waited on me that, while I did not seek the honor, I felt it my duty, as a citizen of North Platte, to accept it, on condition that there were no strings on me; that although I was a Democrat, I was broad enough to ignore politics; that in any appointments I might make, qualities of the man and his ability to serve the city's interests would come first; that if elected mayor, many radical changes that some might not like would occur; gambling would have to cease; saloon keepers must obey the law. Drunkenness on the streets would not be tolerated, the selling of liquor to minors must stop, nor would they be allowed in saloons. The city marshal and police would be given their orders and obey them or resign. I proposed to make mine, if aided by the council, a business administration, with the view of lifting the city out of debt, and a dollar's value would have to be shown for every one expended.

Enough to say that my election was nearly unanimous. A council of good citizens was elected to aid me.

After election I called the council together at my office for a conference, at which meeting I showed the financial condition of the city—the stipulated amount due the water company as per judgment rendered, and the $7000.00 of floating debt due by the city to our citizens, who were clamoring for their money. I impressed upon the minds of those present our duty to provide payment for same by practising the strictest economy in order to pay 30% to 50% of the floating indebtedness and 25% of the $11,057.90 due the water company during our first year. In order to help this proposition along I proposed to cut my salary in two and asked the members of the council to do the same, to which they all readily agreed. We decided what cut we should make on other city officials and employees. There was some underground objection to these cuts, but we made them, thus saving the city over $750.00 in salaries the first year.

I had a friendly talk with the saloon men and told them that some of them were breaking the law and that they would be expected to quit it—then we would get along—but if they persisted in these violations I should ask that their license be forfeited.

I also had a talk with the leading gamblers. I told them that gambling would not be tolerated for a moment and that

I had instructed the marshal and police to stop it, and that I hoped the gamblers would not force me to extremes, otherwise I should cause them all the trouble they wanted. Tucker of Ogallala, of dance house fame and an undesirable citizen, who had killed his third man, offered to pay into the city treasury $50.00 per month for the privilege of running a "quiet little joint," as he called it, and said he would make it $100.00 per month and put up a bond of sufficient amount, guaranteeing all a square deal and make good any loss from robberies or losses that might occur in this place, if we would give him some exclusive rights and privileges. I told him his proposition would not be considered for a moment and that the best thing he could do would be to quit the game or leave the city. After a period of thirty days, he concluded to pack up and leave. I happened to be over at the depot when he boarded the train. He bade me good-bye and said he would like to put a bullet through me before he left.

To show the bankrupt state of the city's funds and its credit among our merchants, the street commissioner needed a few planks to repair a broken culvert. The lumber dealer refused to furnish them unless I personally guaranteed the payment of the bill. I did this and we got the planks.

In justice to the members of the council and every city official and every employee, I will give them credit for aiding me in protecting the city's interests in every manner they could. Our city marshal and police had their hands full in watching the gamblers and the hoodlums. They defied the marshal and one day all set upon him, intending to kill him, but they did not know their man. Honest, fearless Dick H. Davis took their abuse and their beating. He could and would have been justified in killing the whole gang that set on him but did not do so, showing not only his nerve but his good judgment. All were arrested and given the full penalty of the law. His fearless course not only frightened them but public opinion became so strong against this element that the ringleaders, like Tucker, left the city.

The saloon keepers, with a few exceptions, were keeping their promises.

The churches and good citizens of North Platte assisted me and the city officials in our efforts to stamp out these evils and it was not many months before our good efforts became manifest.

The Fourth of July of this year was a great day. The merchants put heart and soul into the carnival. The secret orders also assisted greatly. I believe I am the only mayor North Platte ever had, who succeeded in getting all the ministers (including the Catholic priest, whom I placed beside the Methodist minister), to ride in one carriage. The amusements were all moral and attractive. The fireworks in the evening were appreciated by the great crowd that witnessed them. The Volunteer Fire Department took special interest in making the celebration a grand success. What pleased me most was that everything passed off without accident.

By the reduction of salaries and the practising of the strictest economy, we saved our taxpayers nearly $800.00 the first year's administration, enabling us to pay one-fourth of the water company's judgment and nearly 50% of the floating indebtedness, besides establishing the city's credit. Gambling had ceased, hoodlum gangs had been broken up, owing to the earnest efforts of the city marshal, Dick Davis, and his aids.

As the spring election approached, I was again urged to become a candidate for the office of mayor. I did not want a second term except to complete the work I had mapped out: namely, to reduce taxes and to put the city's finances in proper business shape, to uplift its moral standards and use my every effort to make our city better, bigger and more progressive. I tried to be the mayor of the city, seeking the welfare of every citizen, and not of a faction or entrenched interests. I believed then and believe now and always shall believe that the people should own all their utilities that God has given them, and if any profit, it should be applied to the reduction of taxes.

I had neglected my private business* but was urged to accept a second term by so many good people that I thought it my duty to serve. The result was I was re-elected by a good majority. I again called the members of the council for a conference and suggested we all serve without pay, the same as the members of the school board. This proposition was tabled, but the members agreed to cut their salaries 50%, the same as the last term. I am ashamed to say they failed to do so. I was the only one who made the reduction. Although my council did not reduce their salaries, they gave the city valuable assistance in the economical management of its affairs and at the end of the second term we paid another one-fourth of the water company's judgment against the city and nearly all the floating indebtedness and further established the city's credit on a solid basis. Taxes were further reduced and the rich and poor got a square deal. We made many improvements in our crossings, bettered the condition of our streets and alleys, and built up our fire department. Not a dollar was wasted or misappropriated. I had done my duty fearlessly and without favor to my friends or punishment to my enemies. I could have been nominated for a third term but I declined the honor.

I look back upon my two terms as mayor of North Platte with some degree of satisfaction.

To show that I did not please everyone, about this time I received a threatening letter, telling me I would be killed and my building on Front Street blown up if I did not deposit $500.00 in gold by a certain time on a certain night at a certain place upstairs in the rear of my building. Not wishing to have my life ended and my building blown up so abruptly, on the afternoon of the evening I had to make the deposit

* After the dissolution of the Equitable Farm and Stock Improvement Co., the writer opened a real estate office and in the year 1900 went into partnership with Edward R. Goodman (later his son-in-law). In a few years a prosperous business was established which necessitated taking in a third partner. Two years before the writer's death Newton E. Buckley (also a son-in-law) was asked to come into the firm under the present name of Bratt, Goodman and Buckley.

of the $500.00 in gold I went to the bank and carried back in my hands, up Dewey Street and into my office on Front Street, a sack resembling that amount in gold, which at eight o'clock that evening I carried up my hall by the front stairs and deposited in the place designated in the letter. That afternoon I smuggled into a room three men, who with three loaded guns, took their places on an elevated table, from which they could easily kill any one who tried to pick up that sack of gold. In reality this sack of gold was a sack of iron washers. Enough to say, the man did not come for the sack of gold. The threat may have been a joke or the writer may have meant it. I thought I knew the writer, the writing bearing a great resemblance to a signed letter that I happened to have in my possession. I had this party shadowed for several weeks but failed to get sufficient evidence to connect him with writing and mailing me the letter, hence I will call it a joke.

In conclusion, I will state that in writing this autobiography I have endeavored to confine myself to facts recorded at the time or shortly after they occurred, the same jotted down in notes, memorandum or diary if I happened to have that with me. Sometimes these were written under difficulties in tent, wagon box, ranch, or on the open prairie, if not on my field desk; perhaps on a cracker box, the cook's bread board, the end gate or seat of a wagon, the skirts of my saddle or on an ox yoke. These facts are what I have seen and done in years of earnest activity, often at the risk of my life. The night was never too dark or stormy, the distance too great, the river too deep, too wide or too swift for me to tackle it. Confidence in my ability to make it never left me. I knew and felt an Infinite Protector with me always. I believed an Indian could not kill me or do me bodily harm. The Guardian Angel, often referred to in these chapters, always seemed to be with me; filled me with courage and confidence that I would come through in safety. In leaving home both mother and father, in saying the last good-bye, whispered to me that their constant prayer would be for my safety. I often thought I heard that earnest prayer when things seemed to be going against me. I would hear a voice say: "You will come out all right. God is your protector." I was not a saint, a "goody-goody" fellow, nor a hypocrite. I liked the good and had no use for the bad. I did not drink, smoke or gamble. I always thought, and still think, that a man ought to be as pure as a woman. I have often been criticised for these so-called "shortcomings" in my early education, but it is now too late to make the change. I have passed my seventieth birthday and will, no doubt, get through the rest of my life without these accomplishments.

I have met and talked with many of our old employees who have made good. Again, I sometimes meet some less fortunate. Drink, cards and other weaknesses have been their curses. These often ask me for aid, sometimes a meal, a night's lodging or railroad fare. I usually give these, which they promise to return, but they forget, poor fellows! They are to be pitied. I listen to their stories, give them the benefit of the doubt, and if I cannot find them work, help them to their destination.

If I knew the addresses of these old associates, who have shared these hardships with me, I would gladly mail them a copy of this book, if printed before I pass "under the wire." It would remind them of many familiar scenes.

While there were many hardships, there were some sunny spots in this fascinating frontier life; every day, every hour something new and interesting: the beautiful scenery, the great rivers stocked with fish, the lofty mountains with peaks covered with perpetual snow, the great plains and broad valleys dotted with the antelope, deer, elk, buffalo, often the river brush and quaking asp groves being the home of the bear, coyotes and wolves. To a lover of nature, it seemed sacrilegious to break into this paradise. No wonder the Indian considered the "pale face" his natural enemy, intruder and trespasser on his domain. But it is the old story—"The survival of the fittest." Progress and civilization were bound to conquer. The Indian fought hard and died hard. Spotted

Tail expressed his meaning truthfully and vividly on his return trip to his people from Washington, D. C., when speaking of the large number of white people, he picked up a handful of sand, saying the whites were like those grains of sand—it was impossible to count them. His people would not believe him. Some said he spoke falsely, others claimed he had been bribed and a few called him a coward because he refused to continue war on the whites. One of his bands threatened to waylay and kill him on his return through Scotts bluff. He was sent back to his people in a United States ambulance with a military escort, but instead of riding through the bluffs, gun in hand he walked over the top of them.

In their many years of war with the whites, the Indians met with some success as in the Phil Kearny, Custer and other massacres, but later they were compelled to surrender. Disease and other causes have greatly depleted their number. The older Indians have never taken kindly to reservation life. When first given the white man's clothes, they cut the seats out of the pants. When houses were built for them to live in, consumption took them rapidly. The younger generations have been and are being educated at schools in the East and on the reservations. At first these made little improvement among them. They, however, are now doing better. The government has sent practical farmers and stock raisers among them, including many competent, good women teachers among the squaws, who are teaching them to properly care for their homes and families, teaching them domestic science, and since their land has been allotted them, it is wonderful to note the progress they are making. Even some of these college graduate teachers, sent out by the government to instruct them, are in such love with their work that they have condescended to marry full-blooded Indians. A few years hence the full-blooded Indian will exist in history only. Prejudice against him is rapidly vanishing. With a little more civilization and education, the Indian will take his place among our best type of citizens and even to-day they are preferable to many illiterate, criminal foreigners who are coming to our shores.

The pioneers and earlier settlers have well and faithfully performed their mission. Much honor is due them for the important part they have taken in the civilization of the Red Man and the settlement of this vast Western empire. Mark the change in a few short years. Law and order have taken the place of the vigilance committee. The desperado has either met his fate or become good. The church and Sunday school have driven out the frontier gambling halls and lewd dance houses, and while we have some bad people with us yet, I believe the world is growing better.

I am now taking life easier than I used to, living happily with my family, children and grandchildren. I expect to live many years yet. My purse has always been open, and ever will be, to help fight for the interests of my fellow citizens. When the final summons comes I shall be ready to obey it without fear for the future.

With love for all and malice toward none, when death shall come, I desire that my brother Sir Knights Templar shall take charge of my remains and deposit them tenderly in the grave. My spirit will go back to the God who gave it but will be with you and the loved ones through eternity.

DEDICATED TO MY BELOVED WIFE,
CHILDREN AND GRANDCHILDREN